Legal Answer Book for Managed Care

Aspen Health Law Center
Patricia Younger, J.D.
Cynthia Conner, LL.L.
Kara Kinney Cartwright, J.D.
Susan M. Kole, J.D.

An Aspen Publication®
Aspen Publishers, Inc.
Gaithersburg, Maryland
1995

This publication is designed to provide accurate and authoritative information in regard to the Subject Matter covered. It is sold with the understanding that the publisher is not engaged in rendering legal, accounting, or other professional service. If legal advice or other expert assistance is required, the service of a competent professional person should be sought. (*From a Declaration of Principles jointly adopted by a Committee of the American Bar Association and a Committee of Publishers and Associations.*)

Library of Congress Cataloging-in-Publication Data

Younger, Patricia A.
Legal answer book for managed care / Patricia Younger, Cynthia Conner, Kara Kinney Cartwright.
p.   cm.
Includes bibliographical references and index.
ISBN 0-8342-0700-1
1. Managed care plans (Medical care) — Law and legislation — United States.
2. Insurance, Health — Law and legislation — United States.
I. Conner, Cynthia.   II. Cartwright, Kara Kinney.   III. Title.
KF1183.Y68   1995
344.73'022247.30422—dc20
95-15098
CIP

Editorial Resources: Ruth Bloom

Library of Congress Catalog Card Number: 95-15098
ISBN: 0-8342-0700-1

Printed in the United States of America

1   2   3   4   5

Table of Contents _____

Introduction _____

As a result of federal and state health care reform initiatives, consumer demand, and economic necessity, the delivery of health care in America has changed significantly in the past five years. Delivery of health care is no longer dominated by fee-for-service medicine and acute care facilities; increasingly, managed care systems and networks of providers provide a full range of health care services to beneficiaries under contracts with employers or third party payers. This process of managing health care involves a myriad of activities, including financing, purchasing, delivering, measuring, and documenting. All of the different professionals involved in these activities will benefit from the overview of the managed care process offered in the *Legal Answer Book for Managed Care*.

This *Legal Answer Book for Managed Care* is designed to provide quick and authoritative answers to a broad spectrum of questions concerning the numerous legal issues involved in managed health care. The book covers the various types of managed care organizations, including health maintenance organizations, management service organizations, physician–hospital organizations, and preferred provider organizations. Also provided is an overview of state and federal legislation governing managed care organizations and their activities, antitrust issues, managed care contracting, utilization review, ERISA issues, and the application of federal tax-exempt provisions to managed care entities. The answer book is intended to be a handy reference that provides comprehensive and accessible information on all of these issues. The reader should be aware, however, that the law varies from state to state and will also vary with time as a result of new legislation and court opinions.

The Health Law Center is grateful to the attorneys on its staff, all of whom contributed to this book through their writing and research. The Center would also like to acknowledge Merrilee Hagaman for her help on several of the introductory chapters of the book, and Robert McAdams, Jr., of the law firm of Baker and Hostetler, for reviewing the manuscript.

How To Use This Book _____

This *Answer Book* attempts to use simple language and avoid complex terminology when possible, although technical language that is necessary and appropriate to describe legal concepts may appear at various points in the book.

CITATIONS

Citations of authority are provided as research aids for those who need to pursue particular items in greater detail.

QUESTION NUMBERING

The question numbering system is simple. Questions are numbered consecutively within each chapter.

LIST OF QUESTIONS

The List of Questions is intended to help the reader locate areas of immediate interest.

INDEX

At the back of the book is an Index, provided as a further aid to locating specific information. All references in the index are to question numbers rather than page numbers.

TABLE OF CASES

A Table of Cases follows the index at the back of the book. The cases are listed alphabetically, followed by the number of the question in which the case is referenced.

ABBREVIATIONS

Due to the breadth of the subject area, various terms are either abbreviated or designated by acronyms throughout the book. Generally, the first time each such abbreviation is used, it follows the full term with which it is associated in the text.

List of Questions _____

1—Managed Care Organizations, Provider Formations, and Affiliated Entities

2—Overview of Laws Applicable to Managed Care

3—Antitrust Laws Relevant to Managed Care

4—Utilization Review

5—ERISA

6—Liability

7—Contracting

8—Credentialing and Peer Review

9—Fraud and Abuse

10—Special Issues for Tax-Exempt Organizations in Managed Care

1

Managed Care Organizations, Provider Formations, and Affiliated Entities

Managed care is a broad term used to describe a health care delivery system that attempts to manage the cost and quality of health care, as well as access to health care. Examples of managed care organizations include health maintenance organizations (HMOs), preferred provider organizations (PPOs), and physician–hospital organizations (PHOs). Originally, the different types of managed care organizations were distinct and mutually exclusive of one another. Today, however, the differences among HMOs, PPOs, PHOs, and other managed care organizations are becoming less clear. In fact, many managed care organizations are hybrids of several specific types of managed care organizations.

A simplistic concept that illustrates the relationship between managed care organizations is the continuum of integration. In progressing from one end of the continuum to the other, new and greater elements of control and accountability are added, which tend to increase both the complexity and the overhead required to operate the plan. At the same time, greater potential control of cost and quality is achieved. For example, on one end of the continuum is managed indemnity, a variation on a traditional insurance plan in that there is precertification of elective admissions and large case management of catastrophic cases. Further along the continuum are point-of-service plans and preferred provider organizations (PPOs), which provide consumers with a more expansive choice of physicians. Toward the end of the continuum are closed panel HMOs.

This chapter provides a general overview of the different types of managed care organizations, along with a discussion of the advantages and disadvantages of the different types. Because delineations between the organizational models are not always clear, and due to regional variations in terminology, the following descriptions are not definitive, but serve as a baseline for an understanding of managed care concepts.

TYPES OF MANAGED CARE ORGANIZATIONS

Health Maintenance Organizations

Q.1:1   What is a health maintenance organization (HMO)?

An HMO is an organized health care system that both finances and delivers health care services to its enrollees or subscribers. An HMO generally contracts with selected health care providers to arrange for the provision of comprehensive health care services for its covered members, who prepay a fixed amount for care. HMOs are the most restrictive type of managed care organizations. A member must receive health care from a participating provider for the HMO to pay for the cost of the health care services. A covered member must choose a primary care physician (a gatekeeper) from a panel of participating providers and must receive health care from this gatekeeper unless the gatekeeper authorizes the member to receive specialist or in-hospital care. The HMO provides incentives for a primary care physician to limit the number of referrals to specialists or hospital care. These incentives are created under the assumption that fewer referrals will result in lower costs.

Q.1:2   What are the basic characteristics of an HMO?

The basic characteristics of an HMO are:

- *Select provider panel.* HMOs contract with selected providers in a community to provide health care services for covered individuals. Providers are selected to participate on the basis of their cost efficiency, community reputation, and scope of services.
- *Gatekeeper.* Covered members of an HMO are required to select a primary care physician (gatekeeper) and must receive their health care from this gatekeeper unless the gatekeeper authorizes specialist or in-hospital care.
- *Utilization review.* HMOs are responsible for the evaluation of the appropriateness, necessity, and efficiency of health care services to its covered members.

Q.1:3   How does an HMO differ from traditional health insurance?

Traditional health insurance consists of an indemnity plan, where the insurer either reimburses covered individuals for medical expenses or compensates providers for services performed. Under a traditional plan, physicians are typically paid after performing a particular service, commonly known as a fee-for-service arrangement. HMOs, on the other hand, generally compensate providers on a prepaid, fixed-fee basis. This payment arrangement is known as *capitation*.

An HMO is a combination of a health insurer and health care delivery system. HMOs are responsible not only for covering the cost of care, but also for arranging for the provision of health care services through affiliated providers. HMOs, unlike traditional health insurance plans, must ensure that enrollees have access to health care providers and that members receive quality health care that satisfies individual members' health care needs.

Q.1:4   Are there different types of HMOs?

Yes. There are five common HMO models:

1. staff,
2. group practice,
3. network,
4. individual practice association (IPA), and
5. direct contract.

The models differ largely in the types of relationships and control they have over the panel of participating physicians. HMO models also differ in payment methods, utilization review requirements, subscriber choice, and subscriber benefits.

Q.1:5   What is a staff model HMO?

In a staff model HMO, the participating physicians are HMO employees. The HMO typically pays the physicians on a salary basis, with bonus or incentive payments based on performance and profits. Staff models must employ physicians in all common specialties to offer a wide range of services. Staff models may, however, contract with nonemployee specialists whose services are needed on an infrequent basis. Staff model HMOs may be categorized as closed panel HMOs because physicians must be employees in order to participate; the panel is closed to community physicians.

Staff model physicians usually practice in one or a limited number of ambulatory care facilities. These facilities resemble outpatient clinics and contain physician offices and ancillary support facilities (e.g., laboratory and radiology) to support the health care needs of the HMO's beneficiaries. Staff model HMOs usually contract with hospitals and other inpatient facilities in the community to provide nonphysician services for beneficiaries.

Q.1:6   What are the advantages of the staff model HMO?

Advantages of the staff model HMO include:

- greater degree of control over physician practice patterns
- greater ability to manage and control utilization of health services
- convenience resulting from the provision of comprehensive services at one location

Q.1:7   What are the disadvantages of the staff model HMO?

Disadvantages of the staff model HMO include:

- cost of developing and implementing fixed salary expenses for staff physicians and support staff
- need to construct new ambulatory service facilities to expand services into new areas
- limited choice of participating physicians
- members may dislike outpatient clinic setting

Q.1:8   What is a group model HMO?

In a group model HMO, the HMO contracts with a multispecialty physician group practice. (See **Question 1:37** for definition of group practice.) Unlike the staff model HMO, the participating physicians are employed by the group practice and not by the HMO. Group practice physicians are responsible for providing health care services to the HMO's members. The group may contract on a flat-fee basis to provide physician services to HMO members, or the group may contract to provide services on a cost basis.

Group model HMOs are also closed panel HMOs because physicians must be members of the group practice to participate in the HMO. The HMO is closed to physicians who are not in the group.

Q.1:9   Are there different categories of group model HMOs?

Yes. There are two main categories.

1. *Captive group.* In this model, the physician group practice exists solely
   to provide services to the HMO's beneficiaries and does not provide
   services to patients who are not HMO members. The HMO may have
   recruited physicians to form the group practice in order to provide
   services to HMO members. Usually, the HMO provides administrative services to the group practice.
2. *Independent group model.* In this model, the HMO contracts with an
   existing independent multispecialty physician group to provide physician services to its members. The independent physician group
   may be the sponsor or owner of the HMO, as well as participating in
   other HMOs. Typically, the independent physician group continues
   to provide services to non-HMO members while it participates in the
   HMO. Even if the group has an exclusive relationship with the HMO,
   this relationship usually does not prevent the group from engaging
   in non-HMO business.

Q.1:10   What are the advantages of the group model HMO?

Advantages of the group model include:

- *Utilization management.* Utilization management is facilitated by the
  integration of physician practices and the provision of broad services
  at its facilities.
- *Reduced need for capital.* Since group model HMOs do not have to
  support the large fixed salary costs that staff models do, they may need
  less capital.

Q.1:11   What are the disadvantages of the group model HMO?

Disadvantages of the group model include:

- *Limited consumer choice.* Potential HMO members have a limited choice
  of participating physicians.
- *Restricted geographic access.* The limited number of office locations for
  participating medical groups restricts geographic coverage.
- *Clinic setting.* Some potential HMO members find the clinic setting
  undesirable.

Q.1:12   What is a network model HMO?

In a network model, the HMO contracts with more than one group practice to provide physician services to the HMO's members. (See **Question 1:37** for a definition of group practice.) In contrast to staff and group model HMOs, network models may be either closed or open panel plans. If the network model HMO is a closed panel plan, it will contract with only a limited number of existing group practices. If it is an open panel plan, participation in the group practices will be open to any physician who meets the HMO and group credentialing criteria. In some cases, network model HMOs will assist independent primary care physicians with the formation of primary care groups for the sole purpose of participating in the HMO's network.

Q.1:13   What are the advantages and disadvantages of the network model HMO?

The network model HMO has an advantage over the staff and group model HMOs in that broader physician participation allows it to offer a greater variety of providers. Network model HMOs possess many of the disadvantages associated with staff and group model HMOs. (See **Questions 1:7** and **1:11**, respectively.)

Q.1:14   What is an individual practice association (IPA) model HMO?

An individual practice association (IPA) model HMO contracts with an association of physicians—the IPA—to provide physician services to their members. (See **Question 1:36** for a definition of IPA.) The physicians remain individual practitioners, retain their separate offices and identities, and continue to see non-HMO patients. The physicians also maintain their own offices, medical records, and support staff. IPA model HMOs are open panel plans because participation is open to all community physicians who meet HMO and IPA selection criteria.

Generally, IPAs include physicians from all specialties. Broad participation of physicians allows the IPA to provide all necessary physician services through participating physicians and minimizes the need for its physicians to refer HMO members to nonparticipating physicians.

The HMO may contract with an IPA that has been established independently by community physicians. This type of IPA often has contracts with more than one HMO on a nonexclusive basis. The HMO may also work with community physicians to create an IPA, recruiting participating physicians. The HMO's contract with this type of IPA is usually on an exclusive basis because of the HMO's leading role in forming the IPA.

Q.1:15 Can hospital staff membership affect a physician's IPA eligibility?

Yes. In a community-wide IPA, physicians may participate without regard to the hospital in which they are affiliated. In a hospital-based IPA, however, physicians from only one or two hospitals are eligible to participate in the IPA. HMOs sometimes prefer this format because a hospital-based IPA can restrict its panel to physicians who are familiar with each other's practice patterns—familiarity that can make the utilization management process easier. In addition, an HMO can limit the impact of a termination of one of its IPA agreements to a smaller group of physicians by using several hospital-based IPAs.

Q.1:16 How does IPA model HMO compensation work?

Most HMOs compensate their IPAs on a flat-fee basis. The IPA then compensates its participating physicians on either a fee-for-service basis or a combination of fee for service and flat fees. In the fee-for-service variation, IPAs pay all their participating physicians on the basis of a fee schedule or a usual, customary, or reasonable (UCR) charge approach and withhold a portion of each payment for incentive and risk-sharing purposes.

Under the flat fee, or capitation approach, IPAs pay their participating primary care physicians a fixed amount per subscriber per month and pay their specialist physicians on the basis of a fee schedule or UCR. The primary care capitation payments vary, depending on factors such as HMO members' age and sex. The IPA typically withholds a portion of both the capitation and fee-for-service payments for risk sharing and incentive purposes.

Q.1:17 What are the advantages of the IPA model HMO?

Advantages of the IPA model HMO include:

- *Demand for less capital.* This type of HMO requires less capital to establish and operate than the staff, group, and network model HMOs.

- *Broad range of consumer choice.* Potential HMO members have a broad choice of participating physicians who practice in their private offices.

Q.1:18   What are the disadvantages of the IPA model HMO?

Disadvantages include:

- *Increased physician bargaining power.* The development of an IPA creates an organized forum for physicians to negotiate as a group with the HMO, a disadvantage from the HMO's perspective. The IPA offers the negotiating benefits of a group practice, while allowing individual physicians to contract directly with managed care plans. Physicians joined in IPAs are generally immune from antitrust restrictions on group activities because they accept combined risk through capitation payments.
- *Difficulty with utilization management.* The process of utilization management is generally more difficult in an IPA model HMO than in staff and group models because physicians remain individual practitioners with little sense of being a part of the HMO. As a result, IPA model HMOs may devote more administrative resources to managing inpatient and outpatient utilization than their staff and group model counterparts.

Q.1:19   What is a direct contract HMO?

Direct contract model HMOs contract directly with individual physicians to provide physician services to their members. With the exception of that relationship, direct contract model HMOs are similar to IPA model plans.

Direct contract model HMOs attempt to recruit broad panels of community physicians to provide physician services as participating providers. These HMOs usually recruit both primary care and specialist physicians and typically use a primary care case management approach (also known as a gatekeeper system).

Like IPA model plans, direct contract model HMOs compensate their physicians on either a fee-for-service or a primary care capitation basis. Primary care capitation is used somewhat more commonly by direct contract model HMOs because it helps limit the financial risk the HMO assumes. Unlike IPA model HMOs, direct contract models retain most of the financial risk for providing physician services; IPA model plans transfer this risk to their IPAs.

Q.1:20 What are the advantages of the direct contract model HMO?

Advantages of the direct contract model HMO include:

- *Broad range of consumer choice.* Potential HMO members have a broad choice of participating physicians who practice in private offices.
- *Reduction of physician bargaining potential.* Since the HMO contracts directly with individual physicians, physician bargaining power is dramatically reduced.

Q.1:21 What are the disadvantages of the direct contract model HMO?

Disadvantages include:

- *Additional risk exposure.* The direct contract model HMO assumes additional financial risk for physician services in comparison with the IPA model HMO. This additional risk exposure can be expensive if primary care physicians generate excessive referrals to specialist physicians.
- *Difficulty in recruiting physicians.* It can be more difficult and time consuming for a direct contract model HMO to recruit physicians because it lacks the physician leadership inherent in an IPA model plan. It is difficult for nonphysicians to recruit physicians, as several direct contract model HMOs have discovered in their attempts to expand into new markets.
- *Difficulty with utilization management.* Since all physician contact is on an individualized basis, utilization management may be more difficult in direct contract model HMOs. There also may be little incentive for physicians to participate in utilization management programs.

Q.1:22 What is a specialty HMO?

A specialty HMO provides care only within a specialized medical practice area. Specialty HMOs have developed in areas such as mental health and dental care as alternatives to traditional indemnity insurance. Specialty HMOs are not widespread, however, because most state HMO laws require a broad range of coverage.

Preferred Provider Organizations

Q.1:23 What is a preferred provider organization (PPO)?

Preferred provider organizations supply networks of health care providers to employer health benefit plans and health insurance carriers who wish to purchase health care services for covered beneficiaries. Typically, participating providers in PPOs agree to abide by utilization management and other procedures implemented by the PPO and to accept the PPO's reimbursement structure and payment levels. In return, PPOs often limit the size of their participating provider panels. Although PPO enrollees may usually seek care from providers outside the network, the PPO provides incentives for enrollees to use participating providers.

Q.1:24   How does a PPO differ from an HMO?

PPOs are less restrictive than HMOs. An HMO enrollee must choose a participating provider for health care to be covered. A PPO enrollee may choose a nonparticipating provider and still be covered, although individuals who receive health care services from nonparticipating providers pay higher levels of coinsurance or deductibles.

Q.1:25   What are the basic characteristics of a PPO?

The key characteristics of a PPO are:

- *Selected provider panel.* PPOs typically contract with selected providers in a community, including hospitals, physicians, and other diagnostic facilities. Providers are selected to participate on the basis of their cost efficiency, community reputation, and scope of services. Some PPOs assemble massive databases of information about potential providers, including costs by diagnostic category, before they make their contracting decisions.
- *Negotiated payment rates.* Most PPO participation agreements require participating providers to accept the PPO's payments as payment in full for covered services (except for applicable coinsurance or deductibles). Providers are willing to accept lower rates due to the increase in patient volume that PPO membership generates. PPOs attempt to negotiate payment rates that provide them with a competitive cost advantage relative to charge-based payment systems. These negotiated payment rates usually take the form of discounts from charges, all-inclusive per diem rates, or payments based on diagnosis-related groups.
- *Rapid payment terms.* Some PPOs are willing to include prompt payment features in their contracts with participating providers in return

for favorable payment rates. For example, a PPO may commit to pay all clean claims submitted by its providers within 15 days of submittal in return for an additional 5 percent discount from charges.

- *Utilization management*. Many PPOs implement utilization management programs to control the utilization and cost of health services provided to their covered beneficiaries. In the more sophisticated PPOs, these utilization management programs resemble those operated by HMOs.
- *Consumer choice*. Unlike traditional HMOs, PPOs generally allow covered beneficiaries to use non-PPO providers instead of PPO providers when they need health services. Higher levels of beneficiary cost sharing, often in the form of higher copayments, typically are imposed when PPO beneficiaries use non-PPO providers.

Q.1:26   Are there different PPO models?

Yes. The three basic PPO models are:

1. *Provider sponsored plans* are sponsored and promoted by health care providers. One or more hospitals or even a group of physicians may sponsor the plan. The sponsors may or may not be organized as a distinct legal entity.
2. *Carrier sponsored plans* involve the direct contracting of insurance companies with providers to provide health care services.
3. *Broker model plans* involve the use of independent companies that establish a network of health care providers and then provide insurance companies and self-insured employers with access to the network.

Q.1:27   What is a primary care PPO?

A primary care PPO, also known as a capitated PPO or a primary care network (PCN), has the following characteristics:

- Primary care physicians are reimbursed at a fixed rate per member per month (PMPM) or on another performance-based basis.
- There is often an amount withheld from physician compensation that is paid contingent upon achievement of utilization or cost targets.
- The primary care physician acts as a gatekeeper for referral and institutional medical services.

- The member retains some coverage for services provided that either are not authorized by the primary care physician or are delivered by nonparticipating providers. Such coverage typically is significantly lower than coverage for authorized services delivered by participating providers.

Q.1:28   What is a preferred provider arrangement (PPA)?

A PPO is sometimes referred to as a PPA. The definitions of the two terms are typically the same; however, the term PPA implies that PPO-type activities take place within an informal arrangement among providers and payers, rather than within a distinct organization.

Q.1:29   What is an exclusive provider organization (EPO)?

An EPO has a similar structure to that of a PPO. An EPO, however, does not have the element of consumer choice that a PPO does; EPO beneficiaries are required to receive all of their health care services from the provider panel. The EPO does not offer any coverage for services received from other providers.

Q.1:30   How does an EPO differ from an HMO?

Some EPOs are similar to HMOs in that they require a gatekeeper to authorize the use of a specialist. However, even if there is a gatekeeper arrangement, EPOs are regulated by insurance laws rather than federal and state HMO laws.

Q.1:31   What are the advantages and disadvantages of an EPO?

An EPO has the advantage of cost saving and is generally implemented by an employer. On the other hand, an EPO has the disadvantage of lack of enrollee choice. Due to the restriction on consumer choice, few employers implement an EPO as their sole health care benefits program.

Point-of-Service Plans

Q.1:32   What is a point-of-service (POS) plan?

A POS plan is a hybrid plan. POS enrollees belong to both an HMO and a traditional indemnity insurance plan. Enrollees may choose whether to seek care within the HMO or to opt out when it becomes necessary to receive health care services—at the point of service. Enrollees may choose a different provider each time health care is needed. Thus, POS plans are sometimes called open ended HMOs, swing-out HMOs, self-referral options, and multiple option plans. Some POS plans require that certain services, such as eye care, dental care, and prenatal care be obtained from the provider panel.

Although a PPO allows enrollees to select a participating or outside provider at the point of service, the term *point of service* usually refers to plans with an HMO feature.

Q.1:33 What is a dual-option POS plan?

A dual-option POS plan offers subscribers a choice between an HMO (or HMO-like) plan and an indemnity plan at the point of service. The indemnity coverage typically incorporates higher deductibles and coinsurance to encourage members to use HMO services.

Q.1:34 What is a triple-option POS plan?

Triple-option POS plan enrollees may choose to receive health care under any of the following coverage types at the point of service:

- HMO
- PPO
- indemnity plan

Typically, the HMO option offers the highest reimbursement, and indemnity offers the least.

Q.1:35 What are the advantages and disadvantages of a POS plan?

POS plans have the advantage of offering more consumer choice. On the other hand, due to the wide variety of services offered, costs are higher. There is also some uncertainty with regard to the regulatory requirements for POS plans, since some plans are regulated by state insurance laws, while others are regulated by HMO laws. Some states require entities that offer POS plans to have both an HMO and an insurance license.

Provider Group Formations

Q.1:36   What is an independent practice association (IPA)?

An IPA is a legal entity composed of physicians organized for the purpose of negotiating contracts to provide physician services to health plan subscribers. For example, an IPA might contract with an HMO to provide medical services to HMO members. IPA members may be compensated by health plans on either a capitated or fee-for-service basis, depending on the type of plan. The physicians maintain their own private practices and do not share services such as claims, billing, scheduling, and accounting.

Q.1:37   What is a group practice?

A group practice is a physician group that is completely integrated economically. The physicians, organized as a professional organization, share costs and revenues and work at one or a limited number of locations. The physicians also share facilities, equipment, medical records, and support staff. Group practices usually focus on either primary or specialty care.

Q.1:38   What is a group practice without walls (GPWW)?

A group practice without walls, also known as a clinic without walls (CWW), is a single legal entity consisting of a group of physicians. Although the physicians share administrative and management costs, they maintain their own practice locations instead of working together in a group environment.

Not all GPWWs are integrated to the same extent. Less integrated models resemble IPAs, with physicians sharing administrative services, but maintaining separate billing. In more integrated GPWWs, the legal entity may employ the physicians, purchase certain assets from the individual practices, or set compensation schedules.

Q.1:39   What is a management services organization (MSO)?

An MSO, sometimes called a medical service organization or a management services bureau (MSB), is a corporation that provides management and administrative services to physicians or physician groups or other affiliated providers, such as a hospital. Although the MSO provides office space, equipment, personnel, and administrative services, the physician continues to own and manage clinical aspects of the practice. The MSO may be hospital affiliated, a hospital–physician joint venture, physician owned, or investor owned. The organization performs services such as practice management, marketing, managed care contracting, recruitment, contracting management information system (MIS) development, purchasing, facilities development, accounting, billing, and personnel management. Sometimes an MSO even provides capital to enable physicians to expand their practices.

Q.1:40 What are the advantages of an MSO?

The advantages of an MSO can be numerous. The primary reason for the development of an MSO is access to managed care plans. An MSO can aggregate physician participation for managed care contracting. In addition, it can improve practice efficiencies by conducting utilization review.

Further, the MSO provides physicians with the benefits of a medical group but allows them to retain their independence.

An MSO is useful in physician recruitment because physicians can contract with the MSO to run their practice. The costs of opening and operating a medical practice also can be made more certain.

An MSO can also be a first step toward an integrated delivery system. An MSO that initially provides limited services to a few physicians may grow in terms of both the range of services and the number of physicians served [Paul R. DeMuro, *Management Services Organizations*, TOPICS IN HEALTH CARE FINANCING, Spring 1994, at 19–27].

Q.1:41 What organizational forms might an MSO take?

An MSO may take several forms:

- *Freestanding.* This type of MSO might be developed by a group of private individuals, including physicians and other investors.
- *Hospital-affiliated.* A hospital-affiliated MSO might be an MSO that the hospital owns as a for-profit subsidiary.
- *Physician-affiliated.* This type of MSO might be owned by a group of physicians.

- *Joint venture.* An example of a joint venture MSO is one partially owned by a hospital or hospitals and physicians or physician groups.
- *HMO-affiliated.* An MSO owned by an HMO falls into this category [Paul R. DeMuro, *Management Services Organizations*, TOPICS IN HEALTH CARE FINANCING, Spring 1994, at 19–27].

Q.1:42   What is an integrated delivery system (IDS)?

IDS, integrated health care system (IHS), community care network (CCN), and organized system of care (OSC) are terms encompassing the types of managed care organizations that offer a full continuum of care. While a basic IDS provides at least physician and hospital services to patients, more sophisticated systems provide additional services, such as home health, hospice, skilled nursing, preventive medicine, mental health, rehabilitation, and long-term care.

Thus, the term IDS may be used to describe the following types of MCOs, among others:

- PHO (See **Question 1:44** for a definition of PHO.)
- hospital affiliated with an IPA or group practice
- medical foundation affiliated with a hospital (See **Question 1:46** for a definition of medical foundation.)

Q.1:43   What are the advantages of an IDS?

Each type of IDS has its particular advantages, as discussed in the following sections. Generally, an MCO that offers both physician and hospital services has greater influence over payers, provides more efficient health care, and has more capital than a physician group or single provider.

Q.1:44   What is a physician–hospital organization (PHO)?

A PHO, sometimes called a medical staff–hospital organization (MeSH), is a joint venture between a hospital and a number of physicians. It is formed to facilitate managed care contracting with managed care plans and employers and to improve cost management and services.

PHOs vary in their structure. A PHO may contract with an individual physician or it may contract with a physician group, such as an individual practice association (IPA). An open panel PHO contracts with a hospital's entire physician staff, while a closed panel PHO employs its own credentialing criteria. Physicians usually retain their individual practices.

The most successful PHOs are those in which the physicians own 50 percent of the entity and the hospital owns the other 50 percent, and each group has an equal voice, although this arrangement may present problems regarding tax-exempt status of nonprofit hospitals.

PHO activities include utilization review, quality assurance, physician credentialing, and the development of fee schedules. Due to physician referrals, fraud and abuse issues often arise in the area of PHOs. Antitrust issues are also common. (The topics of fraud and abuse, and antitrust, are discussed in depth in **Chapter 9** and **Chapter 3**, respectively.)

Q.1:45 What is the difference between a PHO and an MSO?

In a PHO arrangement, the PHO itself, rather than physicians, contracts with the HMOs. In an MSO, the physician or physician group and not the MSO contracts with the payers. The MSO assumes full risk for the practice between the physician group and the MSO owners.

Q.1:46 What is a medical foundation?

A medical foundation, also known as a foundation for medical care (FMC), is a corporation that owns and operates entire physician practices. A medical foundation may be a hospital affiliate or subsidiary that contracts with a physician group to provide medical services. Some commentators prefer the terms *physician–hospital organization* or *integrated delivery system* for foundations affiliated with a hospital.

The foundation owns the facilities, equipment, clinical assets, and supplies that the physician group uses. The foundation also hires all nonphysician personnel and manages nonclinical services such as billing and purchasing. Medical foundations may also conduct utilization review and peer review.

There are at least three types of medical foundations:

- The freestanding medical foundation is not hospital or system owned, although it may have close clinical and contractual links with a hospital or system. Freestanding medical foundations are tax-exempt organizations that often have a strong research and education purpose.
- The hospital-affiliated tax-exempt clinic is an affiliate of the hospital or health system. Affiliation may be for managed care contracting or

other shared purposes, for example, to provide a primary care base or operate an ambulatory care center.

• The hospital-owned medical foundation may directly own the medical foundation as a subsidiary. This model provides for greater control of the medical group practice through the professional services arrangement [Russell C. Coile, Jr., *Year 2000 Scenario for Physician–Hospital Organizations*, TOPICS IN HEALTH CARE FINANCING, Summer 1994, at 75–83].

Q.1:47 Why is a foundation attractive to physicians?

A foundation is attractive to physicians for several reasons. A tax-exempt medical foundation has access to capital through its affiliated hospital, does not pay property and income taxes, and may receive tax-deductible donations. Thus, the foundation offers physicians more capital, and more reliable incomes, than would be available in other group formations. Additionally, when the physician group sells its practice assets to the foundation, physician owners may make a sizable gain on the sale of their assets. Because the foundation administers the physician's practice, the physician is relieved of paperwork and may concentrate on practicing medicine. Finally, through the foundation's hospital affiliation, physicians may have access to the hospital's contracts and increased leverage with payers [Robert A. Waterman, *Nonprofit Medical Care Foundations*, TOPICS IN HEALTH CARE FINANCING, Spring 1994, at 13–18].

Q.1:48 Why is a foundation attractive to hospitals?

Many hospitals face intense competition, focused on obtaining or keeping managed care contracts. A hospital affiliated with a medical foundation may be more appealing to payers due to its size, stability, and visibility in the community. Second, the foundation, not the hospital, owns the payer contracts. Thus, even if some members of the group leave, the foundation can retain the contracts and much of the business. Third, the nonprofit foundation may perform research and charitable activities, contributing to the charitable mission of the tax-exempt hospital. Fourth, the foundation model facilitates cooperation between the hospital and physicians. Finally, a hospital with an affiliated physician group that guarantees employment may improve recruiting of physicians [Robert A. Waterman, *Nonprofit Medical Care Foundations*, TOPICS IN HEALTH CARE FINANCING, Spring 1994, at 13–18].

Q.1:49 What is an integrated health organization (IHO)?

An IHO is a type of IDS that operates as a single organization. An IHO contracts with payers to provide comprehensive health services to patients. The organization employs all staff members, enters into all payer contracts, owns or leases all assets, collects all revenue, and assumes all responsibility for providing health care services.

Q.1:50 What is a limited liability company (LLC)?

An LLC is a form of business organization that is becoming a favored legal format for health care entities. Its basic characteristic is that it provides the owners of a business entity the same protection from liability that a corporation affords its stockholders, while also treating the owners as partners for purposes of federal and state income tax.

Operationally, the LLC most resembles a partnership. The partners or owners are referred to as members in many state statutes. Under state law, the authority of the members may be the same as in a general partnership, in that each member is an agent of the LLC and has the authority to bind the LLC to contracts. In many states, however, the LLC may include a limitation statement in its organizing documents that indicates to third parties that the members do not have the authority to bind the LLC. Although state statutes also vary in the scope of the limitations possible for the liability of members, this limitation is the cornerstone of the LLC concept [Martha Nathanson, *Home Health Care Answer Book: Legal Issues for Providers* (Gaithersburg, MD: Aspen Publishers, Inc., 1995)].

OTHER ENTITIES IN THE MANAGED CARE ARENA

Q.1:51 What is a utilization management firm?

A utilization management firm, sometimes called a utilization review organization (URO), is an organization that contracts with managed care organizations and performs utilization review for them toward the goal of reducing health care expenditures. The firm evaluates the efficiency, necessity, and appropriateness of health care services by reviewing admission rates, provided services, lengths of stay, and referrals to specialists. Refer to Chapter 5 for an extensive discussion of this subject.

Q.1:52   What is a case management firm?

Employers and insurers contract with case management firms to reduce the cost of potentially expensive health care by coordinating a patient's care. The firm identifies cases that will become catastrophic, negotiates services and reimbursement with providers who can treat the patient's condition, develops a treatment protocol for the patient, and monitors the treatment.

Q.1:53   What is a third party administrator (TPA)?

A TPA is a firm that contracts with managed care organizations to perform administrative services, such as claims processing and membership services.

2

Overview of Laws Applicable to Managed Care

Managed care organizations (MCOs) are hybrids, performing functions that were once divided between health care providers and insurers. As a result, MCOs must be familiar with laws and regulations that apply to health care providers, as well as laws directed at insurers. Both the health care and insurance industries are heavily regulated by federal, state, and local governments, creating an onerous burden for MCOs. In addition, legislatures are focusing on MCOs, enacting laws directed specifically at preferred provider organizations (PPOs) and health maintenance organizations (HMOs), for example.

Because managed care regulation is dynamic, it is not possible to provide an exhaustive discussion of federal and state legislation. Rather, this chapter illustrates the breadth of regulation applicable to MCOs.

FEDERAL LAW

Q.2:1 What areas of federal law affect managed care?

Implementing a managed care program requires familiarity with many areas of federal regulation. Important areas of compliance include:

- employment laws (see **Question 2:2**)
- laws governing business relationships (see **Question 2:3**)
- regulation of health care services (see **Question 2:4**)
- benefits law (see **Question 2:5**)
- tax laws (see **Question 2:6**)
- laws directed at MCOs (see **Questions 2:7–2:9**)

Q.2:2   How do federal employment laws affect MCOs?

Like every employer, a managed care organization must comply with federal employment laws. Currently, no major aspect of the employment relationship is free from detailed federal regulation. Federal labor laws fall into three main categories:

1. Equal employment laws deal with employment discrimination on the basis of race, color, religion, national origin, age, sex, disability, and sexual orientation.
2. Labor standards laws establish minimum standards that employers must maintain with respect to working conditions. The principal laws in this field deal with minimum wages, maximum hours, equal pay for equal work, child labor, and safety and health.
3. Labor relations laws establish the rights and duties of employers, unions, and employees in relationship to each other; they are sometimes called labor-management or collective bargaining laws.

Detailed federal regulations, issued primarily by the Equal Employment Opportunity Commission and the National Labor Relations Board, outline employers' rights and duties under these laws. Employers that fail to comply may be subject to agency enforcement, private lawsuits, or both.

Q.2:3   How do federal laws restrict business relationships between MCOs?

As MCOs continue to experiment with new relationships between health care providers and other entities, MCOs must contend with long-standing federal rules that restrict these relationships as follows:

- *Antitrust laws.* The purpose of antitrust laws, simply stated, is to engender competition by prohibiting monopolies and other restrictive trade practices. This purpose is in conflict with a basic premise of managed care—that coordination between health care providers can provide high quality, cost-effective care. Thus, MCOs should carefully examine the antitrust ramifications before entering into relationships with providers or other MCOs. The three most important federal antitrust statutes are the Sherman Act, the Clayton Act, and the Federal Trade Commission (FTC) Act. (See **Chapter 3** for a detailed discussion of antitrust law.)

- *Fraud and abuse laws.* Fraud and abuse refers to legislation directed at curtailing improper conduct that increases Medicare and Medicaid costs. For MCOs, there are two types of fraud and abuse provisions that are particularly important: (1) Medicare and Medicaid antikickback legislation, and (2) physician self-referral restrictions. These federal prohibitions examine whether the purpose of a managed care arrangement is to enhance revenues, rather than provide needed services. (See **Chapter 9** for a complete discussion of fraud and abuse.)

Q.2:4   What are some examples of health care services regulated by the federal government?

Nearly every aspect of health care services is regulated. Laboratories must meet testing standards; pharmacies must comply with controlled substance laws; and medical waste must be properly disposed. Health care providers that participate in Medicare or Medicaid are subject to a detailed federal regulatory scheme with far-reaching effects. MCOs are subject to the same restrictions on health care delivery that traditional health care providers must follow.

Q.2:5   What federal benefits law affects managed care plan administration?

The Employee Retirement Income Security Act (ERISA) is an important, but easily overlooked, source of federal regulation of managed care plans. ERISA applies to activities involving the sponsorship, administration, and servicing of employee health benefit plans, including managed care plans. The statute establishes responsibilities for certain health benefit plan administrators, known as fiduciaries, and outlines claims review procedures. Perhaps most important to managed care plans, however, ERISA shields plans from certain types of liability by superseding state laws that relate to employee benefit plans. (See **Chapter 5** for more information on ERISA.)

Q.2:6   What important federal tax issues should MCOs be alert to?

The tax exemptions traditionally enjoyed by many nonprofit health care providers may be in jeopardy due to private inurement, hospital–physician relationships, compensation arrangements, or unrelated business income. Further, federal tax law may provide exemptions for specific types of organizations, such as HMOs, integrated delivery systems, and independent practice associations (IPAs). MCOs should carefully consider tax-exempt status when implementing a network. (See **Chapter 10** for a detailed explanation of federal tax issues for tax-exempt organizations.)

Q.2:7   What federal regulatory scheme is directed at MCOs?

The federal HMO Act, introduced in 1973, was intended to foster the growth of HMOs, which were considered to be a cost-effective method of health care delivery. The HMO Act establishes a system for federal qualification, which is entirely voluntary. In order to be federally qualified, an HMO must meet federal standards for legal and organizational status, financial viability, marketing, and health service delivery systems, as delineated in the federal HMO Act and its implementing regulations [42 U.S.C. § 300e *et seq*].

Federally qualified HMOs must also provide or arrange for basic necessary health services for their members without limitation as to time, cost, frequency, extent, or kind of services actually provided.

Q.2:8   Why do HMOs seek federal qualification?

Advantages of federal qualification include:

- credibility with employers due to the federal approval;
- the advantage gained by the dual choice mandate, which requires certain employers to offer an HMO option to employees if a federally qualified HMO approaches the employer (although this provision ends in 1995);
- a shortened Medicare risk-contracting process; and
- exemption from certain restrictive state laws.

Q.2:9   Are there drawbacks to federal qualification for an HMO?

Disadvantages of federal qualification include:

- the fee requirement to become federally qualified;
- the requirement to offer certain benefits, making federally qualified HMOs less flexible than state-regulated HMOs; and
- inflexible premium rates.

STATE LAW

Q.2:10   What aspects of managed care do state laws regulate?

- *Employment law.* In addition to federal employment laws, MCOs must comply with state regulation of discrimination, wages, hours, and other employment matters.
- *Contract law.* Contract law, which governs written agreements between individuals and/or entities, has developed at the state level. Contract disputes between providers and MCOs, subscribers and MCOs, and employers and MCOs are heard in state courts, in accordance with state case law. (Refer to **Chapter 7** for a discussion of contract negotiation and typical MCO–provider contract terms.)
- *Regulation of health care services.* Health care is heavily regulated by state governments as well. State licensure requirements impose detailed requirements in areas such as facilities, recordkeeping, and provider qualifications. States have also enacted laws in specific practice areas, such as organ donation and HIV testing.
- *Laws directed at MCOs.* States have responded to the integration of providers and payers more quickly than the federal government. Because HMOs were prevalent at the onset of managed care, most states have passed "HMO Acts" with requirements in diverse areas. (See **Question 2:12**, **Appendix 2-A**, and **Appendix C**.) States have also enacted laws directly regulating PPOs. (See **Questions 2:13–2:16**, **Appendix 2-B**, and **Appendix B**.) Most state legislatures have addressed utilization review, a process integral to managed care. (See **Chapter 4** on utilization review.)
- *Insurance laws.* Because a managed care plan may fall within the regulatory definition of *insurer*, managed care entities must be familiar with state insurance laws. For example, insurance laws may mandate coverage for particular medical procedures, establish standards for claims review, regulate subscriber eligibility, and constrain physician selection criteria.

Q.2:11   What should an MCO do when state and federal law regulate the same activity?

When state and federal law regulate the same activity, state law often imposes a higher standard. In that case, compliance with the higher state standard also satisfies federal law. When state and federal laws are in conflict, however, the general rule is that the federal law supersedes, or pre-empts the state law. When faced with a conflict, managed care administrators should consult an attorney. (See **Chapter 5** for a more detailed discussion of how one federal statute pre-empts state law.)

Q.2:12   What activities do state HMO laws restrict?

Although laws vary between states (see **Appendix 2-A**), the following list illustrates the variety of subjects covered by state HMO Acts:

- entities authorized to operate HMOs
- governing body composition
- mandatory health services
- financial stability
- contracts between HMOs and providers
- enrollee participation in HMO policy making
- coverage information that must be disclosed to subscribers
- enrollment periods
- termination of subscribers
- continuation of benefits
- grievance procedures
- quality assurance
- utilization review
- maintenance and confidentiality of medical records
- rate setting
- advertising and solicitation
- HMO investing
- acquisitions and mergers
- reporting of financial and operational information
- inspections by state regulators

See **Appendix C** for an example of an HMO act.

Q.2:13   What are some examples of state PPO legislation?

Although PPOs are not regulated to the same extent that HMOs typically are, many states (see **Appendix 2-B**) have enacted a few important limitations on PPOs as follows:

- any willing provider (AWP) laws
- freedom of choice laws
- fair reimbursement laws

Q.2:14   What is an AWP law?

An AWP law requires MCOs to allow any provider who meets the terms and conditions of the managed care plan to participate in the plan. AWP laws have been characterized as anti-PPO laws because they can severely limit PPOs' ability to provide cost-effective care by restricting care networks to a small number of health care providers. (See **Appendix A** for a state-by-state discussion of AWP laws.)

Q.2:15   What is a freedom of choice law?

A freedom of choice law focuses on subscribers rather than providers, but serves the same end as an AWP law—opening PPO networks to nonpreferred providers. Freedom of choice laws enable PPO subscribers to self-refer to nonpreferred providers. For example, a health plan subscriber in a freedom of choice state could select a nonparticipating provider and pay no additional copayment or penalty, as long as the provider accepts the plan's preferred provider reimbursement rate. Managed care proponents argue that freedom of choice laws interfere with PPOs' ability to assure quality care and negotiate for discounted services. (See **Appendix A** for a state-by-state description of freedom of choice laws.)

Q.2:16   How does a fair reimbursement law impact PPOs?

Some states have passed laws that limit the price differential that PPOs typically establish between in-network and out-of-network health services. The law may limit the differential to 20 percent, for example, or may prohibit differential payments altogether. These laws limit PPOs' ability to offer incentives to subscribers to seek care within the network.

Q.2:17   What are mandated benefits?

Many states have enacted laws that require insurers and MCOs to provide coverage for specific treatments. Legislators generally mandate benefits in response to public demand for treatments not yet judged by payers to be safe and effective. For example, states have mandated coverage for high-dose chemotherapy in conjunction with autologous bone marrow transplant as a treatment for breast cancer, as well as for other unapproved cancer therapies.

Appendix 2-A

State-by-State List of HMO Laws

The date in parentheses is the effective date of the legislation or regulation, with latest amendments.

	Model/Similar Legis.	Related Legis./Regs.
Alabama	Ala. Code §§ 27-21A-1 to 27-21A-32 (1986).	
Alaska	Alaska Stat. §§ 21-86.010 to 21.86.900 (1990).	
Arizona		Ariz. Rev. Stat. Ann. §§ 20-1051 to 20-1069 (1973/1990) (``Health Care Service Organizations'').
Arkansas	Ark. Stat. Ann. §§ 23-76-101 to 23-76-130 (1975/1987).	
California		Cal. Health & Safety Code §§ 1340 to 1399.64 (1979/1992) (``Knox-Keene Health Care Services Plan''); §§ 1374.60 to 1374.71 (1993) (point-of-service plans).
Colorado	Colo. Rev. Stat. §§ 10-16-401 to 10-16-428 (1992).	
Connecticut		Conn. Gen. Stat. §§ 33-179a to 33-179t (1971/1990) ``Health Care Centers.''
Delaware		Del. Code Ann. tit. 16 §§ 9101 to 9115 (1982); See also: tit. 18 §§ 6401 to 6406 (1987) (Dept. of Public Health).

Source: Reprinted with permission from Model Health Maintenance Organization Model Act, National Association of Insurance Commissioners, copyright 1994, 1995.

D.C.	No Action to Date	
Florida		Fla. Stat. §§ 641.17 to 641.3921 (1985/1991).
Georgia	Ga. Code Ann. §§ 33-21-1 to 33-21-28 (1979/1986).	
Guam	No Action to Date	
Hawaii	No Action to Date	
Idaho		Idaho Code §§ 41-3901 to 41-3934 (1974/1985).
Illinois	215 Ill. Comp. Stat. 125/1-2 to 125/6-19 (1974/1994).	
Indiana	Ind. Code §§ 27-13-1-1 to 27-13-33-2 (1994).	Ind. Code §§ 27-8-7-1 to 27-8-7-18 (1979/1987) (``Proposed Health Care Delivery Plans'') (repealed eff. 7-1-95).
Iowa	Iowa Code §§ 514B.1 to 514B.32 (1973).	
Kansas	Kan. Stat. Ann. §§ 40-3201 to 40-3227 (1974/1991).	
Kentucky		Ky. Rev. Stat. §§ 304.38-010 to 304.38-210 (1982/1990).
Louisiana	La. Rev. Stat. Ann §§ 22:2001 to 22:2026 (1986/1989).	
Maine	Me. Rev. Stat. Ann. tit. 24-A §§ 4201 to 4226 (1975/1994).	Me. Rev. Stat. Ann. tit. 24-A §§ 4202-A, 4204-A, 4207-A (1992) (point-of-service provisions).
Maryland		Md. Ann. Code art. 19 §§ 701 to 734 (1982/1993) (Health Code).
Massachusetts		Mass. Gen. Laws ch. 176G §§ 1 to 17 (1976/1986).
Michigan		Mich. Comp. Laws §§ 333.21001 to 333.21098 (1982/1990) (Public Health Code).
Minnesota	Minn. Stat. §§ 62D.01 to 62D.30 (1973/1988) (Dept. of Health).	
Mississippi	Miss. Code Ann. § 41-7-401 et seq. (1986/1994) (Dept. of Health).	
Missouri	Mo. Rev. Stat. §§ 354.400 to 354.550 (1983).	
Montana	Mont. Code Ann. §§ 33-31-101 to 33-31-405 (1987/1991).	
Nebraska	Neb. Rev. Stat. §§ 44-3292 to 44-32,180 (1990).	
Nevada		Nev. Rev. Stat. §§ 695C.010 to 695C.350 (1973/1991).

New Hampshire		N.H. Rev. Stat. Ann. §§ 420-B:1 to 420-B:22 (1977/1990).
New Jersey	N.J. Rev. Stat. §§ 26:2J-1 to 26:2J-30 (1973) (Dept. of Health).	
New Mexico	N.M. Stat. Ann. §§ 59A-46-1 to 59A-46-32 (1985/1994).	
New York		N.Y. Pub. Health Law §§ 4400 to 4413 (1976/1987).
North Carolina	N.C. Gen. Stat. §§ 58-67-1 to 58-67-185 (1979/1992).	N.C. Admin. Code tit. 11 ch. .1401 to .1404 (1994) (point of service).
North Dakota	N.D. Cent. Code §§ 26.1-18.1-01 to 26.1-18.1-25 (1993).	
Ohio	Ohio Rev. Code Ann. §§ 1742.01 to 1742.39 (1976/1991).	
Oklahoma		Okla. Stat. tit. 63 §§ 2501 to 2510 (1975/1988) (Dept. of Public Health).
Oregon		Or. Rev. Stat. §§ 750.003 to 750.075 (1985).
Pennsylvania		40 Pa. Cons. Stat. §§ 1551 to 1567 (1981); *See also*: Pa. Admin. Code tit. 31 §§ 301.201 to 301.204 (statement of policy on point of service).
Puerto Rico		P.R. Laws Ann. tit. 26 §§ 1901 to 1927.
Rhode Island	R.I. Gen. Laws §§ 27-41-1 to 27-41-34 (1983/1991).	
South Carolina	S.C. Code Ann. §§ 38-33-10 to 38-33-300 (1988/1991).	
South Dakota		S.D. Codified Laws Ann. §§ 58-41-1 to 58-41-97 (1974).
Tennessee	Tenn. Code Ann. §§ 56-32-201 to 56-32-225 (1986/1987).	
Texas	Tex. Ins. Code Ann. art. 20A.01 to 20A.35 (1975/1989).	
Utah		Utah Code Ann. §§ 31A-8-101 to 31A-8-408 (1986/1991) (includes point-of-service provision).
Vermont	Vt. Stat. Ann. tit. 8 §§ 5101 to 5113 (1979/1993) (Most of model).	
Virgin Islands	No Action to Date	
Virginia	Va. Code §§ 38.2-4300 to 38.2-4821 (1986/1990).	
Washington		Wash. Rev. Code Ann. §§ 48.46.010 to 48.46.920 (1975/1990) (parts of model).

West Virginia	W.Va. Code §§ 33-25A-1 to 33-25A-29 (1977/1991).	
Wisconsin		Wis. Stat. §§ 609.91 to 609.98 (1985/1989); *See also*: § 628-36 (2m) providing that Commissioner may make rules for HMOs.
Wyoming	Wyo. Stat. §§ 26-34-101 to 26-34-128 (1986).	

Appendix 2-B

State-by-State List of PPO Laws

The date in parentheses is the effective date of the legislation or regulation, with latest amendments.

	Model/Similar Legis.	Related Legis./Regs.
Alabama	No Action to Date	
Alaska	No Action to Date	
Arizona	No Action to Date	
Arkansas	Bulletins 9-85 and 9-85A (1985).	
California		Cal. Ins. Code §§ 10133 to 10133.5, 10180, 742, 10402 to 10402.1 (1983); *See also:* Cal. Admin. Code tit. 10 §§ 2240 to 2240.4 (1984).
Colorado	No Action to Date	
Connecticut	No Action to Date	
Delaware	No Action to Date	
D.C.	No Action to Date	
Florida		Fla. Stat. §§ 627.6471 to 627.6473 (1992).
Georgia	Ga. Code Ann. §§ 33-30-20 to 33-30-27 (1988/1992)	*See also:* Ga. Admin. Comp. Ch. 120-2-44 (1989).
Guam	No Action to Date	
Hawaii	No Action to Date	
Idaho	No Action to Date	
Illinois		215 Ill. Comp. Stats. 5/370f to 5/370q (1984/1987).
Indiana		Ind. Code §§ 27-8-11-1 to 27-8-11-5 (1984/1988).
Iowa	Iowa Admin. Code §§ 191-27.1 to 191-27.7 (1991).	

Source: Reprinted with permission from Preferred Provider Model Arrangements Act, National Association of Insurance Commissioners, copyright 1993.

Kansas	No Action to Date	
Kentucky		806 Ky. Admin. Regs. 18:020 (1986).
Louisiana		La. Rev. Stat. Ann. §§ 40:2201 to 40:2205.
Maine		Me. Rev. Stat. Ann. tit. 24-A §§ 2333 to 2340; 2670 to 2678 (1986/1987); Me. Ins. Reg. ch. 360 (1990).
Maryland		Md. Ann. Code art. 50 §§ 655 to 660 (1990).
Massachusetts	Mass. Gen. Laws ch. 176I (1989).	*See also*: 211 Code of Mass. Reg. 51.01 to 51.16 (1989).
Michigan		Mich. Comp. Laws §§ 500.3405, 500.3631, 500.3709 (1984/1989).
Minnesota		Minn. Stat. § 62E.101 (1991).
Mississippi	No Action to Date	
Missouri	No Action to Date	
Montana	Mont. Code Ann. §§ 33-22-1701 to 33-22-1707 (1987/1993).	
Nebraska		Neb. Rev. Stat. § 44-4101 to 4113 (1984/1990).
Nevada		Nev. Rev. Stat. § 689B.061 (1987); Nev. Admin. Code §§ 689B.110 to 689B.210 (1990/1992).
New Hampshire		N.H. Rev. Stat. Ann. §§ 420-C:1 to 420-C:7 (1987).
New Jersey	No Action to Date	
New Mexico	N.M. Stat. Ann. §§ 59A-22A-1 to 59A-22A-7 (1993).	
New York		See N.Y. Bulletin (May 1987).
North Carolina		N.C. Gen. Stat. §§ 58-50-50 to 58-50-55 (1985/1987).
North Dakota	N.D. Cent. Code §§ 26.1-47-01 to 26.1-47-07 (1987).	
Ohio	No Action to Date	
Oklahoma	No Action to Date	
Oregon		Or. Rev. Stat. § 743.531 (1985/1989).
Pennsylvania		Pa. Admin. Code tit. 31 §§ 152.1 to 152.25 (1987).
Puerto Rico	No Action to Date	
Rhode Island	No Action to Date	
South Carolina	No Action to Date	
South Dakota	No Action to Date	
Tennessee	No Action to Date	
Texas		Tex. Admin. Code §§ 3.3701 to 3.3705 (1986/1990).

Utah		Utah Code Ann. §§ 31A-22-617 to 31A-22-618 (1985).
Vermont	No Action to Date	
Virgin Islands	No Action to Date	
Virginia		Va. Code §§ 38.2-3407, 38.2-4209 (1986).
Washington	No Action to Date	
West Virginia	No Action to Date	
Wisconsin		Wis. Stat. § 609.20 (1985); § 628.36(2)(a) (1975/1992); *See also:* Wis. Admin. Code § INS 3.48 (1986/1990).
Wyoming		Wyo. Stat. § 26-22-503 (1985/1990).

3

Antitrust Laws Relevant to Managed Care

FEDERAL ANTITRUST LAWS

Q.3:1   Is health care antitrust enforcement regulated at the state or federal level?

The managed health care industry is regulated by both federal and state antitrust laws. A majority of the state laws mirror the relevant federal statutes (see **Questions 3:11–3:14** on state law).

Q.3:2   What major federal antitrust laws are applicable to the health care industry?

There are three principal federal antitrust statutes applicable to the health care industry: the Sherman Act [15 U.S.C. §§ 1 & 2], the Clayton Act [15 U.S.C. §§ 13-19], and the Federal Trade Commission Act [15 U.S.C. § 45]. Also relevant are amendments to the Clayton Act: the Robinson–Patman Act [15 U.S.C. § 13(a)], which prohibits certain practices that result in discriminatory pricing, and the Celler–Kefauver Act [15 U.S.C. § 18] relating to the Clayton Act's provisions concerning corporate mergers.

Q.3:3   What sort of activity is prohibited by the Sherman Act?

The Sherman Act prohibits concerted actions that constitute unreasonable restraints of trade. Section 1 of the Sherman Act provides:

> [E]very contract, combination in the form of trust or otherwise, or conspiracy, in restraint of trade or commerce among the several States, or with foreign nations, is hereby declared to be illegal.

Monopolization and attempted monopolization also are prohibited by the Sherman Act. Section 2 of the Sherman Act provides:

> Every person who shall monopolize, or attempt to monopolize, or combine or conspire with any other person or persons, to monopolize any part of the trade or commerce among the several States, or with foreign nations, shall be deemed guilty of a felony.

Q.3:4   What are the elements of restraint of trade under the Sherman Act?

The elements of restraint of trade under Section 1 of the Sherman Act are: (1) a concerted action by distinct entities (2) that has an unreasonably anticompetitive effect (3) on interstate commerce.

Q.3:5   What are the elements of monopolization under the Sherman Act?

The elements of monopolization under Section 2 of the Sherman Act are:

- market power, generally defined as the power to control prices or exclude competition in a given market; a proxy for market power is a market share of at least 50 percent; and
- willful acquisition or maintenance of that power as distinguished from growth or development arising from a superior product, business acumen, or historic accident.

Q.3:6   What are the elements of attempted monopolization under the Sherman Act?

The elements of attempted monopolization under Section 2 of the Sherman Act are to: (1) intend to monopolize, (2) act in furtherance of that intent, and (3) have a dangerous probability of success (market share greater than 35 percent).

Q.3:7   What sort of activity is prohibited by the Clayton Act?

The Clayton Act addresses specific practices of single entities that would tend to lessen competition or create a monopoly. Section 3 [15 U.S.C. § 14] prohibits exclusive dealing arrangements, tying sales, and requirement contracts involving the sale of commodities, where the effect may be to substantially lessen competition. Section 7 [15 U.S.C. § 18] prohibits mergers, joint ventures, consolidations, or acquisitions of stock or assets where the effect may be to substantially lessen competition or tend to create a monopoly or to otherwise unreasonably restrain trade. In addition, Section 7a [15 U.S.C. § 18a], popularly known as the Hart–Scott–Rodino Act of 1976, requires that certain proposed mergers and acquisitions involving a threshold level of stock/assets receive FTC/Department of Justice approval before consummation. (See **Question 3:72** on premerger notification.) Section 2 of the Clayton Act, which originally prohibited price discrimination in sales of commodities, was amended by the Robinson–Patman Act [15 U.S.C. § 13], which now serves that purpose.

Q.3:8   How do the prohibitions of activity under the Sherman Act differ from similar prohibitions under the Clayton Act?

Under the Sherman Act, an activity generally must have an actual adverse effect on competition before it is considered illegal; however, under the Clayton Act, an activity that might substantially lessen competition may be illegal. The Clayton Act therefore addresses practices in their incipience that, if carried to their logical conclusion, would lead to a monopoly.

Q.3:9   What sort of activity is prohibited by the Federal Trade Commission Act?

The Federal Trade Commission Act (FTC Act) [15 U.S.C. § 45] declares that unfair methods of competition and unfair or deceptive acts or practices are illegal.

Q.3:10 How does the FTC Act relate to other federal antitrust laws?

The broad proscription against unfair methods of competition was intended to ensure that antitrust enforcement would not be limited to the specific activities prohibited by the Clayton Act. Not surprisingly, the FTC Act has been interpreted as broader than the Sherman or Clayton Acts [*FTC v. Brown Shoe Co.*, 384 U.S. 316, 321 (1966)]. Most Sherman Act violations also are violations of the FTC Act.

STATE ANTITRUST LAWS

Q.3:11   To what extent do the states regulate antitrust activity?

The majority of states have state antitrust laws modeled on the Sherman Act. In addition, many of those states have laws that mirror the FTC Act's prohibitions on unfair methods of competition and unfair or deceptive practices.

Q.3:12   Are there any special considerations with respect to the application of state antitrust laws to the health care industry?

Yes, a current trend among the states has been the enactment of legislation that exempts hospitals from state antitrust laws. Such legislation is a response to the fast-paced evolution of health care, which often requires cooperation between entities that could be challenged as antitrust violations without the protection of specific exemptions. The state action immunity doctrine may prove beneficial under federal law as well, as it should result in reducing duplicative antitrust enforcement efforts by exempting from federal antitrust scrutiny activities that are approved and/or supervised by the states.

Q.3:13   What states have enacted legislation providing antitrust relief to hospitals?

The following states have exemptions for hospitals engaging in collaborative ventures: Colorado, Idaho, Kansas, Maine, Minnesota, Montana, Nebraska, New York, North Carolina, North Dakota, Ohio, South Carolina, Tennessee, Texas, Washington, and Wisconsin.

Other states have enacted antitrust exemptions for specific health care providers or activities. For example, Florida permits providers to become part of a rural health network and allows specific activities within that context; Georgia permits mergers only for specified hospitals; and Oregon has a law that applies specifically to heart and kidney transplant services.

Q.3:14   What are some provisions typically included in a state law exempting hospitals from antitrust laws?

In Colorado, for example, the antitrust exemption law applies to hospitals, parents, subsidiaries, and controlled facilities. It permits sharing, allocating, consolidating, or referring of patients, personnel, instructional

programs, support services, and medical, diagnostic or therapeutic facilities, services, or procedures. Negotiations that are intended to culminate in a cooperative agreement must be filed with the Cooperative Health Care Agreements Board. A preliminary description of negotiations also must be filed. A public hearing is required. The board must approve agreements that it finds are likely to improve cost effectiveness, availability, quality, and delivery of hospital health care services, and that are consistent with other state statutory health care policies and programs. There is continuing state supervision in that the parties must notify the board of the progress of negotiations at least once every six months. In addition, the parties must submit annual reports providing information that enables the board to evaluate the impact of the agreement on availability, cost effectiveness, quality, and delivery of hospital or health care services or to determine whether such parties have complied with the terms of the agreement [Colo. Rev. Stat. §§ 24-32-2701 to 2715].

STANDARDS OF REVIEW UNDER FEDERAL ANTITRUST LAW

Q.3:15   What is the per se rule under federal antitrust laws?

The per se rule applies to restraints of trade that are so inimical to competition and so unjustified that they are conclusively presumed to be unreasonable and therefore are illegal. These restraints will not be permitted regardless of any business justification or procompetitive result.

Q.3:16   What sort of antitrust violations are considered per se illegal?

Per se violations of the antitrust laws include: price fixing agreements among competitors, horizontal market allocation, tying, and horizontal group boycotts.

Q.3:17   What is horizontal market allocation?

A horizontal market allocation is a division of markets among two or more actual or potential competitors. Whether such division is along geographic or product lines, it is per se illegal. [*See Palmer v. BBG of Georgia, Inc.*, 111 S. Ct. 401 (1990); *United States v. Topco Associates*, 405 U.S. 596 (1972). *But see Rothery Storage & Van Co. v. Atlas Van Lines, Inc.*, 792 F.2d 210 (D.C. Cir.), *cert. denied*, 479 U.S. 1033 (1982), in which the D.C. Circuit concluded that the standard of per se illegality for horizontal market allocation enunciated in *Topco* has been effectively overruled by subsequent Supreme Court decisions, including *Broadcast Music, Inc. v. Columbia Broadcasting System*, 441 U.S. 1 (1979).]

Q.3:18   What is an example of illegal price fixing in the health care industry?

An agreement between a group of physicians to charge the same fee for certain medical procedures is one example of price fixing in the health care field. (For a more detailed discussion of price fixing, see **Questions 3:33–3:44**.)

Q.3:19   What is an example of an illegal tying arrangement in the health care industry?

Tying arrangements occur when parties conspire to agree to condition the sale of their product or service on the buyer's purchasing another product or service. For example, a hospital would be guilty of a tying arrangement if it refused to allow its physicians to admit patients unless they agreed to use the hospital's laboratory.

Q.3:20   What is an example of a horizontal group boycott in the health care industry?

A group boycott is an agreement between persons or entities not to do business with another person or entity. For example, a group boycott claim might arise when a provider-controlled MCO refuses to admit a provider or decides to terminate a provider, since such action could be viewed as a concerted refusal to deal by the provider members. In a different scenario, an individual physician might allege that a hospital and its medical staff engaged in a group boycott when the hospital's peer review committee acted to exclude the physician from affiliation with the hospital. (For a more detailed discussion of group boycotts, see **Questions 3:45–3:53** on practitioner exclusion.)

Q.3:21   What is the rule of reason under federal antitrust laws?

The rule of reason is a standard of review under which a trade restraint's reasonableness is assessed in light of its nature, purpose, and effect. Under this standard, the courts examine the purpose, operation, and effect of the trade restraint to determine whether the purpose or effect of the agreement is actually to substantially harm competition or whether there are redeeming economic benefits to the arrangement.

Q.3:22   Under the rule of reason, what must be shown to demonstrate the unreasonableness of a particular trade restraint?

There must be a showing of actual and unreasonable harm to competition. Ordinarily, the existence of market power is an essential ingredient in a case seeking to show a restraint of trade under the rule of reason [*Hahn v. Oregon Physicians' Serv.*, 868 F.2d 1022 (9th Cir. 1988), *cert. denied*, 493 U.S. 846 (1989)].

Q.3:23   What is an example of merger activity that would be considered under the rule of reason standard?

A legitimate joint venture is an example of the type of activity that would be considered under the rule of reason. A joint venture can take many forms, but has been defined generally as any collaborative effort of two or more separate firms, short of a merger, with respect to production, distribution, and/or the marketing of products or services that achieves integrational efficiencies. In the health care field, a wide variety of joint ventures have been approved as legitimate, including horizontal joint ventures between physicians and/or hospitals, as well as vertical and conglomerate ventures between physicians/hospitals and (1) durable medical equipment (DME) companies to market DME; (2) home-health businesses to provide home-health service; or (3) managed care plans to offer managed care programs.

Joint ventures often are procompetitive because they allow for expansion into new markets, encourage new products and technologies, and create new economies of scale. However, joint ventures inevitably reduce competition to gain their procompetitive benefits. For that reason, the courts generally apply the rule of reason to legitimate joint ventures, including practices that affect price or exclude competitors. In general, legitimate joint ventures are approved under the rule of reason. A trade restraint resulting from such a venture will usually withstand scrutiny under the rule of reason if the venture's legitimate objectives cannot be accomplished by less restrictive means [*Berkey Photo, Inc. v. Eastman Kodak Co.*, 603 F.2d 263, 303 (2d Cir. 1979), *cert. denied*, 444 U.S. 1093 (1980)]. Moreover, in the health care context, the antitrust enforcement agencies have consistently approved hospital joint ventures. Clearly favoring collaborative efforts over merger, where that is possible, the agencies encourage joint investment in costly equipment, and joint ventures providing inputs (such as laundry services or nurse registries) that tend to lower hospital costs.

MARKET POWER

Q.3:24 What violations of the federal antitrust laws are assessed, in part, by degree of market power?

Violations of Section 2 of the Sherman Act (i.e., monopolization and attempted monopolization) are determined partly by market power. Under Section 7 of the Clayton Act, market power also relates directly to the legality of mergers and joint ventures. Moreover, market power is an element of all of the following violations: illegal price discrimination under the Robinson–Patman Act, illegal tying and exclusive dealing arrangements under Section 3 of the Clayton Act, and illegal, unreasonably restrictive agreements under Section 1 of the Sherman Act.

Q.3:25 How is market power determined?

To determine market power, it is necessary first to identify the market in which the entity exercises power. For antitrust purposes, the relevant market has two components—a product component and a geographical component.

Q.3:26 What is relevant product market?

The term *relevant product market* refers to the product or service at issue and all substantially acceptable substitutes for it. Essentially, the extent of the relevant product market is determined by the entire range of products that are reasonably interchangeable for consumers' use. [*See, e.g., United States v. E. I. Du Pont de Nemours & Co.*, 353 U.S. 586 (1957).] In making this determination, courts also have inquired into commercial realities, such as buyer preferences, physical differences, and established trade practices. [*See, e.g., United States v. Grinnell Corp.*, 384 U.S. 563 (1966).] In addition, consideration should be given to the probability that new competitors will enter the market as a result of price increases.

Q.3:27 What is the relevant product market for MCOs?

The relevant product market for MCOs is the market for health care financing. Broadly defined, this market includes traditional insurers, HMOs, PPOs, IPAs, etc., and their subscriber members. Participants in the market are considered to be purchasers of health care benefits packages.

Q.3:28 What are some of the characteristics of the relevant product market for MCOs?

Characteristics of the market for health care financing include few barriers to entry and great mobility. As a result, the market share necessary to demonstrate market power is extremely high. For example, in *Ball Memorial Hosp. v. Mutual Hosp. Ins., Inc.*, 603 F. Supp. 1077 (S.D. Ind. 1985), *aff'd*, 784 F.2d 1325 (7th Cir.), *reh'g denied, en banc*, 788 F.2d 1223 (7th Cir. 1986), which involved an attempt by 80 Indiana acute care hospitals to stop the implementation of a new PPO offered by Blue Cross/Blue Shield, the court refused to delay the PPO's implementation because the Blues did not possess sufficient market power to warrant antitrust scrutiny of the PPO. Market power results from the ability to cut back the market's total supply and then raise prices due to consumer demand for the product. In this case, the court found that the Blues did not have such power because they furnished a product—health care financing—that others could and did supply easily. The market in health care financing is competitive because the customers can switch companies readily, new suppliers can enter the market quickly, and existing suppliers can expand their sales rapidly, the court explained. Rather than finding the proposed PPO to be an antitrust threat, the court held that blocking its implementation would have an anticompetitive effect. Without the PPO, the court said, buyers of health care financing would have fewer options, and competitors would have one fewer entity with which to compete.

Q.3:29 What is relevant geographical market?

The term *relevant geographical market* refers to "the market area in which the seller operates, and to which the purchaser can practically turn for supplies" [*Tampa Elec. Co. v. Nashville Coal Co.*, 365 U.S. 320, 327 (1961)]. Thus, to ascertain the boundaries of the geographical market (i.e., the area of effective competition), such economic and physical barriers to expansion as transportation cost, delivery limitations, customer convenience, and customer preferences must be considered. [*See, e.g., United States v. Phillipsburg Nat'l Bank & Trust Co.*, 399 U.S. 350, 361 (1970).]

Q.3:30   What factors do the courts consider in determining the geographical market for hospital services?

The primary factors that courts have examined to determine the geographical scope of the market for hospital services are: patient flow statistics, location of physicians who admit patients, determinations of health planners, and public perception. [*See, e.g., United States v. Phillipsburg Nat'l Bank & Trust Co.*, 399 U.S. 350, 361 (1970) (patient flow statistics); *In re American Medical Int'l*, FTC Dkt. No. 9158, Initial Decision (July 27, 1983) (location of physicians who admit patients, and public perception); *United States v. Hospital Affiliates International, Inc.*, 1980-1 Trade Cas. (CCH) ¶ 63,721, at 77,852 n.1 (E.D. La.. 1980) (determinations of health planners).]

Q.3:31   In the managed care context, what factors have the courts considered in determining geographical market?

Some courts have looked to the area from which the managed care system draws members. For example, one court accepted an expert's identification of a three-county area as the relevant geographic market, while another found the Portland, Oregon metropolitan area to be the relevant market. [*Compare Hassan v. Independent Practice Associates*, 698 F. Supp. 679 (D. Mich. 1988), *with Northwest Medical Laboratories, Inc. v. Blue Cross & Blue Shield, Inc.*, 775 P.2d 863 (Ore. Ct. App. 1989), *aff'd*, 794 P.2d 428 (Ore. 1990).] In another instance, a court held that the entire state of Rhode Island was the applicable geographic market [*Ocean State Physicians Health Plan, Inc. v. Blue Cross & Blue Shield*, 883 F.2d 1101 (1st Cir. 1989), *cert. denied*, 494 U.S. 1027 (1990)]. The Seventh Circuit has ruled that the relevant geographic market for nonprofit providers of health care financing is regional, if not national, where rivals had the unrestricted mobility to move into a nonprofit provider's market [*Ball Memorial Hosp., Inc. v. Mutual Hosp. Ins., Inc.*, 784 F.2d 1325 (7th Cir.), *reh'g denied, en banc*, 788 F.2d 1223 (7th Cir. 1986)].

Q.3:32   After identification of relevant markets, what is the next step in antitrust analysis?

After the relevant geographical and product markets have been identified, the market share of the MCO must be determined. Whether the market share is sufficiently high to expose an MCO to antitrust liability depends on the facts of each case.

PRICE FIXING

Q.3:33 What is price fixing?

Price fixing occurs when two or more competitors come together to decide on the price that will be charged for services or goods. Price fixing is considered a per se violation of the federal antitrust laws.

Q.3:34 Does the status (e.g., provider-controlled or non-provider-controlled) of an MCO have any relevance to assessing price-fixing charges against an MCO?

Yes, when providers participate in reimbursement and pricing issues through discussion and negotiation with a non-provider-controlled organization, the antitrust risk is low. The provider-controlled MCO, however, is at a significant risk when setting provider reimbursement rates and bargaining with payers.

The Sherman Act prohibits "contracts, combinations and conspiracies" (concerted action) in restraint of trade. Concerted action refers, for the most part, to joint activity by competitors, that is, horizontal agreements. It follows that if the managed care organization is not controlled by providers, it is not in competition with the providers with whom it is negotiating. Because such negotiations do not involve two competitors getting together to agree on price or other terms, the transaction falls outside the prohibition on concerted action in restraint of trade. This is considered a "vertical" rather than a horizontal agreement. Also, with respect to a purchaser-or-payer-controlled, rather than a provider-controlled organization, if a provider is negotiating reimbursement issues through a non-provider-controlled entity and the provider concludes that the proposed price term is unacceptable, this conclusion will not be considered a horizontal price-fixing attempt or an attempt to boycott.

With regard to provider-controlled organizations, however, there is danger that such entities will be viewed as a horizontal conspiracy between competitors that acts as a mechanism for price fixing.

Q.3:35 What factors demonstrate provider control of an MCO?

Provider control is viewed as a question of fact to be determined on a case-by-case basis, but it is demonstrated most easily when the provider organization owns the plan or selects a majority of the voting members of the plan's governing body. Even though a provider organization selects only a minority of the governing body members, it may be found to control the plan if the minority has the practical ability to make policy. The FTC has indicated, however, it will not likely find control when a provider organization selects fewer than one-fourth of the governing body members and there is no evidence of their dominance over the plan's decision-making process. [See Enforcement Policy with Respect to Physician Agreements to Control Medical Prepayment Plans, 46 Fed. Reg. 48,982 (Oct. 5, 1981).]

Even without organizational control, providers may have practical control of the plan. The FTC has identified the following factors as indicative of control:

- power to vote on plan reimbursement or coverage proposals
- representation on (or selection of) key plan policy-making committees
- delegated authority, including veto or approval power over plan policies
- power to appoint or approve plan management
- financing of plan operations
- interlocking directors, officers, or executives
- absence of other strong interest groups in the governing body [See 46 Fed. Reg. 48,982 (Oct. 5, 1981).]

Legitimate Joint Ventures

Q.3:36   What sort of managed care programs have generally been subject to a rule-of-reason antitrust analysis?

In general, courts have approved capitated programs as legitimate joint ventures subject to rule-of-reason analysis. Under such plans, physician members of the plan share risk through participation in risk-sharing pools. These physicians are encouraged to provide cost-efficient services and preventive health care measures. They are paid a certain fixed amount per patient irrespective of whether a patient is treated. If treatment costs exceed capitated payments, a loss is incurred that can affect payment of withholds and bonuses. Because of the risk sharing inherent in capitation plans and the fact that such plans usually involve the creation of a new product, the courts are likely to view these systems as legitimate joint ventures and to analyze their activities under the rule of reason.

The Federal Trade Commission (FTC) has also specifically analyzed partially integrated plans in which providers practice separately, but combine their efforts and share significant risk in a health care payment plan. The FTC has distinguished such plans from per se illegal price fixing and has determined that they should be evaluated under the rule of reason. According to the FTC, in partially integrated plans (e.g., Blue Shield Plans, IPA-type HMOs),

> unlike in a merger situation, the controlling physicians retain their independent medical practices and therefore at least in part continue to compete with each other for patients in solo or group practices. [Thus], the formation and operation of such a plan may present many of the same antitrust implications as a traditional joint business venture—i.e., pro-competitive effects may result from the creation of a new business entity or from efficiencies achieved by the group, but the integration by competitors may also reduce competition among them or otherwise restrain trade [*Enforcement Policy with Respect to Physician Agreements to Control Medical Prepayment Plans*, 46 Fed. Reg. 48,982 (Oct. 5, 1981)].

Accordingly, in an advisory opinion, the FTC found that an HMO's affiliation with an IPA (see **Question 1:36** on independent practice associations) was a legitimate joint venture in which risk was shared, and therefore the FTC applied the rule of reason to the IPA's determination of maximum fee schedules. The FTC emphasized that the IPA physicians had a clear financial involvement in the HMO's operation, first through their substantial risk assumption via the IPA's acceptance of a capitation payment, and second, through the IPA's partial ownership of the HMO. Under these circumstances, the FTC concluded, the agreements on price by the IPA physicians (i.e., setting maximum allowable fees for services provided to HMO patients and negotiating with the HMO as to a capitation rate derived, in part, from the physicians' agreed-upon fee levels) are to be distinguished from per se illegal price fixing, and therefore subject to rule-of-reason analysis [*Health Plus of Michigan*, advisory opinion issued March 22, 1984].

Most-Favored-Nation Clauses

Q.3:37 What is a most-favored-nation clause?

Most-favored-nation (MFN) clauses are often found in contracts between managed care organizations and providers. In an arrangement involving an MFN clause, a provider is obligated to render services to a particular purchaser at a price no less favorable than that at which it offers services to its most favored customer. In other words, MFN clauses require the provider to charge the payer a fee at least as low as the lowest fee the provider charges to any patient.

Q.3:38   What are some antitrust concerns related to MFN clauses?

Although MFN clauses enable insurers to better manage costs, they may impede entry into a market by other HMOs. A new market entrant may be able to attract consumers only by cutting fees paid to providers, enabling it to cut premiums. However, if a substantial amount of a provider's business comes from an HMO with an MFN clause, the provider may be unwilling to furnish services at a discount to a new HMO, because the provider then would be required under the MFN clause to offer lower prices to the first HMO's patients. The Assistant Attorney General of the Department of Justice's Antitrust Division has pointed out that the actual effect of MFN clauses when used by a dominant insurer is to require participating physicians to charge other insurance plans and nonplan patients fees that are as high as or higher than the fees the physicians charge the dominant insurer. Thus, MFN clauses can restrain competition because they may cause a large number of participating physicians to refuse to discount their fees [Anne K. Bingaman, Assistant Attorney General, Antitrust Division, "The Importance of Antitrust in Health Care," Speech before Symposium on Antitrust Policy and Health Care Reform (Oct. 5, 1994)].

Q.3:39   Do MFN arrangements with health care purchasers constitute per se illegal price fixing?

No, since MFN clause provisions should not affect physicians' decisions about the level of their fees, courts have generally concluded that such provisions should not be characterized as per se illegal price fixing, but rather should be evaluated under the rule of reason.

Q.3:40   Under what circumstances might an MFN clause constitute a violation of the Sherman Act?

No court thus far has held that an MFN clause violated antitrust laws. However, a California court has recognized the possibility that an MFN clause could rise to the level of an unreasonable restraint of trade, even under circumstances in which the class of consumers was not harmed by the clause, if there was a possibility of demonstrating that the clause could have caused a sufficient number of providers to be unwilling to participate in programs offering less reimbursement than the payer originally imposing the clause. [*See Reynolds v. California Dental Serv.*, 246 Cal. Rptr. 331 (Ct. App. 1988). *See also Reazin v. Blue Cross & Blue Shield, Inc.*, 663 F. Supp. 1360 (D. Kan. 1987), *aff'd*, 899 F. 2d 951 (10th Cir.), *cert. denied*, 497 U.S. 1005, where the court held that an MFN clause used by Blue Cross—which had 60 percent of the relevant market—served to prevent competing insurance companies from offering lower rates, thereby effectively controlling prices.]

Q.3:41 How have the agencies approached MFN clauses in the managed care context?

The Department of Justice's Antitrust Division began to express increasing concern about the antitrust implications of MFN clauses in 1988 and has been active in this area since (the FTC appears to have yielded enforcement to the Division). The Division has investigated the use of MFN clauses by several health plans, such as Blue Cross's MFN clauses in contracts with hospitals. These arrangements raise antitrust concerns when Blue Cross is the dominant managed care entity in the relevant region. The clause is considered anticompetitive because hospitals are unwilling to offer a lower price to smaller companies, since they would also have to offer a lower price to Blue Cross. In other cases, the Division has challenged the use of MFN clauses by a dental service plan in Arizona, and a nationwide vision care insurer headquartered in California. [*See United States v. Delta Dental Plan*, 7 Trade Reg. Reptr. (CCH) ¶ 50,767 (D. Ariz. Aug. 30, 1994), and, *United States v. Vision Service Plan* (D.C. Dec. 15, 1994) (proposed consent decrees).] MFN clauses are not necessarily illegal and have been analyzed by the Division under the rule of reason. From the MFN clause cases thus far investigated by the Division, it is clear that the implementation of MFN clauses by health plans and networks with substantial market power will be subject to careful scrutiny by the Division.

Balance-Billing Bans

Q.3:42 What is balance billing?

Balance billing refers to the practice of a provider billing a patient for all charges not paid for by the insurance plan, even if those charges are above the plan's usual, customary, and reasonable (UCR) fee, or are considered medically unnecessary.

Q.3:43 Is balance billing a common reimbursement practice for MCOs?

No, managed care plans and service plans generally prohibit providers from balance billing, except for allowed copayments, coinsurance, and deductibles. Participation agreements with insurers that set levels of reimbursement below the hospital's usual charges often contain provisions that prohibit the hospital from billing covered patients for the difference between charges and the combined amount of insurer reimbursement, member copayments, and deductibles. The provisions, otherwise known as no balance billing clauses, typically state that a provider may not bill a plan member for any balance of the payment owed by the managed care plan regardless of the reason for nonpayment.

Q.3:44 Does a prohibition on balance billing violate antitrust laws?

Because no balance-billing provisions protect the insurer's subscribers from costs that they did not anticipate, such a ban should be permissible under the antitrust laws in most cases. For example, the First Circuit has held that a ban on balance billing imposed by an insurer with a dominant market share and virtually unanimous participation by physicians did not amount to an unreasonable restraint of trade in violation of the Sherman Act [*Kartell v. Blue Shield*, 749 F.2d 922 (1st Cir. 1984), *cert. denied*, 471 U.S. 1029 (1985)]. The court viewed the insurer as a purchaser of physicians' services for its insured, rather than as a third force preventing willing buyers and sellers from independently reaching price/quality agreements. The court ruled that the insurer's use of monopsony power to obtain lower than competitive prices did not violate Section 2 of the Sherman Act because the law is aimed at "protecting consumers against prices that were too high, not too low," and because a legitimate buyer is entitled to use its market power to keep prices down [749 F.2d at 931].

PRACTITIONER EXCLUSION AND PEER REVIEW ISSUES

Excluding Providers and Exclusive Dealing

Q.3:45 When health care providers are excluded from managed care systems, are antitrust laws implicated?

Yes, providers who are excluded from managed care systems may bring group boycott charges alleging that the exclusion constituted an illegal restraint of trade.

Q.3:46   To establish an illegal group boycott, what must be shown?

To establish a group boycott, there must be more than one actor, anticompetitive intent or the absence of legitimate reasons for the conduct, and a certain degree of market power.

Q.3:47   Are group boycotts generally considered to be per se violations of the Sherman Act?

Yes, a group boycott has traditionally been considered inherently anticompetitive and, therefore, a per se violation of the Sherman Act. The U.S. Supreme Court has identified three characteristics as indicative of a per se illegal group boycott: the boycott cuts off access to a supply, facility, or market necessary to enable the victim to compete; the violator possesses a dominant market position; and the practices are not justified by plausible arguments that they enhance overall efficiency or competition [*Northwest Wholesale Stationers, Inc. v. Pacific Stationery & Printing Co.*, 472 U.S. 284 (1985)].

Q.3:48   Are group boycotts in the managed care context reviewed under the same per se rule?

Exclusions in the managed care context are not always reviewed under the per se rule. In a recent case, the First Circuit explained that "per se condemnation is not visited on every arrangement that might, as a matter of language, be called a group boycott or concerted refusal to deal" [*U.S. Healthcare, Inc. v. Healthsource, Inc.*, 986 F.2d 589 (1st Cir. 1993)]. In that case, the court of appeals upheld an exclusive contract that required primary care physicians to do business with only one HMO. A competing HMO claimed it had been unsuccessful in recruiting physicians in New Hampshire because the primary care physicians were unwilling to drop their exclusive contract with the HMO. The court agreed with the lower court's rule-of-reason analysis of the case and with its determination that competition was not lessened by the exclusivity provision, and therefore concluded that no antitrust violation occurred. While conceding that the provision prohibited primary care physicians from participating with other HMOs, the court nonetheless did not view the exclusivity arrangement as a per se illegal group boycott. The court observed that the term *illegal group boycott* has been principally reserved for cases in which competitors agree with each other not to deal with a supplier or distributor if it continues to serve a competitor whom they seek to injure. The court declared that the per se illegal boycott label is no longer broadly applied to condemn "a joint venture among competitors in which participation was allowed to some but not all. . . . although such a restriction might well fall after a more complete analysis under the rule of reason" [986 F.2d at 594].

Q.3:49   Is a single provider's unilateral decision not to do business with someone an illegal group boycott?

No, an illegal group boycott involves more than one entity. Thus, if a single individual or entity makes a unilateral decision not to do business with someone, that refusal is not illegal unless it amounts to monopolization. [*See, e.g., United States v. Colgate & Co.*, 250 U.S. 300 (1919); *Monsanto v. Spray-Rite Serv. Corp.*, 465 U.S. 752, *reh'g denied*, 466 U.S. 994 (1984).]

Q.3:50   If a legitimate joint venture makes a unilateral decision to exclude a provider, are antitrust laws implicated?

Yes, when a legitimate joint venture excludes a provider, the conduct is subject to rule-of-reason antitrust analysis because it involves an agreement of refusal to deal between two or more entities.

Q.3:51   To what extent does degree of market share indicate that an exclusive agreement constitutes a per se illegal group boycott?

Before the per se rule will be applied to an agreement to exclude providers, the entities involved in the exclusive arrangement must have sufficient market share. Exclusive dealing is not per se illegal, but rather, an unreasonable anticompetitive effect must be shown before exclusive dealing will be held to be illegal. [*See, e.g., Jefferson Parish Hosp. Dist. v. Hyde*, 466 U.S. 2 (1984); *Tampa Elec. Co. v. Nashville Coal Co.*, 365 U.S. 320 (1961).] Thus, where the sufficiency of market share is questionable, the courts will examine an exclusive arrangement under the rule of reason. Under that rule, the question of whether the conduct of exclusive dealing constitutes an illegal restraint of trade is evaluated by balancing the competitive and anticompetitive effects of such action.

Q.3:52   What constitutes sufficient market power to apply the per se rule to an exclusive agreement?

An exact market-share threshold for application of the per se rule to an exclusive arrangement has not been determined. However, both the U.S.

Supreme Court and the Department of Justice have suggested that a 30 percent market share does not present sufficient market power to make such action illegal. [*See, e.g., Jefferson Parish Hosp. Dist. v. Hyde*, 466 U.S. 2 (1984); *Health Care Trends—U.S. Officials' View*, 7 Trade Reg. Rep. (CCH) ¶ 50,025 (Nov. 14, 1989) (proposed "safe harbor" from antitrust violations for physician-controlled HMOs and PPOs with "less than 35 percent of the providers in [the relevant] market.")] (For a more detailed discussion of antitrust safety zones established for exclusive and nonexclusive health care networks, see **Questions 3:73–3:85** on Statements of Enforcement Policy and Analytical Principles Relating to Health Care and Antitrust, U.S. Department of Justice and the Federal Trade Commission, Sept. 27, 1994.)

Q.3:53   Does exclusion of a specific group of providers constitute a violation of antitrust laws?

Exclusion of a specific group of providers may amount to an antitrust violation. In one case, for example, the Ninth Circuit concluded that a fee-for-service, physician-controlled IPA's exclusion of podiatrists, taken together with reimbursement policies that discriminated against podiatrists because they were nonmembers, can constitute an illegal group boycott under Section 1 [*Hahn v. Oregon Physician Serv.*, 868 F.2d 1022 (9th Cir.), *cert. denied*, 493 U.S. 846 (1989)]. In another case, a provider-controlled Blue Cross's refusal to pay for services rendered by clinical psychologists unless they were billed through physicians was found to be an illegal group boycott under a rule-of-reason analysis [*Virginia Academy of Clinical Psychologists v. Blue Shield of Virginia*, 624 F.2d 476 (4th Cir. 1980), *cert. denied*, 450 U.S. 916 (1981)]. The exclusion of chiropractors from a Blue Cross plan, however, was held not to be a conspiracy to restrict the practice of chiropractic in the relevant market. The court applied the rule of reason and concluded that Blue Cross's decision to offer a health care package without coverage of chiropractic services had a procompetitive effect in that it offered consumers a choice between health care cost reimbursement packages [*Johnson v. Blue Cross & Blue Shield*, 677 F. Supp. 1112 (D.N.M. 1987)].

Peer Review

Q.3:54   How does a peer review system operate?

The peer review system, as implemented in the hospital setting, operates through a group of physicians authorized to evaluate the competence of fellow medical professionals. Peer review committees use specific standards to evaluate medical competence. Hospital bylaws typically authorize peer review committees to impose sanctions on physicians who provide substandard care. Such sanctions include warnings, continued practice only under supervision, or termination of hospital staff privileges. (For a more detailed discussion of peer review, see **Chapter 8**.)

Q.3:55   How do antitrust laws relate to the peer review process?

When a peer review committee takes action against a colleague, antitrust concerns usually arise because the peer review committee members are often direct competitors of the physicians they censure. Competition among physicians has become more important as health care has become more competitive. Moreover, changes in the Medicare and reimbursement systems have forced hospitals to fill staff positions only with those physicians who can provide quality care in a cost-effective manner. These circumstances (increased competition among physicians and institutional focus on cost-effectiveness) often provide the excluded or censured physician with a basis for alleging antitrust violations under Sections 1 and 2 of the Sherman Act. [*See* Lisa J. Acevedo, *To Review or Not To Review: Antitrust Liabilities and Peer Review Protections*, 27 J. HEALTH & HOSP. L. 321 (November 1994).]

Q.3:56   What is the Health Care Quality Improvement Act?

The Health Care Quality Improvement Act of 1986 (the HCQIA) is a federal law that grants immunity to peer review activity and seeks to improve the quality of health care through reporting requirements. The HCQIA was enacted in part as a response to numerous antitrust suits against participants in peer review and credentialing activities. (For a more detailed discussion of the HCQIA as it relates to credentialing, see **Questions 8:22–8:26**.)

Q.3:57   How does the HCQIA impact upon the risk of antitrust liability in peer review cases?

The HCQIA provides those assisting in review activities limited immunity from damages that may arise as a result of adverse decisions that affect a physician's medical staff privileges. In this way, the HCQIA is intended to encourage continued participation in peer review activities by reducing the risk of financial liability arising from potential antitrust litigation.

Q.3:58　Are there any standards that must be met to apply the HCQIA's immunity provisions?

Yes, to be covered by the immunity provisions, the individual or body must have participated in the peer review process in some way. The scope of coverage includes individual witnesses and providers of information as well as hospitals, other providers of health care services, and professional societies, assuming that these entities are engaged in formal peer review activities intended to promote the quality of care. Also, the immunity provisions apply only if the following requirements have been satisfied:

- The challenged peer review action must have been taken in the reasonable belief that the action was in the furtherance of quality health care,
- The action must have been taken after reasonable efforts to obtain the facts of the matter,
- The entity must have afforded the affected physician adequate notice and hearing procedures, and
- There must be a reasonable belief that the action was warranted.

(For a discussion of the HCQIA's notice and hearing requirements, see **Questions 8:28–8:33.**)

MERGERS AND ACQUISITIONS

Q.3:59　What characterizes a horizontal merger?

A horizontal merger involves similar or identical businesses at the same level of the market. When competitors on the same marketing level merge, this sort of horizontal transaction is likely to attract the most attention from government agencies responsible for enforcing antitrust statutes because a combination of competitors creates more risk of harmful anticompetitive effects than other forms of corporate growth and expansion.

Q.3:60   How do the courts evaluate whether a horizontal merger violates antitrust laws?

The courts have concluded that there is no single qualitative or quantitative factor from which it can be determined whether a horizontal merger is permissible. [*See, e.g., Brown Shoe Co. v. United States,* 370 U.S. 294 (1962).] Recognizing a congressional intent to preserve competition by preventing undue market concentration, the courts have focused primarily on the likelihood that the consolidation will substantially lessen competition. In this regard, the courts have observed that the competitive evil of a horizontal merger is that it places great economic power in the hands of a few businesses, which in turn restricts business opportunities for smaller firms. Ultimately, however, the courts' primary concern has been the impact of the horizontal merger on market conditions. [*See, e.g., United States v. Continental Can Co.,* 378 U.S. 441, 458 (1964); *United States v. Bethlehem Steel Corp.,* 168 F. Supp. 576 (S.D.N.Y. 1958).]

In assessing the impact of a merger on market conditions, the critical evaluative factors are the market share controlled by the merged firm and the degree of concentration in the relevant market [*Brown Shoe Co. v. United States,* 370 U.S. 294 (1962)]. Concentration measures the degree to which a market contains only a few firms with large market shares, as opposed to a market containing many firms, each with small shares.

However, the courts also have indicated that measuring market concentration and degree of market share is only the starting point in merger analysis. The U.S. Supreme Court has emphasized that market share statistics are "not conclusive indicators of anti-competitive effects" [*United States v. General Dynamics Corp.,* 415 U.S. 486, 498 (1974). *See also United States v. Citizen & Southern Nat'l Bank,* 422 U.S. 86 (1975)].

Another factor considered in merger analysis is the extent to which there are barriers to market entry. If there are few barriers, mergers that result in large market shares may have little or no anticompetitive effect. [*See United States v. Tidewater Marine Serv., Inc.,* 284 F. Supp. 324 (E.D. La. 1968).] On the other hand, in a concentrated industry or in an industry in which there are regulatory barriers to entry (e.g., the hospital industry), even a small increase in market share through merger is more likely to be challenged as adversely affecting the market. [*See United States v. Aluminum Co. of America,* 377 U.S. 271, *reh'g denied,* 377 U.S. 1010 (1964).] Thus, it is important to recognize that, even if the surviving merged company would possess a nondominant share of the market, the merger may be enjoined.

Another factor that is frequently considered in a horizontal merger assessment is indication of a trend toward market concentration in the relevant industry. For example, even if the relevant market would remain competitive after a merger, the courts have invalidated the merger if it appears to be one of a series of events that will lead to concentration in the industry over time. [*See, e.g., United States v. Von's Grocery Co.*, 384 U.S. 270 (1966).]

Q.3:61 Have the agencies outlined their approach for analyzing mergers?

Yes, the Department of Justice, in conjunction with the Federal Trade Commission, issued the *1992 Horizontal Merger Guidelines*, which revised prior 1984 *Guidelines* outlining methods for assessing the legality of a merger, including examination of the merging firms' market shares and evaluation of concentration in the relevant market before and after the merger. To calculate market concentration, the Department of Justice uses the Herfindahl-Herschman Index (HHI), which is the sum of the square of each firm's market share in the relevant market. [*See 1992 Horizontal Merger Guidelines (1992 Merger Guidelines), reported at* 57 Fed. Reg. 41,552 (Sept. 10, 1992).]

Q.3:62 What other factors are considered in analyzing a horizontal merger under agency guidelines?

Other factors considered under the *1992 Merger Guidelines* are the nature of the product, the terms of the sale, the ease of entry into the market, and the availability of information on transactions in the market. The courts appear to agree that the most important factor in assessing a merger (other than market share) is ease of entry into the relevant market. [*See, e.g., United States v. Waste Management, Inc.*, 743 F.2d 976 (2d Cir. 1984); *United States v. Calmar, Inc.*, 612 F. Supp. 1298 (D.N.J. 1985), where the courts indicated that high market share is virtually irrelevant if entry is sufficiently easy).] With respect to market entry, the *Guidelines* provide: "[A] merger is not likely to create or enhance market power . . . if entry into the market is so easy that market participants, after the merger, either collectively or unilaterally would not profitably maintain a price increase above pre-merger levels. . . . In markets where entry is easy . . . the merger raises no antitrust concerns" [*1992 Merger Guidelines*, at § 3.0].

In the context of the health care financing market, however, some courts have held that entry is so easy that anticompetitive effects arising from a merger are impossible [*Ball Memorial Hosp., Inc. v. Mutual Hosp. Ins., Inc.*,

784 F.2d 1325 (7th Cir.), *reh'g denied, en banc,* 788 F.2d 1223 (7th Cir. 1986)], while other courts have disagreed [*Reazin v. Blue Cross & Blue Shield, Inc.,* 663 F. Supp. 1360 (D. Kan. 1987), *aff'd,* 899 F.2d 951 (10th Cir.), *cert. denied,* 497 U.S. 1005 (1990)].

This is currently an unsettled area of law, however. The courts have yet to consider a case requiring an analysis of entry by managed care organizations under the *1992 Merger Guidelines.*

Q.3:63   Have the agencies outlined their approach to horizontal mergers between health care providers?

Yes, the Department of Justice and the FTC first issued six statements regarding their antitrust enforcement policies in relation to merger and other joint activities among health care providers. [*See Statements of Antitrust Enforcement Policy in the Health Care Area,* U.S. Department of Justice and the Federal Trade Commission, Sept. 15, 1993.] The statements create "antitrust safety zones" that present circumstances under which the agencies will not challenge the conduct on antitrust grounds. In 1994, the statements were revised, but no changes were made to the enforcement policy with respect to safety zones for hospital mergers. [*See Statements of Enforcement Policy and Analytical Principles Relating to Health Care and Antitrust,* U.S. Department of Justice and the Federal Trade Commission, Sept. 27, 1994.] (For a more detailed discussion of these statements, see **Questions 3:73–3:85.**)

The statement on hospital mergers creates a safety zone for mergers in cases in which one of the merging hospitals is small. Absent extraordinary circumstances, the agencies will not challenge a merger between two general acute care hospitals where one of the merging hospitals has fewer than 100 licensed beds, has an average daily inpatient census of fewer than 40 patients, and is more than five years old. In explaining the justification for such a safety zone, the agencies pointed out that they had challenged only eight of the more than 200 hospital mergers that had occurred in 1987.

As for hospital mergers falling outside the safety zone, the agencies have indicated that they will follow the *1992 Merger Guidelines.* However, the agencies have pointed out that, in applying the Herfindahl-Herschman Index (HHI) equation and related analysis to specific hospital mergers, they often have concluded that a merger will not result in a substantial lessening of competition in situations in which market concentration otherwise might raise an inference of anticompetitive effects. Such situations include transactions in which the agencies found:

- the merger would not increase the likelihood of the exercise of market power either because of the postmerger existence of strong competitors or because the merger hospitals were sufficiently differentiated;
- the merger would allow the hospitals to realize significant cost savings that could not be realized otherwise; or
- the merger would eliminate a hospital that was likely to fail, with its assets exiting the market. [*See 1994 Statements of Enforcement Policy Relating to Health Care and Antitrust*, at Statement 1.]

Q.3:64 What characterizes a vertical consolidation?

A vertical consolidation occurs when a supplier and a customer combine, often resulting in a deviation from the normal market forces of supply and demand. Unlike a horizontal business combination, a vertical merger or acquisition does not eliminate a competitor. Rather, it unites a supplier and a customer and is a means of assuring availability of supplies and increasing sales of a manufacturer's product.

Q.3:65 What are the antitrust implications of a vertical consolidation?

In the case of a vertical consolidation, either the supplier or the customer is removed from a segment of the market, which deprives its rivals of an opportunity to compete for that company's business. If the size of the market foreclosed in this manner is substantial, the vertical consolidation may violate antitrust laws. In analyzing the antitrust implications of a vertical consolidation, the primary questions are whether the transaction has deprived a competitor from a source of supply and whether it has closed access to the market by a competitor or potential competitor. [*See Fruehauf Corp. v. FTC*, 603 F.2d 345 (1979).]

Q.3:66 How do the courts evaluate whether a vertical consolidation violates antitrust laws?

With the exception of vertical price-fixing agreements, vertical consolidations are tested under the rule of reason. In essence, the test of legality with respect to vertical consolidations involves an examination of various economic factors to determine whether the arrangement is the type that Congress sought to proscribe by the antitrust laws. The courts have indicated that whether a particular vertical consolidation is permissible depends in part on the degree of market foreclosure, but that this is not a sole determinant of competitive effect. In analyzing vertical mergers, the courts have focused primarily on the following seven factors:

1. market share foreclosed to competitors
2. nature and purpose of the vertical arrangement
3. actual and probable effect on local industry and small businesses
4. level and trend of concentration in the market and the market shares of the participating companies
5. trend toward vertical integration and consolidation in the industry
6. barriers to entry
7. economies of scale

Also, an unlawful anticompetitive effect may be found when a competitor is forced out of business as a result of a vertical consolidation. [*See, e.g., United States Steel Corp. v. FTC*, 426 F.2d 592 (6th Cir. 1970); *United States v. Kennecott Copper Corp.*, 231 F. Supp. 95 (S.D.N.Y. 1964), *aff'd*, 381 U.S. 414 (1965).]

Q.3:67   What is the failing company defense?

The failing company defense provides a complete defense to an otherwise illegal merger under Section 7 of the Clayton Act, which prohibits mergers that may substantially lessen competition or otherwise unreasonably restrain trade, if all elements of the defense are satisfied at the time of the merger. The courts created the defense on the theory that the acquisition of a failing company does not substantially lessen competition. [*See International Shoe Co. v. FTC*, 280 U.S. 291 (1930).]

Q.3:68   How have the courts and/or agencies construed the failing company defense?

The failing company defense has been construed narrowly and has been applied only if the company probably would have been unable either to meet its financial obligations in the near future or to reorganize successfully. The doctrine as defined by the courts has been held to require that:

- the acquired company's resources be so depleted that insolvency is almost certain, and there is no hope of revitalization;
- the acquiring company be the only available purchaser for the failing company; and

* the acquired firm has made a substantial but unsuccessful good faith effort to obtain alternate buyers.

[*See, e.g., United States v. General Dynamics Corp.*, 415 U.S. 486 (1974); *Citizen Publishing Co. v. United States*, 394 U.S. 131 (1969); *United States v. Reed Roller Bit Co.*, 274 F. Supp. 573 (W.D. Okla. 1967); *In re The Pillsbury Co. and Fox Deluxe Foods*, 93 F.T.C. 967, 1032 (1979).]

In addition, the *1992 Merger Guidelines* apply standards similar to those traditionally used by the courts in assessing a failing company defense. Before the defense will apply, the failing company must have made unsuccessful good faith attempts to obtain reasonable alternative offers of acquisition [*1992 Merger Guidelines*, at § 5.1].

Q.3:69 What is an efficiencies defense?

A defense based on the efficiency and/or procompetitive effects of a merger has been created judicially in accordance with the legislative history of the 1950 amendments to the Clayton Act (e.g., the Celler–Kefauver Act, codified at 15 U.S.C. § 18). Supporters of these amendments, which deal with antitrust analysis of corporate mergers, noted that competition may be enhanced as a result of certain mergers. Thus, the defense is based on the theory that efficiencies and cost savings created by a merger should militate in favor of the merger. [*See, e.g., Brown Shoe Co. v. United States*, 370 U.S. 294 (1962).]

Q.3:70 Have the courts been generally receptive to the efficiencies defense in antitrust cases?

No, even though the U.S. Supreme Court, in dictum, has recognized possible procompetitive effects when two smaller firms merge to improve their ability to compete with a large, dominant competitor [*United States v. Von's Grocery Co.*, 384 U.S. 270 (1966)], the defense nonetheless has rarely been invoked successfully and has faced significant legal hurdles. [*See, e.g., FTC v. Procter & Gamble Co.*, 386 U.S. 568 (1967); *United States v. Philadelphia Nat'l Bank*, 374 U.S. 321 (1963); *Marathon Oil Co. v. Mobil Co.*, 669 F.2d 366 (6th Cir. 1981), *cert. denied*, 455 U.S. 982 (1982).]

Q.3:71 Have the agencies indicated their approach to mergers that enhance efficiency (i.e., procompetitive effects)?

Yes, in the *1984 Horizontal Merger Guidelines*, the Department of Justice indicated that efficiency would be considered not as a defense, but rather as a mitigating factor relevant to the Department's determination of whether to initiate legal action against a particular merger. However, the Department of Justice stated in those *Guidelines* that efficiencies would be considered only upon "clear and convincing evidence" [*1984 Horizontal Merger Guidelines, reported at* 49 Fed. Reg. 26,823 (June 29, 1984)].

In its *1992 Merger Guidelines*, the Department of Justice indicated that the presence of efficiencies may grow in significance as a factor in merger analysis. Accordingly, the *1992 Merger Guidelines* no longer require "clear and convincing evidence" for invoking the efficiencies defense, but instead state only that the burden of proof with regard to efficiencies is on the merging parties. The Department has recognized that a merger's primary benefit is its potential for enhancing efficiency and that it might refrain from challenging a suspect merger if the merging parties meet their burden of proof in showing that the merger would produce substantial cost savings through economies of scale, integration of production facilities, plant specialization, lower transportation costs, or other efficiencies in specific business activities. In addition, the Department indicated that, under certain circumstances, it might take into account reductions in general selling and administrative or overhead expenses [*1992 Merger Guidelines,* at § 4].

Thus, under the *Guidelines,* it is possible that certain hospital acquisitions could be justified on the grounds of efficiency. However, the Department has also stated that it will reject efficiency claims if equivalent results are achievable by other means, that is, the expected net efficiencies must be greater than the competitive risks identified in the *Guidelines* [*1992 Merger Guidelines,* at § 4].

Q.3:72   To what extent are entities required to provide advance notice of a proposed merger to the agencies?

The Hart–Scott–Rodino Act [15 U.S.C. § 18a], otherwise known as Section 7A of the Clayton Act, requires premerger notification to the FTC and the Department of Justice if a hospital to be acquired has total assets of $10 million or more and the acquiring company has annual assets or annual net sales of $100 million or more, or if the acquired hospital has annual net sales or total assets of $100 million or more and the acquiring company has total assets or annual net sales of $10 million or more. Essentially the same rules apply to acquisitions by hospitals, with the additional condition that an acquiring hospital must notify the agencies of a merger if, as a result of the acquisition, it would hold 15 percent or more of the voting securities or assets of the acquired company, or if it would hold an aggregate total amount of the voting securities and assets in excess of $15 million. Thus, the premerger notification requirement applies only to comparatively large acquisitions. When it applies, the acquisition may not be consummated until after the expiration of either a 30-day waiting period, or a 15-day waiting period in the case of a tender offer.

AGENCY STATEMENTS ON HEALTH CARE ANTITRUST ENFORCEMENT

Q.3:73 How have the federal agencies clarified their approach to health care antitrust enforcement?

In September 1993, the Department of Justice and the Federal Trade Commission issued six statements regarding health care antitrust enforcement. The statements were intended to resolve uncertainty for hospitals and health care providers who are attempting to increase efficiency and reduce costs by instituting beneficial mergers and joint ventures. The agency statements established "antitrust safety zones," activities that will not be challenged by either agency, absent extraordinary circumstances. Significantly, the agencies pledged to respond to queries regarding whether specific conduct is within a safety zone within 90 days [*Statements of Antitrust Enforcement Policy in the Health Care Area*, Sept. 15, 1993].

A year later, the agencies issued nine statements of their health care antitrust enforcement policies and analytical principles relating to mergers and various joint activities. These policy statements supersede those issued in 1993. The policy statements address: (1) mergers among hospitals; (2) hospital joint ventures involving high technology or other expensive health care equipment; (3) hospital joint ventures involving specialized clinical or other expensive health care services; (4) providers' collective provision of non-fee-related information to purchasers of health care services; (5) providers' collective provision of fee-related information to purchasers of health care services; (6) provider participation in exchanges of price and cost information; (7) joint purchasing arrangements among health care providers; (8) physician network joint ventures; and (9) analytical principles relating to multiprovider networks [*Statements of Enforcement Policy and Analytical Principles Relating to Health Care and Antitrust*, U.S. Department of Justice and the Federal Trade Commission, Sept. 27, 1994].

Q.3:74   To what extent do the agencies intend to challenge hospital mergers?

The 1994 policy statement on hospital mergers makes no significant changes from the previous statement, continuing the safety zone for small mergers. Hospital mergers between two general acute care hospitals will not be challenged if one of the merging hospitals is at least five years old, has fewer than 100 beds, and has fewer than 40 inpatients per day on average. Hospital mergers that fall outside the antitrust safety zone are not necessarily anticompetitive and will be analyzed following the five steps in the *1992 Merger Guidelines*. (See preceding **Questions 3:59–3:63** on horizontal consolidations.)

Q.3:75   Are there certain types of hospital joint ventures that the agencies are unlikely to challenge?

Yes, the agencies are unlikely to challenge hospital joint ventures involving specialized clinical or other expensive health care services, as well as joint ventures involving high-technology or other expensive hospital equipment. The agencies state that most hospital joint ventures to provide specialized clinical or other expensive health care services do not create antitrust problems. The agencies set out the appropriate antitrust analysis. They did not, however, provide a safety zone for such ventures stating that they need more expertise in evaluating the cost of, demand for, and potential benefits from such joint ventures before they can articulate a meaningful safety zone. The agencies emphasize that the absence of a safety zone for such collaborative activities does not imply that they create any greater antitrust risk than other types of collaborative activities.

The 1994 statements also provide a safety zone for joint ventures among hospitals to purchase, operate, and market the services of high-technology or other expensive medical equipment if the joint venture included only those hospitals whose participation is needed to support the equipment. This extends to joint ventures involving existing, as well as new high-technology or other expensive health care equipment. A joint venture that includes additional hospitals will not be challenged if the additional hospitals could not support the equipment on their own or through the formation of a competing joint venture. The agencies state that most hospital joint ventures for this purpose do not create antitrust problems, but rather create procompetitive efficiencies that benefit consumers. If such a joint venture falls outside the safety zone, it does not necessarily raise significant antitrust concerns and will be analyzed under the rule of reason.

Q.3:76 To what extent do the agencies intend to challenge providers' collective provision of information to purchasers of health care services?

The agencies will not challenge providers' collective provision of under-lying medical data that may improve purchasers' resolution of issues relating to the mode, quality, or efficiency of treatment. They will not challenge, absent extraordinary circumstances, a medical society's collec-tion of outcome data from its members about a particular procedure that they believe should be covered by a purchaser and the provision of that information to the purchaser. The agencies also will not challenge provid-ers' development of suggested practice parameters that may provide useful information to patients, providers, and purchasers. In providing medical data, providers may collectively engage in discussions with pur-chasers about the scientific merit of the data. Providers who collectively threaten or actually refuse to deal with a purchaser because they object to the purchaser's administrative, clinical, or other terms governing the provision of services run a substantial antitrust risk.

The agencies state that providers' collective provision to purchasers of health care services of factual information about the providers' current or historical fees or other aspects of reimbursement, such as discounts or alternative reimbursement methods, are unlikely to raise significant anti-trust concerns. To qualify for the safety zone, the collection of information to be provided to purchasers must satisfy the following conditions:

- the collection is managed by a third party (e.g., a purchaser, govern-ment agency, health care consultant, academic institution, or trade association);
- although current fee-related information may be provided to purchas-ers, any information that is shared among or is available to the compet-ing providers furnishing the data must be more than three months old; and
- for any information that is available to the providers furnishing data, there are at least five providers reporting data upon which each disseminated statistic is based, no individual provider's data may represent more than 25 percent on a weighted basis of that statistic, and any information disseminated must be sufficiently aggregated such that it would not allow recipients to identify the prices charged by any individual provider.

This safety zone is intended to ensure that an exchange of price or cost data is not used by competing providers for discussion or coordination of provider prices or costs. There are various activities that fall outside the safety zone. For example, the safety zone does not apply to collective negotiations between unintegrated providers and purchasers in contemplation or in furtherance of an agreement among the providers on fees or other terms or aspects of reimbursement, or to an agreement among unintegrated providers to deal with purchasers only on agreed terms. Also outside the safety zone is providers' collective provision of information or views concerning prospective fee-related matters. These activities are not necessarily illegal but will be reviewed on a case-by-case basis.

Q.3:77   To what extent do the agencies intend to regulate the exchange of price and cost information among providers?

The agencies will not challenge provider participation in written surveys of (1) prices for health care services, or of (2) wages, salaries or benefits of health care personnel if:

- the survey is managed by a third party (e.g., a purchaser, government agency, health care consultant, academic institution, or trade association);
- the information provided by survey participants is based on data more than three months old; and
- there are at least five providers reporting data upon which each disseminated statistic is based, no individual provider's data represents more than 25 percent on a weighted basis of that statistic, and any information disseminated is sufficiently aggregated such that it would not allow recipients to identify the prices charged or compensation paid by any particular provider.

Exchanges of price and cost information that fall outside the safety zone will be evaluated to determine if the information exchange has an anticompetitive effect that outweighs any procompetitive justification for the exchange.

Q.3:78   Is there a safety zone covering certain joint purchasing arrangements among health care providers?

Yes, joint purchasing arrangements among health care providers fall within a safety zone if: (1) the purchases account for less than 35 percent of the total sales of the purchased product or service in the relevant market; and (2) the cost of the products and services purchased jointly accounts for less than 20 percent of the total revenues from all products or services sold by each competing participant in the joint purchasing arrangement.

For joint purchasing arrangements that fall outside the safety zone, the agencies have delineated factors that mitigate competitive concerns. Antitrust concern is lessened: (1) if members are not required to use the arrangement for all their purchases of a particular product or service; (2) when negotiations are conducted on behalf of the joint purchasing arrangement by an independent employee or agent who is not also an employee of a participant; and (3) when the likelihood of anticompetitive communications is lessened where communications between the purchasing group and each individual participant are kept confidential and are not discussed with, or disseminated to, other participants.

Q.3:79 To what extent do the agencies intend to challenge physician network joint ventures?

There is a safety zone for an exclusive physician network joint venture comprising 20 percent or less of the physicians in each physician specialty with active hospital staff privileges who practice in the relevant geographic market and share substantial financial risk. In relevant markets with fewer than five physicians in a particular specialty, an exclusive physician network joint venture otherwise qualifying for the antitrust safety zone may include one physician from that specialty, on a nonexclusive basis, even though the inclusion of that physician results in a physician network joint venture consisting of more than 20 percent of the physicians in that specialty.

There is also a safety zone for a nonexclusive physician network joint venture comprising 30 percent or less of the physicians in each physician specialty with active hospital staff privileges who practice in the relevant geographic market and share substantial financial risk. In relevant markets with fewer than four physicians in a particular specialty, a nonexclusive physician network joint venture otherwise qualifying for the antitrust safety zone may include one physician from that specialty even though the inclusion of that physician results in a physician network joint venture consisting of more than 30 percent of the physicians in that specialty.

In determining whether a physician network joint venture is exclusive or nonexclusive, the agencies will examine the following indications of nonexclusivity, among others:

- viable competing networks or plans with adequate provider participation currently exist in the market;
- providers in the network actually participate in other networks or contract individually with health benefits plans, or there is other evidence of their willingness and incentive to do so;
- providers in the network earn substantial revenue outside the network;
- absence of any indications of significant departicipation from other networks in the market; and
- absence of any indications of coordination among the providers in the network regarding price or other competitively significant terms of participation in other networks or plans.

Physician network joint ventures will be reviewed under a rule of reason and will not be considered per se illegal either if the physicians in the joint venture share substantial financial risk or if the combining of the physicians into a joint venture enables them to offer a new product producing substantial efficiencies.

Q.3:80 Do the enforcement statements address how the agencies intend to approach multiprovider networks?

Yes, one statement is devoted to the agencies' outline of the analytical principles that will be used to assess multiprovider networks. Multiprovider networks are defined as ventures among providers that jointly market their services to health benefits plans and other purchasers. They vary substantially as to providers included, contractual obligations imposed on those providers, and the efficiencies likely to be realized by the network. In discussing these networks, the agencies address integration, market definition, and competitive effects. The focus will be on the effect a multiprovider network will likely have on competition. If the network involves agreements among competitors that restrict competition, the agencies will decide whether the competitors are sufficiently integrated through the network to be evaluated under the rule of reason rather than being held per se illegal. Under the rule of reason, they will determine the markets in which the multiprovider network could affect competition and will then evaluate the network's overall competitive effects.

Q.3:81 With respect to integration, how can a multiprovider network avoid violating antitrust laws?

In multiprovider networks that include direct competitors, the competitors must either avoid price and market (or service) allocation agreements by making unilateral decisions on the prices they will charge and the markets they will serve, or they must assure that joint decisions are necessarily related to significant economic integration among them. Substantial financial risk sharing among competitors in a multiprovider network is evidence of integration. Thus, for a network to avoid an antitrust challenge based on joint pricing, members of the network must share substantial financial risk (like capitation). The joint price also must be reasonably necessary to achieve the efficiencies the venture seeks. A price agreement that involves substantial risk sharing is subject to a rule of reason. An agreement among competitors in a multiprovider network on service allocation or specialization that is reasonably related to significant economic integration is also subject to the rule of reason.

Another way for a network to avoid antitrust challenge on joint pricing grounds is to simply avoid joint pricing agreements. Setting up a messenger-model network is one way to avoid joint pricing agreements. This involves a third party relaying to purchasers information that is obtained individually from providers in the network about the prices the participants are willing to accept and conveying to providers any contract offers made by purchasers.

Q.3:82 How do the agencies intend to define the market in analyzing multiprovider networks?

The product markets for analyzing the competitive effects of multiprovider networks will likely include both the market for networks, if there is a distinct market for networks, and the market for service components of the network that are or could be sold separately outside the network.

The relevant geographic market for each relevant product market affected by the multiprovider network will be determined through a fact-specific analysis that focuses on the location of reasonable alternatives.

Q.3:83 How do the agencies intend to analyze the competitive effects of multiprovider networks?

The horizontal and vertical competitive effects of an integrated multiprovider network will be evaluated under the rule of reason. For networks requiring horizontal analysis, the agencies will define the relevant markets, consider concentration in those markets, and evaluate a multiprovider network's likely overall competitive effects considering all market conditions. Determining concentration in markets affected by the formation of a multiprovider network is one factor, but the conclusion will be based on a more comprehensive analysis. In evaluating competitive effects, the agencies are interested in the ability and willingness of third-party purchasers to switch between different health care providers or networks. The agencies will also examine whether the competing providers in the network are dealing exclusively through the network. Exclusive arrangements may raise antitrust concerns.

For networks requiring vertical analysis, a key concern is the extent to which the network's arrangements with its provider members will foreclose competition by impeding the formation and operation of competing networks. Vertical exclusive arrangements that restrict the providers in one market from dealing with non-network providers that compete in a different market or that restrict network members' dealings with insurers will be examined to determine the degree to which the arrangement limits the ability of other networks or health benefits plans to compete in the market.

The following factors will be considered in determining if a network is nonexclusive:

- viable competing networks or plans with adequate provider participation currently exist in the market;
- providers in the network actually participate in other networks or contract individually with health benefits plans, or there is other evidence of their willingness and incentive to do so;
- providers in the network earn substantial revenue outside the network;
- the absence of any indications of substantial departicipation from other networks in the market; and
- the absence of any indications of coordination among the providers in the network regarding price or other competitively significant terms of participation in other networks or plans.

Q.3:84   How do the agencies intend to analyze the exclusion of particular providers from multiprovider networks?

The rule of reason will be used in analyzing the exclusion of providers from a multiprovider network. The focus is whether the exclusion reduces competition among providers in the market and harms consumers, not whether a particular provider has been harmed. Exclusions may either raise competitive concerns or have procompetitive effects.

Q.3:85   Do the agencies intend to consider efficiencies resulting from a multiprovider network?

Yes, the agencies will balance potential anticompetitive effects of the multiprovider network against the potential efficiencies associated with its formation and operation. The greater the likely anticompetitive effects, the greater the likely efficiencies must be. Efficiencies include cost savings associated with the assumption of financial risk, as well as reduced administrative costs, improved utilization review, improved case management, quality assurance, and economies of scale.

4

Utilization Review

DEFINITIONS

Q.4:1   What is utilization management?

Utilization management is an essential element of managed care. It is a broad term, referring to methods of coordinating providers and provider services by monitoring treatment quality, identifying quality and cost-efficient providers, identifying and minimizing inappropriate use of services or facilities, and making medical necessity determinations on which payers rely to make coverage and payment decisions. Utilization management is comprised of several elements, including utilization review, treatment and discharge planning, and case management activities. Physician profiling and adoption of clinical practice guidelines are other aspects of utilization management.

Q.4:2   What is case management?

Case management is an increasingly important aspect of utilization management. It involves identifying at an early stage those patients who could be more cost effectively treated in an alternative setting or at a lower level of care without negatively affecting the quality of care. Case management therefore attempts to manage both quality and cost. Case management is usually employed in catastrophic or high-cost cases.

Q.4:3   What is utilization review?

Utilization review is a central element of utilization management. It is a process for evaluating the medical necessity of nonemergency care. Third party payers generally refuse to pay for medical treatment that is not medically necessary. There are three kinds of utilization review:

1. Prospective review is performed before the initiation of treatment. At that time, if the review reveals that the treatment is not medically necessary, the payer will indicate that it will not pay for the medical care.
2. Concurrent review is performed during the course of treatment. It entails monitoring whether the care continues to be appropriate and necessary. If the care is found not to be necessary, the payer will refuse to pay for additional care.
3. Retrospective review is performed after the treatment has been completed. If the review indicates that the medical care was not necessary, the insurer will deny the claim.

Most insurance companies and managed care organizations rely on prospective and concurrent utilization review to determine whether care is necessary and what level of care is appropriate. Utilization review has become an accepted and essential part of cost containment.

Q.4:4   What is the usual chronology of the utilization review process?

1. A physician proposes a course of medical treatment.
2. A first-line utilization reviewer, typically a registered nurse, reviews the patient's diagnosis, symptoms, test results, and other relevant medical information and determines whether the patient meets the eligibility criteria the utilization reviewers have adopted for the proposed treatment. The first-line reviewer will either authorize or deny authorization for the proposed treatment.
3. If the first-line reviewer denies authorization, a second-line reviewer determines whether the patient is eligible for the proposed treatment and either authorizes or denies authorization accordingly. The second-line reviewer is usually a physician, as nurses are rarely permitted to deny care.
4. If the second-line reviewer denies coverage for the proposed treatment, the treating physician or patient may appeal the decision.

Q.4:5   What is a utilization review organization?

A utilization review organization (URO) is a private entity that provides utilization review services to managed care organizations.

STATE REGULATION OF UTILIZATION REVIEW

Q.4:6   Do state laws regulate utilization review?

Yes. In recent years, the regulation of utilization review (UR) has increased dramatically. Most states have enacted laws regulating utilization management companies and practices. See **Appendix 4-A** for a state-specific listing of UR laws.

Q.4:7   What entities are regulated by state UR laws?

The applicability of UR laws varies from state to state. States may exempt workers compensation plans or plans governed by the Employee Retirement Income Security Act. Other laws do not apply to internal utilization review programs, such as those administered by hospitals, home health agencies, or HMOs. A few states offer a narrow exemption for internal review programs, exempting only those that do not deny or approve coverage for medical services. Even exempt organizations may be required to register in a state, however. Further, because some state statutes include no exemptions, it is important for managed care organization (MCO) administrators to examine the laws of each state in which the MCO does business.

Q.4:8   What kind of authorization do states require?

States have developed more than one approach to regulating utilization reviewers. Some states merely require reviewers to register with a regulating agency (such as the Department of Health) by providing information.

Many states require certification, sometimes called accreditation. In order to be certified, reviewers must meet the state's standards in areas such as education, training, and experience. In some states, the certification process is waived for reviewing entities that are accredited by an approved organization. (See **Questions 4:17–4:27.**)

Finally, some states require utilization reviewers to be licensed. Licensure states may also waive their requirements for privately accredited reviewers.

Q.4:9   Do state laws govern specific UR practices?

State laws govern many aspects of the UR process, including:

- who may review care
- appeals of adverse decisions
- disclosure of coverage criteria

Q.4:10   How do state laws address who may deny coverage?

Although states require varying levels of physician involvement in the UR process, adverse coverage decisions must be made by a physician in many states. Other states merely require physician oversight of reviewers.

Q.4:11   Do state laws limit utilization review to certain specialties?

Some states require that utilization review be performed by a physician in the same specialty as the treating physician. Others allow a looser approximation, requiring a physician in a relevant or similar specialty.

Q.4:12   What do state laws require concerning appeals of coverage determinations?

State laws usually require MCOs to allow subscribers and/or their treating physicians to appeal adverse UR decisions. Most states require utilization reviewers to inform subscribers of appeal procedures at the time of the denial.

Q.4:13   Can state laws require UROs to reveal their coverage criteria?

Some states require UROs to provide subscribers with specific reasons for a coverage denial, including UR criteria. A few states require public access to UR standards. Many states require UR entities to disclose review criteria to physicians upon request.

Q.4:14   Do state laws address the development of clinical criteria?

Some states require that the criteria be reviewed by board-certified physicians whose names must be furnished upon request. Others regulate the validity of the criteria by requiring them to be clinically valid or periodically reviewed.

Q.4:15   Do state laws address the confidentiality of medical information?

Yes. Most laws indicate that utilization review agents must ensure confidentiality and must establish procedures to accomplish this. Medical information confidentiality requirements are also found in other areas of the law—in statutes concerning substance abuse treatment or mental health programs, general medical record statutes, and the doctor–patient privilege, for example.

Q.4:16   What are the consequences of failing to comply with state regulations regarding utilization review?

Failing to comply may result in significant fines. For example, a California health plan was fined $500,000 for violating state regulations in connection with the plan's refusal to refer a child with a rare cancer to a specialist. The regulations required health plans to refer patients when consistent with good professional practice; make services, including specialists, accessible; and to ensure that care decisions are not made for the purpose of financial gain [*Commissioner of Corporations v. Takecare Health Plan*, No. 933-0290 (Cal. Dept. of Corp. Nov. 17, 1994)].

PRIVATE ACCREDITATION OF UTILIZATION REVIEW ORGANIZATIONS

Q.4:17   Are there private organizations that guide the activities of UROs?

Yes. These organizations provide more detailed standards than those contained in most state statutes. The leading accreditation organizations for utilization review are the Utilization Review Accreditation Commission (URAC) and the National Committee for Quality Assurance (NCQA). The following discussion focuses on NCQA standards.

Q.4:18   What entities does NCQA accredit?

NCQA accredits organizations that either provide, or arrange to provide, comprehensive health services to enrolled members through a defined benefits package and an organized delivery system. To be eligible for accreditation, the organization must also be located in the United States and must comply with state and federal laws and regulations, including licensure requirements.

Q.4:19 What activities does NCQA examine?

NCQA reviews an organization's activities in the following areas: quality management and improvement, utilization management, credentialing, members' rights and responsibilities, preventive health services, and medical records. The discussion in this chapter is limited to accreditation standards in the area of utilization management.

Q.4:20 Under the NCQA standards, who may deny authorization for treatment?

Every denial must be reviewed by a physician. Further, board-certified physicians with appropriate specialties must be consulted as needed.

Q.4:21 Do NCQA standards address the validity of the UR criteria?

Yes. The UR decision protocols must be written and must be based on reasonable medical evidence. There must be a mechanism for updating the review criteria periodically.

Q.4:22 Who must have access to the criteria, according to the NCQA?

The criteria must be available to participating physicians who request it.

Q.4:23 What procedural requirements do the NCQA standards establish for UR?

Utilization reviewers must make an effort to obtain all information necessary for the review. A consultation with the treating physician is required, where appropriate. The UR decision must be made in a timely manner, relative to the urgency of care. If authorization is denied, the reviewer must provide the health plan subscriber with clear documentation, including the reasons for denial and information on the appeals process.

Q.4:24   How does NCQA accredit MCOs that delegate UR activities to UROs?

MCOs that perform internal UR and MCOs that contract with outside UROs are subject to the same accreditation standards. Under the NCQA standards, accreditation reviewers consider delegated activity, as well as nondelegated activity.

Q.4:25   Does NCQA require additional information from MCOs that delegate UR activities to UROs?

Yes. Delegating MCOs must provide a written description of the delegated activity, how the delegate will be accountable, how often the delegate will report to the MCO, and how the delegation will be evaluated. The NCQA will also seek evidence of approval of the delegate's program and evaluation of regular reports.

Q.4:26   Why should a URO seek accreditation?

A URO may be found negligent if it deviates from the standard of care for utilization review organizations, that is, if it acts unreasonably, given the circumstances. The standard of care is continuing to evolve, however, as courts are only beginning to decide cases against UROs. Courts may rely on accreditation standards, such as those promulgated by URAC and NCQA, to establish the standard of care. Thus, a URO that adopts policies and procedures consistent with accepted accreditation standards organization may be less likely to be held liable.

Further, several state utilization review statutes allow state agencies to exempt accredited utilization reviewers from certification requirements.

Q.4:27   Why should an employer or MCO require URO accreditation?

A managed care organization that follows a policy of associating only with accredited UROs may have some protection from liability for negligently selecting a utilization review organization. (See **Questions 4:52–4:54** for a discussion of negligent selection.)

LIABILITY ARISING FROM THE UTILIZATION REVIEW PROCESS

The Legal Relationship between MCOs and UROs

Q.4:28   What is the significance of the legal relationship between an MCO and a URO?

A subscriber injured as a result of a utilization review decision may decide to file a lawsuit to recover for the injury. The subscriber must initially determine which entity or entities may be legally responsible for the injury.

If the MCO implements an internal utilization review program, the subscriber may sue the MCO. If the MCO has contracted with a URO for utilization review services, however, the subscriber may sue only the URO, sue the MCO for negligently selecting the URO, or attempt to establish a legal relationship between the MCO and URO such that the MCO can also be held liable for the URO's conduct.

Q.4:29   What legal relationships can lead to MCO liability for URO activities?

An MCO can be held liable for URO activities under the legal theories of ostensible agency or vicarious liability. An MCO also can be directly liable for negligently selecting a URO that causes injury to a subscriber. (See **Questions 4:52–4:54** for a discussion of negligent selection.)

Q.4:30   Under what circumstances might an MCO be held liable for URO activities under ostensible agency?

Ostensible agency, also known as apparent agency, is a legal doctrine that imposes liability based on the appearance of an agency relationship, even if the relationship does not actually exist. (Refer to **Chapter 6** for more information on ostensible agency.) Whether a court will consider a URO an ostensible agent of the managed care organization turns on the reasonable perceptions of the subscribers. If the managed care organization fails to clarify in some manner that the URO is not an agent of the managed care organization, a subscriber reasonably believes that the URO is the managed care organization's agent, and the subscriber relies on this perception to his or her detriment, then the URO may be considered to be the ostensible agent of the managed care organization, and the managed care organization will be liable for the URO's actions. It is therefore important for the relationship between the managed care organization and the URO to be clearly spelled out in all documents, including marketing materials.

Q.4:31   When will an MCO be held liable for the acts of a URO under the doctrine of vicarious liability?

An MCO will only be held liable for URO conduct on the basis of vicarious liability if the court finds an employer/employee relationship between the entities. (Refer to **Chapter 6** for a discussion of factors the courts may consider in assessing the relationship.)

Although a managed care organization that contracts with a URO may be liable for negligently selecting the URO if it does not adequately investigate the quality of the services provided by the URO, the managed care organization must be careful to monitor the URO, without controlling the URO, to avoid allegations that the URO is an employee.

Q.4:32   Can the legal relationship be established by state law?

Yes. At least one state has enacted legislation holding insurers liable for inappropriate benefits denials by UROs [Colo. Rev. Stat. 10-4-115].

General Liability Principles

Q.4:33   What legal theories can a subscriber use to sue for denial of a claim?

Although the law in this area is continuing to develop, there are three basic legal theories emerging: negligent denial (**Questions 4:35–4:39**), breach of contract (**Questions 4:40–4:45**), and bad faith denial (**Questions 4:46–4:51**).

Q.4:34   What conduct might lead to MCO liability?

Liability arising from the UR process can arise from several sources, including failure to adequately gather information prior to making a decision as to medical necessity, failure to initiate a meaningful dialogue between UR personnel and the treating physician, failure to inform members of their right to appeal an adverse UR decision, and failure to issue a timely UR decision.

Negligent Utilization Review

Q.4:35 What must a subscriber show to recover for negligent utilization review?

Generally, the subscriber must prove the MCO had a duty to exercise reasonable care when making coverage decisions, the MCO breached that duty, and the breach caused injury to the subscriber. The subscriber may point to a breach of care in either the design of the utilization review process or in the execution of the process. The injury may be either a monetary injury (where the subscriber is responsible for paying for the treatment) or a physical and emotional injury (when the subscriber did not undergo the treatment, or where treatment was delayed due to the denial).

Q.4:36 What test do courts use to determine whether negligent utilization review occurred?

The test for negligence of any kind is called *the standard of care*. Although the language that individual courts use to describe the standard of care for utilization review varies, courts will generally hold that reviewers should act with the same level of care used by other reviewers under the same circumstances.

Q.4:37 What is the first case that addressed negligent utilization review?

The first reported case involving liability for utilization review, *Wickline v. State of California*, 239 Cal. Rptr. 810 (Ct. App. 1986), *review dismissed, remanded*, 741 P.2d 613 (Cal. 1987), provides an example. The patient in that case underwent surgery to replace a section of the artery that supplied blood to her right leg. Prior to surgery, her physician had obtained authorization from Medi-Cal (California's Medicaid program) for the surgical procedure and ten days of hospitalization. The patient had several post-surgical complications, however, and on the tenth day of her hospitalization, her physician concluded that an additional eight days of hospitalization were medically necessary. Two other physicians who had participated in the patient's care concurred.

The physician's request for an extension of the patient's stay was reviewed by a nurse employed by Medi-Cal. Because she did not agree with the necessity of the eight-day extension, she referred the case to a Medi-Cal physician/consultant. The physician/consultant authorized an additional four days only. He did not contact the attending physician or any other vascular specialist, nor did he rely on any information other than that provided on the request form before making his decision.

All three physicians involved in the patient's care knew they could attempt to obtain a further extension of the patient's hospital stay by telephoning the Medi-Cal consultant, but none of them did so. The patient was discharged when her authorized stay expired. She was admitted as an emergency patient a few weeks later, however, and her leg had to be amputated to save her life. The patient subsequently sued Medi-Cal, alleging that the amputation was due to her premature discharge from the hospital.

The question the court faced was whether a third party payer of health care services can be held legally responsible when medically inappropriate decisions result from defects in design or implementation of the cost-containment mechanism of utilization review. Because the discharge decision in this case was within "the usual standard of medical practice in the community," as required by the regulations governing the Medi-Cal program, the court held that Medi-Cal did not breach the standard of care and was not liable for the subsequent unfavorable medical outcome, largely because the treating physicians did not appeal the adverse decision. In an opinion that alarmed the managed care community, however, the court held that utilization review decisions can be a basis for liability. The court stated:

> The patient who requires treatment and who is harmed when care which should have been provided is not provided should recover for the injuries suffered from all those responsible for the deprivation of such care, including, when appropriate, health care payers. Third party payers of health care services can be held legally accountable when medically inappropriate decisions result from defects in the design or implementation of cost containment mechanisms, as, for example, when appeals made on a patient's behalf for medical or hospital care are arbitrarily ignored or unreasonably disregarded or overridden.

Q.4:38 How do utilization review entities defend against negligence suits?

A common argument made by utilization review entities is that the reviewer did not cause the member's injuries because refusing to cover a course of treatment is not equivalent to obstructing access to treatment. In other words, they argue that a reviewer should not be liable for any injury that results from the patient's decision not to pursue the treatment regardless of authorization, because coverage and treatment decisions are independent. This argument has met with mixed success in the courts.

Q.4:39 What is an example of negligent UR?

In a Georgia case, a federal trial court ruled that an insurance company could be held liable for failing to verify coverage. A hospitalized subscriber needed immediate cardiac bypass surgery. A hospital administrator repeatedly tried to obtain confirmation of coverage from the subscriber's insurance company, but was unsuccessful. The hospital discharged the subscriber, who underwent the surgery 32 days later at a second facility. The subscriber sued the insurer for negligently failing to confirm coverage, claiming that his condition deteriorated during the waiting period, causing him to become disabled and to sell his business at a loss. The insurance company argued that it could not be liable because it had no duty to confirm coverage [*Mimbs v. Commercial Life Ins. Co.*, 832 F. Supp. 354 (S.D. Ga. 1993)].

The court ruled that the subscriber had stated a valid claim. Insurers have "a duty imposed by law not to defeat the insured's ability to obtain needed medical services and thereby cause harm to the health or life of the insured by negligently failing" to verify coverage, according to the court. The court concluded that, because the refusal to verify coverage may have caused additional damage to the subscriber's heart, the suit should proceed to trial.

Breach of Contract

Q.4:40 What must a subscriber show to recover for denial of a claim based on breach of contract?

A subscriber must show that the managed care organization was obliged under the subscriber's policy to cover a particular course of treatment but refused to do so, thus breaching the coverage contract. The subscriber must also show that the breach caused a legal injury.

Q.4:41 What are the arguments in a typical breach of contract suit?

In most breach of contract suits, the dispute centers on contract language. The subscriber argues that a particular medical treatment is covered under the contract, while the payer argues that the treatment is excluded. Thus, it is crucial for payers to carefully draft subscriber contracts.

The subscriber may also argue that the contract exclusion does not apply to the subscriber—because the subscriber did not have notice of the exclusion, for example.

Finally, payers may argue that the refusal to cover a treatment did not cause the subscriber's injury because the subscriber was free to seek medical care independent of coverage. This argument only applies to additional physical injuries and medical costs, however, and not to the cost of the improperly excluded treatment.

Q.4:42 Which subscribers are likely to bring breach of contract suits?

Recently, patients denied coverage for procedures under experimental or investigational contract clauses are suing for coverage. Much of the litigation concerning coverage for high-dose chemotherapy with autologous bone marrow transplant (HDC–ABMT) and for breast cancer is based on breach of contract claims. One study offers an explanation for the number of suits filed contesting coverage for this treatment. Researchers at Duke University reviewed 533 cases and found insurers' coverage decisions inconsistent, even for similar patients. This inconsistency may generate litigation because insurers who are unable to point to a universally applied criteria for denial are susceptible to suit. The study noted that coverage denials were frequently reversed when the patient hired an attorney [William P. Peters and Mark C. Rogers, *Variation in Approval by Insurance Companies of Coverage for Autologous Bone Marrow Transplantation for Breast Cancer*, 330 NEW ENG. J. MED. 473, 477 (Feb. 17, 1994)].

The particular treatments that lead to litigation change over time. Advancing medical technology creates new treatments that will be sought by subscribers before insurers and MCOs are willing to provide coverage. Older treatments lead to less litigation, as clinical data regarding the efficacy of a particular treatment either results in increased coverage or less demand for the treatment. State insurance laws may also reduce litigation over a particular treatment by requiring coverage.

Q.4:43   What form should an exclusion for investigative or experimental treatment take?

According to one commentator, the minimum requirements for an effective exclusion clause in a coverage agreement should contain "sound criteria for making the determination that a procedure, drug, device or treatment is experimental or investigative; a description of the decision-making process; and a grant of discretion to the decision maker to interpret and construe the terms of the exclusion" [Jacqueline M. Saue, *Challenges to Exclusions by Private Payors for "Experimental or Investigational" Procedures—The Insurer's Perspective* presented at Legal Issues in Medical Technology, Apr. 7-8, 1994, National Health Lawyers Association].

Health plans have developed a variety of strategies for excluding experimental treatments. The experimental exclusion may be a separate contract clause or may be set forth in a definition of medically necessary treatments covered by the plan. Subscriber contracts may or may not differentiate between experimental and investigational procedures. Many health plans link treatment coverage to Food and Drug Administration (FDA) approval, as FDA approval is based on scientific proof of safety and efficacy and usually establishes a conservative standard. Other plans cover a treatment if studies reported in medical literature sufficiently establish its usefulness. Plans that defer to experts in the field run the risk of unintentionally expanding coverage, as physicians connected with pioneering a new treatment are likely to agree that it will benefit a patient.

Q.4:44   What are the disadvantages of specifically listing excluded treatments?

Advancing technology makes it necessary to continuously update the list of exclusions, making subscriber notification a daunting task. Periodic lists of newly excluded treatments may also have a negative impact on subscribers' perception of the plan's coverage.

Q.4:45   What are examples of breach of contract cases based on the exclusion of experimental treatments?

Two cases demonstrate the importance of carefully drafting subscriber contracts. In *Harris v. Mututal of Omaha*, a federal appeals court upheld an insurer's refusal to cover high-dose chemotherapy with autologous bone marrow transplant (HDC-ABMT) for a subscriber with advanced breast cancer. The insurer relied on its general exclusion of services that are "investigational or experimental or are mainly for research purposes." The plan went on to define experimental or investigational treatments as those that are the subject of FDA clinical trials or for which reliable evidence shows that the consensus of expert opinion is that the treatment requires further study to determine safety and efficacy. The plan defined reliable evidence as published reports in authoritative medical literature, the protocol for study of the treatment, or the informed consent form for the treatment. The court noted that the protocol for HDC–ABMT for breast cancer stated that the treatment was in the clinical trial stage, the subscriber would have been required to sign an informed consent form stating that HDC–ABMT for breast cancer is part of a clinical trial, and 18 published articles indicated that the treatment requires additional clinical research. A physician's oral testimony that the protocol was outdated and an unpublished paper stating that the treatment was no longer investigative could not be considered because they did not constitute "reliable evidence" under the contract, the court ruled. Because the treatment was excluded by the contract, the court concluded, the insurer was not required to pay for the treatment [992 F.2d 706 (7th Cir. 1993)].

In a second breast cancer case, a federal trial court ordered a health insurance plan to pay for the treatment because the contract did not effectively exclude it. A subscriber sought coverage for high-dose chemotherapy with peripheral stem cell rescue (HDC–PSCT), a treatment in which high doses of chemotherapy are followed by the reintroduction of the patient's own previously harvested stem cells. The plan denied coverage, citing its contract, which listed chemotherapy as a covered hospital service but excluded certain transplants. The subscriber sued. The court ruled that because the contract covered chemotherapy, the primary treatment, it necessarily covered PSCT, a supportive and necessary part of the course of treatment. Although medical literature characterized PSCT as a transplant, the court continued, the procedure involved only the patient's own blood and therefore was not excluded. Although the contract gave the plan discretion to interpret its terms, the court reversed the plan's decision, finding it arbitrary and capricious [*Calhoun v. Complete Health Care*, 860 F. Supp. 1494 (S.D. Ala. 1994)].

Bad Faith

Q.4:46   What is bad faith?

Many courts have held that insurance companies owe their insureds a duty of good faith and fair dealing in evaluating claims. A bad faith action is one in which a subscriber claims that the insurer, MCO, or URO breached its duty of good faith and fair dealing by acting with ill will or self-interest when it denied benefits or authorization to provide covered services.

Q.4:47 What must a subscriber show to recover for bad-faith denial of a claim?

A subscriber alleging bad faith denial must generally show that the insurer or MCO lacked a reasonable basis for denying benefits and that the insurer or MCO knew or recklessly disregarded the lack of a reasonable basis for denying the claim.

Although many jurisdictions characterize bad faith as an intentional wrong, courts have been willing to infer intent from the insurer's conduct.

Q.4:48 What are the legal consequences of denying a claim in bad faith?

The courts have been willing, in bad-faith denial cases, to grant punitive damages. Because the purpose of punitive damages is not to provide compensation for an injury, but to punish the wrongdoer, the monetary penalty can be severe. Some states have adopted statutes that impose penalties, attorney's fees, and cost on insurers who wrongfully deny claims. Many of these laws provide much narrower recovery than what would be available under a common law claim of bad faith.

Q.4:49 What is an example of a verdict that awarded punitive damages for bad faith?

A subscriber obtained an $89 million jury verdict against her insurer, arguing that the insurer denied coverage for HDC–ABMT for breast cancer in bad faith. The case settled for an undisclosed amount following post-trial arguments because neither party expected the verdict amount to be upheld on appeal, according to a press release issued by the insurance company. The complaint alleged that the insurance company acted in bad faith by (1) persuading a physician who had previously recommended the procedure to state that the procedure would not be helpful and (2) requiring a second opinion from a facility that had already determined that it could not perform the procedure, thereby assuring a delay that would make the patient no longer eligible for the procedure [*Fox v. Health Net*, No. 21692, (Cal. Super. Ct. Riverside County, *filed* June 19, 1992, *settled* April 6, 1994)].

Q.4:50 What failures might allow a patient to recover for bad-faith denial?

Insurers have been found liable for:

• failing to contact the member's attending physician to discuss the patient's condition before denying coverage,
• failing to obtain the patient's progress notes,
• failing to follow procedures for claims review before determining that services were not medically necessary, and
• failing to inform a member of the right to appeal an adverse decision and settle disputes through arbitration.

Q.4:51 What should an MCO do to avoid liability for bad-faith denial of claims?

The majority of states have adopted variations of the National Association of Insurance Commissioner's (NAIC) Unfair Claims Settlement Practices Model Regulation, which specifies how insurers should process claims and notify beneficiaries of claim determinations. State laws based on the NAIC model require fair and timely claims evaluations and written notice of claims denials that indicate the basis of denial. Following NAIC procedures, as well as avoiding the conduct outlined in **Question 4:50** may offer some protection from liability.

Negligent Selection

Q.4:52 What is negligent selection?

A subscriber who has been injured as a result of a URO's actions may sue the MCO, without showing an employment or agency relationship between the MCO and URO, under the doctrine of negligent selection. Just as health care entities have a corporate duty to carefully select and monitor physicians, they have a duty to carefully select the URO with which they contract. This duty entails investigating the URO before contracting to ensure that its procedures are adequate and its personnel are qualified. After entering into a contract, the managed care entity should be aware of performance problems associated with the URO. The managed care entity must walk a fine line between monitoring, which is a duty, and controlling, which could create an agency relationship leading to ostensible agency or vicarious liability lawsuits. (See **Questions 4:28–4:32** for a discussion of ostensible agency and vicarious liability. See **Chapter 8** for a discussion of negligent selection of health care providers.)

Q.4:53   What must a subscriber show to recover for negligent selection of a URO?

The subscriber must show that the MCO owed the subscriber a duty to carefully select a utilization review organization, that the MCO breached that duty by failing to act reasonably in selecting the URO, and that the failure to carefully select a URO caused the subscriber's injuries.

Q.4:54   What should an MCO do to avoid liability for negligently selecting a URO?

MCOs selecting a utilization review organization should ensure that the URO meets the following criteria:

- The UR entity or personnel are properly licensed (if required by state law) and comply with the standards of a private accreditation organization. (See **Questions 4:17–4:27**.)
- The utilization review policies and procedures are clear and are followed on a regular basis.
- Proper personnel review the cases (e.g., the initial reviewer may be a nurse, but a denial should be reviewed by a physician reviewer as well).
- Physician reviewers practice in the area of medicine relevant to the cases they review.
- There is discussion with the attending physician prior to rendering a denial.
- The basis of denials and the protocols followed are documented.

- Patients and physicians have the right to appeal denials, and there is a procedure for doing so.
- Medical criteria are based on local practice standards (unless dealing with a specialty hospital).
- Denials are communicated to the patient, and the patient is informed of his or her rights.

Appendix 4-A

State-by-State Utilization Review (UR) Laws

Key to information contained in this survey:

Responsible Agency: Governmental agency responsible for enforcing the law; phone number.

Requirements: Requirements to perform utilization review (licensure, registration, certification, or other pertinent information).

Cost: Cost of obtaining/maintaining UR certification, etc.

Accred. Waiver: Provision granting commissioner authority to waive UR requirements for entities accredited by URAC or other utilization accreditation organization.

Exemptions: Entities exempt from the law. Also will include exemption from fees, if applicable.

Criteria Disclosure: Requirements for UR criteria disclosure.

Reference for Law: Legal citation and year enacted.

Reference for Regs: Citation for Rules and Regulations, if established, and year.

Application Available: Are applications for UR certification available? (AMCRA members may obtain copies of all such applications through the Office of State Health Policy.)

Notes: Any pertinent additional information.

Recent Activity: Recent legislation/regulatory activity.

We have attempted to confirm the information contained herein with the appropriate regulatory body in each state. Supporting documents are available to AMCRA members through the AMCRA's Office of State Health Policy.

Source: Reprinted with permission from *1995 State Managed Care Legislative Resource*, copyright 1994, American Managed Care and Review Association.

ALABAMA

Responsible agency:	Dept. of Public Health
	(205) 613-5366
Requirements:	Registration, Certification
Cost:	$1000 annually
Accred. Waiver:	Application requirements shall not apply to any entity accredited by URAC. However, URAC accredited entities shall file their URAC certification annually with the Dept.
Exemptions:	Workers Compensation
	(Subject to Ala. Code § 25-5-312)
	State licensed HMOs, but only to the extent of providing UR to their own members.
Criteria Disclosure:	No requirements
Reference for Law:	1994 Ala. Acts 786
Application Available:	Yes

ALASKA

No UR law has been enacted.

ARIZONA

Responsible Agency:	Dept. of Insurance
	(602) 542-4236
Requirements:	Registration, Certification
Cost:	$500 initial fee, renewable every 3 years
Accred. Waiver:	URAC/NCQA accredited companies (exempts fee)
Exemptions:	This law grants a full exemption for a UR agent that conducts internal UR for hospitals, home health agencies, clinics, private offices, or other health facilities or entities if the review does not result in the approval or denial of payment for medical services.
Criteria Disclosure:	No requirements
Reference for Law:	Ariz. Rev. Stat. § 20-2301, et. seq (1993)
Application Available:	Yes

ARKANSAS

Responsible Agency:	Dept. of Health
	(501) 661-2771

Requirements:	Certification
Cost:	$1500/biennially paid in advance
Accred. Waiver:	None
Exemptions:	None
Criteria Disclosure:	No requirements
Reference for Law:	Ark. Code Ann. § 20-9-901 et seq. (1988)
Reference for Regs:	Ark. Reg. 43 § 12 (1990)
Application Available:	Yes
Notes:	While the Dept. reported no exemptions, the law provides that certification is not required for those private review agents conducting general in-house UR for hospitals, home health agencies, PPOs, or other managed care entities so long as the review does not result in the approval or denial of payment for medical services for a particular case.

CALIFORNIA

Responsible Agency:	Department of Corporations (213) 736-2741
Requirements:	No licensure or certification requirement. For contested UR decisions, reviewers must possess the "education, training, and relevant expertise that is pertinent for evaluating the specific clinical issues." Applies to HMOs only.
Cost:	N/A
Accred. Waiver:	N/A
Exemptions:	N/A
Criteria Disclosure:	No requirements
Reference for Law:	Chapter 614, Acts of 1994 (SB 1832) (effective January 1, 1995)

COLORADO

Responsible Agency:	Dept. of Insurance (303) 894-7499
Requirements:	None
Cost:	N/A
Accred. Waiver:	None
Exemptions:	Workers Compensation (Subject to Colo. Rev. Stat. § 8-43-501)

Criteria Disclosure: No requirements
Reference for Law: Colo. Rev. Stat. § 10-4-115 (1993)
Application Available: N/A
Notes: The law makes insurance carriers liable for any inappropriate denial of benefits made by a contracted utilization review organization. Additionally, makes carriers, HMOs, and non-profit hospital and health care service corporations responsible for the actions of a utilization review organization acting on behalf of the entity.

CONNECTICUT

Responsible Agency: Insurance Dept.
                          (203) 297-3859
Requirements: Licensure, Certification
Cost: $2500 annually
Accred. Waiver: The Commissioner of Insurance may find that the minimum standards have been met if the UR entity has received accreditation by a UR accreditation organization.
Exemptions: None
Criteria Disclosure: No requirements
Reference for Law: Conn. Gen. Stat. § 38A-226a et seq. (1991)
Application Available: Yes

DELAWARE

No UR law has been enacted.

DISTRICT OF COLUMBIA

Note: D.C. Code Ann. § 36-301 et seq. requires URAC accreditation for firms performing utilization review on Workers Compensation claims.

FLORIDA

Responsible Agency: Agency for Health Care Administration
                          (904) 487-2717

Requirements: Registration, Certification
Cost: $250 annually
Accred. Waiver: None
Exemptions: ERISA plans
        Workers Compensation (Subject to Fla. Stat. ch. 440.13) (1992)
Criteria Disclosure: No requirements
Reference for Law: Fla. Stat. ch. 395.0199 et seq. (1990)
Reference for Regs: Fla. Admin. Code r. 10D-111.001 et seq. (1991)
Application Available: Yes
Notes: Although the Agency reported exemptions for workers' compensation and ERISA, Fla. Stat. ch. 395.002(23) provides that the term "private review agent" does not apply to full-time employees, personnel, or staff of health insurers, HMOs, or hospitals, or wholly owned subsidiaries thereof or affiliates under common ownership, when performing UR for their respective organizations or insureds. For this purpose, health insurers, HMOs, and hospitals, or wholly owned subsidiaries thereof or affiliates under common ownership, include such entities engaged as administrators of self-insurance.

GEORGIA

Responsible Agency: Dept. of Insurance
        Life and Health Division
        (404) 657-6041
Requirements: Registration, Certification
        URAC accreditation required for Certification
Cost: $1000 initial fee, good for 2 years, $500 biennially
Accred. Waiver: None
Exemptions: ERISA plans
        Workers Compensation (Subject to Ga. Code Ann. § 33-7-3)
Criteria Disclosure: No requirements
Reference for Law: Ga. Code Ann. § 33-46-1 et seq. (1990)
Application Available: No
Notes: Regulations were proposed June 1994, and are currently pending.

HAWAII

Responsible Agency: Dept. of Health
        (808) 586-4688

Requirements: Registration
Cost: None
Accred. Waiver: None
Exemptions: None
Criteria Disclosure: Statute requires public access to criteria and standards used in utilization review and managed care activities as they relate to mental health and chemical dependency.
Reference for Law: Haw. Rev. Stat. § 334B-1 et seq. (1991)
Application Available: No

IDAHO

No UR law has been enacted.

ILLINOIS

Responsible Agency: Dept. of Insurance
                         (217) 782-4515
Requirements: None
Cost: N/A
Accred. Waiver: None
Exemptions: None
Criteria Disclosure: No requirements
Reference for Law: Ill. Rev. Stat. Ch. 20, para. 2215/3-5 et seq. (1984)
Application Available: N/A
Notes: This law allows for third party payer utilization review activities.
Recent Activity: Comprehensive UR legislation (HB 4050/HB 4189) was considered in 1994, and is likely to be introduced in 1995.

INDIANA

Responsible Agency: Dept. of Insurance
                         (317) 232-2385
Requirements: Licensure
Cost: $300 application fee
                         $200 annually
Accred. Waiver: The Department may determine that a UR agent satisfies the requirements set forth in this law if the UR agent maintains the accreditation of a UR accreditation organization that has been approved by the Department.

Exemptions: Although the Dept. did not so acknowledge, the law states that it does not apply to entities conducting general in-house UR for hospitals, home health agencies, HMOs, PPOs, and other managed care entities, clinics, private offices, or any other health facility, so long as the review does not result in the approval or denial of an enrollee's coverage for medical services.

Criteria Disclosure: No requirements
Reference for Law: Ind. Code § 27-8-17-1 et seq. (1992)
Reference for Regs: 760 Ind. Admin. Code tit. 1-46 (1992)
Application Available: Yes
Notes: Medical Claims Review Law (amended in 1994, HB 1321) requires that claims review agents base their decisions on the appropriateness of health care services delivered to the enrollee and requires them to include detailed information in each notification of a medical review determination based on the appropriateness of the amount charged for the service.

IOWA

Responsible Agency: Dept. of Insurance
                            (515) 281-4222
Requirements: Payers (Insurers, HMOs, PPOs, etc.) are required to register with the Department. Utilization Review must be conducted in accordance with URAC standards.
Cost: None
Accred. Waiver: None
Exemptions: None
Criteria Disclosure: No requirements
Reference for Law: Iowa Admin. Code r. 191-70.1 (1992)
Application Available: No
Notes: Dept. requires firms performing utilization review on mental health to certify compliance with confidentiality statute.

KANSAS

Responsible Agency: Dept. of Insurance
                            (913) 296-3071
Requirements: Certification (effective 5/95)
Cost: $100 annually

Accred. Waiver:	URAC accredited companies and Kansas City-area UR organizations subscribing to the voluntary guidelines established by the Kansas City private review group.
Exemptions:	This law does not apply to:

1) reviews conducted by any insurance company, HMO, prepaid service plan, ERISA plan or similar entity solely for the purpose of determining compliance with specific terms and conditions of an insurance policy; or
2) a state-licensed Federally qualified HMO which is administering a quality assurance program and performing UR activities for its own members;
3) Workers Compensation (Subject to Kan. Stat. Ann. § 44-501 et seq.)

Criteria Disclosure:	No requirements
Reference for Law:	1994 Kan. Sess. Laws 909
Application Available:	No
Notes:	Currently developing regulations.

KENTUCKY

Responsible agency:	Office of the Inspector General Insurance Licensing and Regulation (502) 564-2800
Requirements:	Registration, Certification
Cost:	$500 biennially
Accred. Waiver:	None
Exemptions:	Workers Compensation
Criteria Disclosure:	No requirement
Reference for Law:	Ky. Rev. Stat. Ann. § 211.461 et seq. and § 311.131 et seq. (1990)
Reference for Regs:	906 Ky. Admin. Regs. 1:080 (1991)
Application Available:	Yes
Notes:	While the OIG only identified workers' compensation as exempted, the statute provides for a limited exemption, stating that no registration shall be required for private review agents conducting in-house UR for hospitals, home health agencies, PPOs, or other managed care entities, clinics, private offices, or any other health facility so long as the review does not result in the approval or denial of payment for medical services for a particular case.

LOUISIANA

Responsible Agency:	Dept. of Health
	(504) 342-5778
Requirement:	Certification
Cost:	$500 initial fee
	$350 biennially
Accred. Waiver:	None
Exemptions:	HMOs
	Workers Compensation (Subject to La. Rev. Stat. Ann.)
	§ 23:1291 (1992)
Criteria Disclosure:	No requirements
Reference for Law:	La. Rev. Stat. Ann. § 40:2721 et seq. 1992
Application Available:	Yes
Notes:	While the Dept. only identified HMOs and workers' compensation as exempt, the statute states that no certificate shall be required for:

1) those private review agents who conduct general in-house UR for hospitals, HMOs, home health agencies, PPOs, other managed care entities, clinics, private offices, or any other health facility, provided the review does not result in the approval or denial of payment for hospital or medical services in a particular case;

2) an HMO which acts as a private review agent, which performs UR exclusively for its own contracted enrollees.

MAINE

Responsible Agency:	Bureau of Insurance
	(207) 582-8707
Requirements:	Licensure, Certification
Cost:	$400 application fee + $100 initial fee
	$100 annually
Accred. Waiver:	None
Exemptions:	HMOs
Criteria Disclosure:	1993 amendment requires that firms submit criteria to the Bureau of Insurance.
Reference for Law:	Me. Rev. Stat. Ann. tit. 24, § 2340 et seq., and tit. 24-A, § 2771 et seq. (1993)
Reference for Regs:	Code Me. R. § 1 et seq. (1991)
Application Available:	Yes
Notes:	While the Bureau only identified HMOs as exempt, the statute states that this law does not apply to an

insurer, nonprofit service organization, HMO, PPO, or an employee of those exempt organizations that performs medical UR services on behalf of commercial insurers, nonprofit service organizations, third-party administrators, or employers.

MARYLAND

Responsible Agency:	Dept. of Health and Mental Hygiene Licensing and Certification (410) 764-4979
Requirements:	Registration, Certification Criteria disclosure with application
Cost:	$1500 biennially
Accred. Waiver:	None
Exemptions:	None
Criteria Disclosure:	As of 1992, private review agents are required to provide specific criteria and standards used in conducting utilization review, upon written request by any person or health facility.
Reference for Law:	Md. Code Ann., Health-Gen. § 19-1301 et seq., §§ 48A-470Y, 48A-477-II
Reference for Regs:	Md. Regs. Code 10.07.19.01-.12
Application Available:	Yes

MASSACHUSETTS

Notes:	Mass. Gen. L. Ch. 6B, § 4 reauthorized as part of hospital rate regulation revisions. Allows third party payers to conduct utilization review. No registration or certification required. (Registration is required for workers' compensation utilization review. Contact the Department of Industrial Accidents at (617) 727-4900 for more information.)

MICHIGAN

No UR law has been enacted.

MINNESOTA

Responsible Agency:	Commission of Commerce and Health (612) 296-9431
Requirements:	Registration

Cost: None
Accred. Waiver: None
Exemptions: None
Criteria Disclosure: No requirement
Reference for Law: Minn. Stat. § 62M.01 et seq. (1992)
Application Available: Yes
Notes: Board of Chiropractic Examiners requires registration for chiropractic reviewers, and an amendment to Minn. Stat. § 62M.01 requires that chiropractic review be performed by a chiropractor.

MISSISSIPPI

Responsible Agency: Dept. of Health
                        Licensing and Certification
                        (601) 354-7300
Requirements: Registration, Certification
Cost: $1000 biennially
Accred. Waiver: None
Exemptions: None
Criteria Disclosure: No requirements
Reference for Law: Miss. Code Ann. § 41-83-1 et seq. (1990)
Application Available: Yes
Notes: While the Dept. reported no exemptions, the statute states that certification not required for those private UR agents conducting general in-house UR for hospitals, home health agencies, PPOs, or other managed care entities, clinics, private physician offices, or any other health facility or entity, so long as the review does not result in the approval or denial of payment for medical services for a particular case. Such general in-house UR is completely exempt from the provisions of this law.

MISSOURI

Responsible Agency: Dept. of Insurance
                        (314) 751-4363
Requirements: Registration, Certification
Cost: $1000 initial fee
                        $500 annually

Accred. Waiver:	None
Exemptions:	This law does not apply to: 1) HMOs performing UR for its own enrollees; and 2) ERISA plans
Criteria Disclosure:	No requirements
Reference for Law:	Mo. Rev. Stat. § 374.500 et seq. (1991)
Reference for Regs:	Mo. Code Regs. tit. 20, § 700-4.1 et seq. (1994)
Application Available:	Yes
Notes:	Board of Chiropractic Examiners requires certification for "Chiropractic Insurance Consultants." $1000 initial certification fee, $500 annual renewal fee.

MONTANA

Responsible Agency:	Dept. of Insurance Licensing Dept. (406) 444-2040
Requirements:	Firms must have a Utilization Review Plan on file with the Commissioner.
Cost:	None
Accred. Waiver:	None
Exemptions:	A general in-house UR for health care provider (including an in-house UR that is conducted by or for a long-term care facility and that is required by Medicare or Medicaid regulations) is exempt from the provisions of this law as long as the review does not directly result in the approval or denial of payment for health care services for a particular case.
Criteria Disclosure:	No requirements
Reference for Law:	Mont. Code Ann. §§ 33-32-101 et seq. 33-32-201 et seq. (1993)
Application Available:	N/A

NEBRASKA

Responsible Agency:	Dept. of Insurance (402) 471-4707
Requirements:	Certification URAC accreditation (or similar body)
Cost:	$300 initial fee $100 biennially

Accred. Waiver: None
Exemptions: This law does not apply to:
1) internal quality assurance programs conducted by hospitals, home health agencies, PPOs, HMOs, or other managed care entities, clinics, or private offices for purposes other than for allowing, denying, or making a recommendation on allowing or denying an enrollee's claim for payment;
2) ERISA plans; or
3) Workers Compensation
Reference for Law: Neb. Rev. Stat. § 44-5401 et seq. (1992)
Application Available: Yes

NEVADA

Responsible Agency: Dept. of Insurance
                         (702) 687-4270
Requirements: Certification
Cost: $250 annually
Accred. Waiver: None
Exemptions: Although the statute provides HMOs with a full exemption from the provisions of this law, state Department of Commerce regulations require HMOs to register with the state in order to engage in UR activity.
Criteria Disclosure: No requirements
Reference for Law: Nev. Rev. Stat. § 683A.375 et seq. (1991)
Reference for Regs: Nev. Admin. Code § 683A.280 et seq. (1992)
Application Available: Yes

NEW HAMPSHIRE

Responsible Agency: Insurance Dept.
                         (603) 271-2261
Requirements: Licensure
                         URAC standards are minimal acceptable standards for licensure
Cost: $500 application fee
                         $100 annually
Accred. Waiver: None
Exemptions: This law does not apply to an insurer, nonprofit service organization, HMO, PPO, or an employee of any of the above that performs medical UR services on behalf of same. However, any person, partnership, or

corporation which performs UR services, but which is exempt from licensure, shall register with the Department of Insurance. Upon registration, such person, partnership, or corporation shall be considered a licensee for all the purposes of this law, but shall not be required to file an application for licensure or pay any licensure fees.

Criteria Disclosure:	No requirements
Reference for Law:	N.H. Rev. Stat. Ann. § 420-E:2 et seq. (1993)
Reference for Regs:	Anticipated November 1994 completion
Application Available:	No

NEW JERSEY

Notes: Prior to 1992, the Dept. of Health certified a utilization review organization for each region of the state to make binding decisions on in-patient DRG admissions. Legislation approved in 1992 overturned this system, and is still in effect. The state does not currently regulate utilization review.

NEW MEXICO

Notes: 1994 enacted legislation (SB 862, amending N.M. Stat. Ann. § 61-6-6) defines the "practice of medicine" to include utilization review activities. Although it is still unclear how the law is to be implemented, it may have the practical impact of prohibiting UR conducted by anyone other than a New Mexico-licensed physician.

NEW YORK

Recent Activity: UR certification legislation was considered in 1994.

NORTH CAROLINA

Responsible Agency: Dept. of Insurance
(919) 715-0526

Requirements:	Registration
	Every payer must present to the Commissioner certification that the UR agents they contract with are in compliance with the statute.
Cost:	None
Accred. Waiver:	None
Exemptions:	ERISA plans
Criteria Disclosure:	No requirements
Reference for Law:	N.C. Gen. Stat. § 58-50-60 (1989)
Reference for Regs:	N.C. Admin. Code tit. 11, r. 12.0903 et seq. (1991)
Application Available:	No
Notes:	While the law states that payers must report to the Commissioner, the Department of Insurance has recently required UROs to submit reports of UR activity and be certified by the Department.

NORTH DAKOTA

Responsible Agency:	Insurance Dept.
	(701) 224-2440
Requirements:	Registration, Certification 1993 amendment requires the submission of a client list, concurrence of a physician trained in the relevant specialty on final appeal, and to allow providers to request that a UR agent furnish them with a copy of the medical review criteria.
Cost:	$10 annually
Accred. Waiver:	The Insurance Commissioner may find that the standards in this law have been met if the UR agent has received approval or accreditation by a UR accreditation organization.
Criteria Disclosure:	See requirements above
Reference for Law:	N.D. Cent. Code § 65-01-02 (1993)
Application Available:	Yes

OHIO

Recent Activity:	1994 proposed legislation (HB 526) mandates that only a state licensed UR agent may conduct UR in the state.

OKLAHOMA

Responsible Agency:	Insurance Dept.
	(405) 521-6619

Requirements:	Registration, Certification
Cost:	$500 annually
Accred. Waiver:	None
Exemptions:	No certificate is required for those private review agents conducting general in-house UR for hospitals, home health agencies, PPOs, or other managed care entities, clinics, private offices, or any other health facility or entity, so long as the review does not result in the approval or denial of payment for medical services for a particular case.
Criteria Disclosure:	No requirements
Reference for Law:	Okla. Stat. Ann. tit. 36, § 6551 et seq. (1991)
Application Available:	Yes

OREGON

Responsible Agency:	Insurance Dept. (503) 986-1180
Notes:	Or. Rev. Stat. § 743.556 establishes utilization review criteria for chemical dependence and mental conditions.

PENNSYLVANIA

Notes:	Pennsylvania Code Chap. 68, Title 31, Part 2 requires registration for firms conducting automobile insurance utilization review.
Recent Activity:	Legislation proposed regarding UR in the state.

RHODE ISLAND

Responsible Agency:	Dept. of Health (401) 277-2566
Requirements:	Certification
Cost:	$3000 biennially
Accred. Waiver:	Except for UR activities performed to determine the necessity and appropriateness of substance abuse and mental health care, the Department shall waive the requirements of this law (except for sections 12-9, 12-

12, and 12-14) for a review agent that has received, maintains, and provides evidence of accreditation from URAC or any other organization approved by the Director of the Department of Health.

Criteria Disclosure:	No requirements
Reference for Law:	R.I. Gen. Laws § 23-17.12-1 et seq. (1992)
Reference for Regs:	R.I. Regs. § 23-17-12.1-UR (1993)
Application Available:	Yes
Notes:	Non-accredited and psych/substance abuse firms are subject to an independent appeals process.

SOUTH CAROLINA

Responsible Agency:	Dept. of Insurance (803) 737-6150
Requirements:	Certification
Cost:	$400 application fee $800 biennially
Accred. Waiver:	None
Exemptions:	HMOs
Criteria Disclosure:	No requirements
Reference for Law:	S.C. Code Ann. § 38-70-10 et seq. (1990)
Application Available:	Yes
Notes:	1) Working on regulations. Possible February 1995 completion;
	2) While the Dept. reported that only HMOs are exempt, the statute states that it does not apply to insurance companies and HMOs licensed and regulated by the S.C. Department of Insurance.

SOUTH DAKOTA

No UR law has been enacted.

TENNESSEE

Responsible Agency:	Dept. of Commerce and Insurance (615) 741-2825
Requirements:	Registration, Certification
Cost:	$1000 annually

Accred. Waiver:	The Insurance Commissioner shall exempt from these standards any UR agent which has received accreditation by URAC.
Criteria Disclosure:	No requirements
Reference for Law:	Tenn. Code Ann. § 56-6-701 et seq. (1993)
Application Available:	Yes
Notes:	While the Dept. reports no other exemptions, the statute states that HMOs licensed and regulated by the Insurance Commissioner are exempt from this law, but only to the extent of providing UR to their own members.

TEXAS

Responsible Agency:	Dept. of Insurance (512) 322-3401
Requirements:	Registration, Certification
Cost:	$2157 initial fee, good for 2 years $2076 renewal every two years
Accred. Waiver:	None
Exemptions:	ERISA plans Workers Compensation (Subject to Tex. Code Ann. § 8308-.01 et seq.) Must send a letter requesting exemption.
Criteria Disclosure:	No requirements
Reference for Law:	Tex. Code Ann. § 21.58A (1991)
Reference for Regs:	Tex. Admin. Code tit. 2819.1701 et seq. (1992)
Application Available:	Yes
Notes:	Firms conducting chemical dependency utilization review must comply with the insurance regulation Title 28 Part I, Chapter 3, Subchapter HH, 28 TAC 3.8001-3.8022. $2157 initial certification, $2076 biennial renewal fee.

UTAH

No UR law has been enacted.

VERMONT

Notes:	1994 H.B. 171 would require licensure for firms conducting utilization review on mental health. Prior to 1995 rules are to be established that include disclosure

of review criteria to patients or providers upon request.

VIRGINIA

Responsible Agency:	Bureau of Insurance
	(804) 371-9741
Requirements:	Certification
Cost:	$500 application fee
	$500 biennially
Accred. Waiver:	None
Exemptions:	HMOs
	ERISA plans
Reference for Law:	Va. Code Ann. § 38-2-5300 et seq. (1990)
Reference for Regs:	Va. Regs. Reg. 37 § 1 et seq. (1991)
Application Available:	Yes

WASHINGTON

No UR law has been enacted.

WEST VIRGINIA

No UR law has been enacted.

WISCONSIN

No UR law has been enacted.

WYOMING

No UR law has been enacted.

5

ERISA

INTRODUCTION

Q.5:1　What is ERISA?

ERISA stands for *Employee Retirement Income Security Act*, a federal law that applies to activities involving the sponsorship, administration, and servicing of employee welfare benefit plans, including health plans [ERISA is codified at 29 U.S.C. §§ 1001 through 1461].

Q.5:2　What is an employee welfare plan?

An employee welfare plan subject to ERISA (commonly known as an ERISA plan) is broadly defined in the statute as:

> ... any plan, fund, or program, which was heretofore or is hereafter established or maintained by an employer or by an employee organization, or by both, to the extent that such plan, fund, or program was established or is maintained for the purpose of providing for its participants or their beneficiaries, through the purchase of insurance or otherwise, (A) medical, surgical, or hospital care or benefits, or benefits in the event of sickness, accident, disability, death, or unemployment, or vacation benefits, apprenticeship or other training programs, or day care centers, scholarship funds, or prepaid legal services or (B) any benefit described in Section 302(c) of the Labor Management Relations Act, 1947 (other than pensions on retirement or death and insurance to provide such pension) [29 U.S.C. § 1002(1)].

Thus, employer-sponsored health plans, including managed care plans, are subject to ERISA.

Q.5:3   What is an employer?

ERISA defines *employer* more broadly than the everyday use of the term. An employer is "any person acting directly as an employer, or indirectly in the interest of an employer in relation to an employee benefit plan; and includes a group or association of employers acting for an employer in such a capacity" [29 U.S.C. § 1002(5)].

Q.5:4   What aspects of plan administration does ERISA regulate?

In addition to reporting and disclosure requirements not discussed in this chapter, ERISA:

- regulates the conduct of plan fiduciaries, requiring them to act in a certain matter with respect to the plan;
- allows ERISA plan beneficiaries to sue ERISA plans for damages, under certain circumstances;
- outlines procedures for claims review, denial, and appeals; and
- pre-empts state laws that relate to ERISA plans.

FIDUCIARIES

Q.5:5   What is a fiduciary?

Generally speaking, a fiduciary is a person under a duty to act primarily for another's benefit. Fiduciaries have special duties of good faith and candor toward the individuals for whom they act. A common example is a trustee. ERISA contains its own definition of fiduciary in connection with employee welfare plans. ERISA states that a person is a fiduciary to the extent that the person:

- exercises any discretionary authority or discretionary control regarding management of the plan or exercises any authority or control involving management or disposition of the plan's assets;
- provides investment advice for a fee or other compensation, direct or indirect, regarding any moneys or other property of such plan, or has any authority or responsibility to do so; or
- has discretionary authority or discretionary responsibility in the administration of the plan [29 U.S.C. § 1002(21)(A)].

Q.5:6   What is a named fiduciary?

ERISA plans must specifically designate, in writing, at least one named fiduciary, identified by job title, or by name, who is responsible for plan operation and administration [29 U.S.C. § 1102(a)]. A plan's named fiduciary is not the only fiduciary, however, as ERISA, federal regulations, and courts rely on activities rather than titles to identify fiduciaries.

Q.5:7   What specific tasks will not create fiduciary status under ERISA?

The Department of Labor, a federal agency, has issued regulations indicating that fiduciary status turns on whether an individual's functions are discretionary or ministerial. According to the agency, fiduciary status will *not* arise from conducting the following ministerial tasks within the framework of policies, interpretations, rules, practices, and procedures made by others:

- applying rules to determine eligibility for participation or benefits
- calculating service and compensation credits for benefits
- preparing employee communications material
- maintaining participants' service and employment records
- preparing reports required by governmental agencies
- calculating benefits
- conducting orientation of new participants and advising participants of their rights and options under the plan
- collecting contributions and applying contributions as provided in the plan
- preparing reports regarding participants' benefits
- making recommendations to others for decisions regarding plan administration [29 C.F.R. § 2509.75-8, D-2]

Q.5:8   Are claims processors considered fiduciaries under ERISA?

The answer to this question depends on the duties of the particular claims processor. A regulation issued by the Department of Labor provides that a party with authority to review and decide upon denied claims is a fiduciary for purposes of ERISA claims review [29 C.F.R. § 2650.503-1(g)]. Claims processors who perform only administrative functions are not fiduciaries, however [29 C.F.R. § 2509-75.8, D-2]. Refer to **Questions 5:26–5:31** for a discussion of ERISA claims review requirements, and to **Chapter 4** for other claims review requirements.

Q.5:9   How have courts interpreted the definition of fiduciary?

Courts have applied ERISA's definition of a fiduciary liberally. The fact that an individual is not named as a fiduciary or does not carry a fiduciary's title is not relevant. What is important is whether the individual or entity has discretionary authority or control over some aspect of the plan, its operations, and administration of its assets. [*See, e.g., Fulk v. Bagley*, 88 F.R.D. 153 (D.N.C. 1980); *Eaves v. Penn*, 587 F.2d 453 (10th Cir. 1978).]

Q.5:10   What entities have courts considered fiduciaries?

Courts have held that the following entities are ERISA fiduciaries:

- insurance companies performing claims processing [*Credit Managers Ass'n v. Kennesaw Life & Accident Ins. Co.*, 809 F.2d 617 (9th Cir. 1987)]
- insurance companies with the power to manage assets where a guaranteed annuity contract is not involved [*Peoria Union Stock Yards Co. Retirement Plan v. Penn. Mutual Life Ins. Co.*, 698 F.2d 320 (7th Cir. 1986)]
- insurance companies with the power to amend unilaterally a provision of a contract [*Ed Miniat, Inc. v. Globe Life Ins. Group, Inc.*, 805 F.2d 732 (7th Cir. 1986), *cert. denied*, 482 U.S. 915 (1987)]
- consulting firms [*McNeese v. Health Plan Marketing, Inc.*, 647 F. Supp. 981 (N.D. Ala. 1986)]

Q.5:11   What MCOs can be considered fiduciaries?

The following MCOs might be considered fiduciaries with respect to a medical plan because they have discretionary authority with regard to plan administration:

- HMOs
- entities acting as agent for and governing the operation of a PPO

- utilization review firms
- other service providers engaged by a plan to assist the plan's fiduciary in evaluating the performance of other fiduciaries if that service provider develops the methodology for evaluation

Q.5:12   Could health care providers be considered fiduciaries?

Generally, it is unlikely that health care providers such as physicians, hospitals, and others practicing directly in the field of medicine would be fiduciaries because their services are provided to the patient, not to the plan. Moreover, it is the delivery of medical care that is purchased by the plan in providing its benefits, as the plan itself cannot deliver medical care. Thus, the practice of medicine is not a matter relating to the operation and administration of the plan. However, quality assurance, utilization review, and other activities provided by hospitals and physicians may be deemed to provide services to the plan in addition to the patient, resulting in some fiduciary responsibility.

Q.5:13   What duties does ERISA impose on fiduciaries?

Any individual or entity who qualifies as a plan fiduciary has the responsibility of a trustee with respect to the plan. Plan fiduciaries have five distinct obligations. ERISA requires a fiduciary to act:

1. solely in the interest of the participants and beneficiaries [29 U.S.C. § 1104(a)]
2. for the exclusive purposes of (1) providing benefits to participants and their beneficiaries and (2) defraying reasonable expenses of administering the plan [*Id.* § (a)(1)(A)]
3. with the care, skill, prudence, and diligence that a prudent person acting in a like capacity and familiar with such matters would use in the conduct of an enterprise of the same character and aims under the same circumstances [*Id.* § (a)(1)(B)]
4. by diversifying the investments of the plan so as to minimize the risk of large losses, unless under the circumstances it clearly is prudent not to do so [*Id.* § (a)(1)(C)]
5. in accordance with the documents and instruments governing the plan insofar as such documents and instruments are consistent with ERISA [*Id.* § (a)(1)(D)]

Q.5:14   What fiduciary conduct does ERISA limit?

In addition to imposing the general duties outlined in the previous question, ERISA prohibits certain transactions. These provisions establish absolute bars to certain kinds of plan transactions and fiduciary conduct unless an exemption applies. There are two types of prohibited transactions. The first type prohibits transactions between a plan and a party in interest. The second type prohibits fiduciaries from taking action when they have a conflict of interest [29 U.S.C. § 1106].

Q.5:15   Can a fiduciary be personally sued by an ERISA plan?

ERISA states that a fiduciary will have personal liability to the plan for a fiduciary breach. Any fiduciary who breaches any of the responsibilities, obligations, or duties imposed upon fiduciaries will be personally liable for any losses to the plan resulting from each breach and must restore to the plan profits the fiduciary made through use of assets of the plan. Further, the fiduciary may be subject to other relief that the court finds appropriate [29 U.S.C. § 1109].

Q.5:16   When can a fiduciary be liable for another fiduciary's conduct?

A fiduciary will be liable for another fiduciary's breach if the non-breaching fiduciary:

- participates knowingly in, or knowingly undertakes to conceal, an act or omission of such other fiduciary, knowing such act or omission is a breach
- enables the other fiduciary to commit a breach by failing to comply with his or her specific fiduciary responsibilities
- has knowledge of the breach by the other fiduciary and does not make reasonable efforts under the circumstances to remedy the breach [29 U.S.C. § 1105(a)]

LIABILITY TO ERISA PLAN BENEFICIARIES

Q.5:17   When may a plan beneficiary sue an ERISA plan?

ERISA allows a plan participant or beneficiary to:

- obtain relief from an administrator's unlawful refusal to provide information to which the participant or beneficiary is entitled [29 U.S.C. § 1132 (a)(1)(A)]
- recover benefits due under the terms of the plan, enforce his or her rights under the terms of the plan, or clarify his or her rights to future benefits [*Id.* § (a)(1)(B)]
- obtain relief for breaches of fiduciary duty [Id. § (a)(2)]
- enjoin any act or practice that violates ERISA or the terms of the plan, or obtain other appropriate equitable relief to redress violations or enforce ERISA provisions or plan terms [*Id.* § (a)(3)]
- sue for interference with ERISA-protected rights [29 U.S.C. § 1140]

Q.5:18   Can beneficiaries sue on any grounds not listed in the statute?

The courts have begun to expand the possible remedies available under ERISA. For example, a few federal appeals courts have recognized a cause of action known as *estoppel* under ERISA. Estoppel is a legal doctrine that prevents a party (the insurer) from refusing a benefit to another party (the beneficiary) because of a statement that the first party (the insurer) made earlier. For example, in a federal appeals court case, a plan participant asked a representative of the insurance company if the plan would cover the medical expenses of a disabled child he and his wife were planning to adopt. The insurer responded that coverage would begin upon commencement of formal legal adoption proceedings. The claims for the child's medical expenses were denied later, however, because hospitalization had begun prior to the date of the coverage. When the beneficiary sued, the court held that estoppel principles may be applied when a beneficiary relies on the interpretations made by a plan fiduciary [*Kane v. Aetna Life Ins. Co.*, 893 F.2d 1283 (11th Cir. 1990), *cert. denied*, 498 U.S. 890 (1990)]. Other federal courts have also allowed estoppel claims in ERISA cases.

Q.5:19   What damages are available to successful claimants under ERISA?

There are three types of damages that courts have addressed in suits by ERISA beneficiaries—contract damages, extracontractual damages, and punitive damages.

Q.5:20   When does a beneficiary obtain contract damages?

A plan beneficiary who successfully sues because benefits were wrongly denied will be awarded damages that are referred to as contract damages—the amount that would have been paid if the contract had properly been enforced.

Q.5:21   Are extracontractual damages available under ERISA?

Extracontractual damages are damages that result from a breach of contract but are not included in the contract. A monetary award for pain and suffering would constitute extracontractual damages, for example. There is a split among the courts as to whether extracontractual damages are available under ERISA. Several federal circuit courts have ruled that this type of damages is not available under ERISA, reasoning that damages not specifically permitted by the statute cannot be awarded [*Harsch v. Eisenberg*, 956 F.2d 651 (7th Cir. 1992), *cert. denied*, 113 S. Ct. 61 (1992); *Novak v. Andersen Corp.*, 962 F.2d 757 (8th Cir. 1992); *Reinking v. Philadelphia Am. Life. Ins. Co.*, 910 F.2d 1210 (4th Cir. 1990)].

A few courts have allowed extracontractual damages in ERISA cases, however. In one case, for example, a plan beneficiary who incurred substantial financial penalties because a plan fiduciary did not make a timely distribution of funds sued the fiduciary, seeking reimbursement for the financial penalties. The court ruled that since ERISA uses trust law principles and extracontractual damages are available under trust law, they are available under ERISA as well [*Warren v. Society Nat'l Bank*, 905 F.2d 975 (6th Cir. 1990), *cert. denied*, 500 U.S. 952 (1991)].

Q.5:22   Can ERISA beneficiaries obtain punitive damages?

Punitive damages, intended not to compensate the claimant, but to punish reckless or intentional bad conduct, generally have not been available under ERISA. The United States Supreme Court has held that punitive damages are not an appropriate remedy under ERISA in a case involving a breach of fiduciary duty. Although the actual ruling was limited to punitive damages for violation of one specific provision of ERISA, the court found that Congress did not intend to allow damages not specifically identified in the statute [*Massachusetts Mut. Life Ins. Co. v. Russell*, 473 U.S. 134 (1985)].

A more recent Supreme Court ruling may have introduced the possibility that punitive damages are available under ERISA, however, by citing the power of the federal courts to provide relief including punitive damages [*Ingersoll-Rand Co. v. McClendon*, 498 U.S. 133 (1990)]. Most lower courts that have considered the issue have refused to award punitive damages.

Q.5:23 What does standard of review mean?

This legal term refers to the amount of deference with which a court will review an earlier determination. For example, an appeals court will typically give a trial court's factual determinations a clearly erroneous standard of review, overturning the lower court's findings only upon a finding of clear error.

Q.5:24 What is the standard of review for an ERISA fiduciary's decisions?

A court examining the decision of an ERISA fiduciary (a claim denial, for example) will apply one of two standards of review, depending on the language of the benefits contract.

1. *De novo:* The court will apply this standard of review if the benefits contract does *not* grant the plan administrator discretion to interpret the plan's terms. Under the *de novo* standard, the court will consider all evidence independently, granting no deference to the administrator's original determinations [*Firestone Tire & Rubber Co. v. Bruch*, 489 U.S. 101 (1989)].
2. *Abuse of discretion/arbitrary and capricious:* The court will apply this standard of review if the benefits contract *does* grant the plan administrator discretion to interpret the plan's terms. Under this standard, the court will overturn the administrator's decision only if the administrator abused his or her discretion, or if the decision was arbitrary and capricious. This is a much more lenient standard of review, making it more difficult for beneficiaries to obtain benefits that were denied by the plan [*Jung v. FMC Corp.*, 755 F.2d 708 (9th Cir. 1985)].

Q.5:25 What role does a fiduciary's financial interest play in determining the standard of review?

Courts have acknowledged that the abuse of discretion standard of review may not be appropriate when the fiduciary's judgment may be affected by financial interests. For example, a fiduciary may benefit financially by denying a beneficiary's claim in cases in which the plan administrator is also the employer. The Supreme Court has held that, in conflict of interest situations, the conflict "must be weighed as a 'facto[r] in determining whether there is an abuse of discretion' " [*Firestone Tire & Rubber Co. v. Bruch*, 489 U.S. 101 (1989), quoting Restatement (Second) of Trusts § 187].

Although courts have described the effect that a conflict of interest has on standard of review in varying terms, the general consensus is that courts will scrutinize the fiduciary's decision more closely when there is a conflict of interest than they would under an abuse of discretion review.

CLAIMS REVIEW

Q.5:26   Does ERISA regulate claims review?

Both ERISA and Department of Labor regulations that implement ERISA specify procedures that must be followed for claims review within ERISA plans. Other legal limitations on claims review are discussed in **Chapter 8.**

Q.5:27   What aspects of claims review do the regulations address?

The regulations contain basic requirements for claims processing, as well as specific procedures for claims denials and appeals.

Q.5:28   What is the overall standard for claims procedures?

The regulations require every ERISA plan to establish and maintain *reasonable* claims procedures. A procedure is reasonable if it:

- is described in the summary plan description,
- does not contain any provision and is not administered in a way that unduly inhibits or hampers the filing or processing of claims,
- provides for written notices to beneficiaries concerning claims processing time limits, and
- complies with claim processing regulations [29 C.F.R. § 2560.503-1(b)].

Q.5:29   What restrictions does ERISA impose on claims denials?

Under ERISA, employee benefit plans must follow two steps when denying a claim:

1. Provide adequate written notice to the plan beneficiary, setting forth the specific reasons for the denial and written in a manner calculated to be understood by the beneficiary; and
2. Afford the beneficiary a reasonable opportunity for full and fair review of the decision denying the claim by a named fiduciary [29 U.S.C. § 1133].

Q.5:30 Do regulations impose more specific requirements for claims denials?

According to the regulations, the plan must notify the beneficiary of the denial within a reasonable period, defined as 90 days or less. The denial must contain:

- the specific reason for the denial,
- specific reference to the pertinent plan provisions on which the denial is based,
- a description of additional information the beneficiary must provide to obtain coverage, and an explanation of why this additional information is necessary, and
- instructions on how to appeal the claim [29 C.F.R. §§ 2560.503-1(e) and (f)].

Q.5:31 How do the regulations impact appeals?

The regulations require ERISA plans to give beneficiaries a reasonable opportunity to appeal, or seek review of, a denied claim. Beneficiaries must be permitted to request an appeal, review pertinent documents, and submit comments in writing. The time limit for requesting an appeal must be at least 60 days. The decision must generally be issued within 60 days of the request for review. The decision must be in writing and must set forth the specific reasons for the denial, including specific references to the pertinent plan provisions on which the decision is based. It must also be written in a manner calculated to be understood by the beneficiary [29 C.F.R. §§ 2560.503-1(g) and (h)].

PRE-EMPTION

Q.5:32 What is pre-emption?

Pre-emption is the legal principle that federal laws take precedence over conflicting state laws. A state law that is pre-empted by a federal law cannot be enforced because doing so would violate the pre-empting federal statute. To the extent that the state law conflicts, it is void.

Q.5:33 What is the ERISA pre-emption clause?

ERISA contains a clause that specifically pre-empts state laws that regulate employee benefit plans. The clause states that ERISA "supersedes any and all State laws insofar as they may now or hereafter relate to any employee benefit plan" [29 U.S.C. §§ 1144(a)].

Q.5:34 What are the elements of ERISA pre-emption?

A managed care organization challenging a state law on pre-emption grounds must show that the law *relates to* an ERISA plan.

Q.5:35 What does *state laws* mean in the ERISA pre-emption clause?

ERISA can pre-empt not only state statutes, but also state common-law claims such as negligence suits.

Q.5:36 How has the Supreme Court interpreted *relates to*?

The pre-emption requirement that a state law relate to an employee benefit plan has been interpreted broadly by the United States Supreme Court. Ruling that ERISA pre-empts a state law requiring employers to provide sick leave to employees unable to work due to pregnancy, the Supreme Court has held that a state law relates to an ERISA plan "in the normal sense of the phrase, if it has a connection with or reference to such a plan" [*Shaw v. Delta Air Lines, Inc.*, 463 U.S. 85 (1983)]. A few years later, the Court held that ERISA pre-empts state law claims for allegedly improper processing of plan benefits, citing the "expansive sweep" and "broad common-sense meaning" of the pre-emption clause [*Pilot Life Ins.*

Co. v. Dedeaux, 481 U.S. 41 (1987)]. In 1990, the Court reiterated that a law relates to an employee benefit plan "even if the law is not specifically designed to affect such plans, or the effect is only indirect" [*Ingersoll-Rand Co. v. McClendon*, 498 U.S. 133 (1990)].

Courts are continuing to define the scope of what relates to an ERISA plan. The remainder of this chapter contains further examples of this analysis.

Q.5:37 What happens when ERISA pre-empts a state law claim?

When ERISA pre-empts a beneficiary's state law claim, the beneficiary must sue under ERISA, which means that recovery generally will be limited to the amount of benefits provided under the plan. When a claim is pre-empted, claimants cannot recover on the basis of state tort or contract law, which often permit more expansive recovery, including damages for emotional distress, and in some instances, punitive damages. (See **Questions 5:17–5:22** for discussion of recovery available under ERISA.)

Q.5:38 In what types of cases is an MCO likely to argue pre-emption ?

MCOs have argued that ERISA pre-empts the following claims:

- negligent claims processing
- negligent credentialing
- medical malpractice

Q.5:39 Does ERISA pre-empt suits for negligent claims processing?

Generally yes, because these suits allege direct liability on the part of the ERISA plan and therefore relate to the plan. *Corcoran v. United Healthcare* is one of the leading cases holding that ERISA pre-empts state law claims based on a plan's direct liability. In this case, the parents of an unborn child who died sued the utilization review service that denied hospitalization coverage for the mother. The woman was employed by a company that contracted with a URO to provide utilization review services for an employee health benefits plan. The woman's physician recommended that she be hospitalized during her last month of pregnancy because she was in a category of high risk, and sought precertification from the URO. The

URO denied the request, instead authorizing 10 hours per day of home nursing care. The fetus went into distress and died during a time when there was no nursing care. The parents sued the URO under state law for wrongful death.

When the URO contended that the case was pre-empted by ERISA, the parents argued that ERISA pre-emption should not apply in this case because it was essentially a malpractice claim against the URO and did not relate to an ERISA plan. The URO countered that it had not made a medical decision, but had merely determined whether the patient was eligible for benefits under the plan, an activity relating to plan administration. The court concluded that the URO does make medical decisions, but went on to rule that the URO makes those decisions in the context of a determination about the availability of benefits under the plan. It therefore held that the state wrongful death action allegedly resulting from the URO's erroneous medical decision is pre-empted by ERISA [*Corcoran v. United Healthcare, Inc.*, 965 F.2d 1321 (5th Cir. 1992), *cert. denied*, 113 S. Ct. 812 (1992)].

Q.5:40   Are negligent credentialing claims pre-empted by ERISA?

Negligent credentialing claims, which are also characterized as negligent selection, supervision, evaluation, or monitoring claims, allege negligent plan administration and therefore are likely to be pre-empted under the *relate to* analysis. One federal trial court ruled that ERISA pre-empted a claim that an HMO negligently selected and employed unqualified personnel, finding it "well settled . . . that state law claims against an HMO for the HMO's own negligence are pre-empted by ERISA" [*Visconti v. U.S. Health Care*, 857 F. Supp. 1097 (E.D. Pa. 1994)].

In another case, a federal trial court held that a patient may not sue an HMO claiming that it negligently administered a health plan's provisions or failed to properly select and monitor its physicians. The court held that ERISA pre-empts claims against an HMO based on its relationship with a physician because such claims involve an examination of how the benefit plan was explained to its members to determine if the HMO held out the physician as its employee. Thus, the court held, such suits relate to the plan [*Dukes v. United States Health Care Sys.*, 848 F. Supp. 39 (E.D. Pa. 1994)].

Q.5:41   Does ERISA pre-empt medical malpractice suits against ERISA plans?

The courts are divided on whether a suit against an ERISA plan based on health care practitioner negligence is pre-empted by ERISA. Federal courts have reached contradictory results on this issue. Suits against ERISA plans based on practitioner negligence may be based on the legal doctrine of vicarious liability (also known as *respondeat superior*) or the doctrine of apparent agency (also known as *ostensible agency*). These doctrines are discussed in **Chapter 6, Questions 6:2–6:12**.

Q.5:42 For what reasons have courts held that ERISA does pre-empt medical malpractice suits?

Courts holding that ERISA pre-empts suits against ERISA plans based on the negligence of health care practitioners have taken more than one approach.

In one case, parents whose child was stillborn sued their HMO, arguing that the HMO was vicariously liable on the basis of HMO physicians' negligent treatment. The federal trial court ruled that the suit was pre-empted by ERISA, because vicarious liability suits relate to ERISA plans. Vicarious liability suits require examination of the agency relationship between the negligent physicians and the ERISA plan, as well as the terms of the plan, the court reasoned. The court also noted that holding HMOs vicariously liable for the negligence of participating physicians would affect ERISA plans by causing HMOs to carry additional insurance and redefine contractual relationships with physicians [*Visconti v. U.S. Health Care*, 857 F. Supp. 1097 (E.D. Pa. 1994)].

Other courts have taken a broader view of this issue. In one case, for example, the court held that ERISA pre-empted a malpractice claim against a prepaid dental program, finding that all of the claims against the dental plan had one central feature—the circumstances surrounding medical care provided under an employer's dental services plan for employees. Therefore, the claims were pre-empted by ERISA [*Altieri v. CIGNA Dental Health, Inc.*, 753 F. Supp. 61 (D. Conn. 1990)].

Q.5:43 For what reasons have courts held that ERISA does not pre-empt medical malpractice suits?

Courts allowing ERISA plan beneficiaries to sue their plans for malpractice typically focus on the distinction between plan administration and medical care. In one case, for example, the court held an HMO liable under an apparent agency theory for the medical decision of a contracting physician. The court ruled that there was no ERISA pre-emption because the malpractice claim was a "run-of-the-mill" state law claim that was not related to denial of rights under an employee benefit plan [*Independence HMO v. Smith*, 733 F. Supp. 983 (E.D. Pa. 1990)].

Similarly, one court ruled that claims against an HMO and physician were not pre-empted because none of the state law claims related to the scope of the HMO's coverage [*Elsesser v. Hospital of the Philadelphia College of Osteopathic Medicine*, Parkview Div., 795 F. Supp. 142 (E.D. Pa. 1992), modified on other grounds, 802 F. Supp. 1286 (E.D. Pa. 1992)].

Q.5:44   What is the savings clause?

ERISA contains a savings clause that saves certain state laws from ERISA pre-emption. The clause provides that no part of ERISA "shall be construed to exempt or relieve any person from any law of any state which regulates insurance" [29 U.S.C. § 1144(b)(2)(A)].

Courts considering whether the savings clause preserves a state law will examine whether the law:

- is directed at the insurance industry
- transfers policyholder risk
- regulates an integral part of the relationship between the insurer and the insured
- applies only to insurers [*Pilot Life Ins. Co. v. Dedeaux*, 481 U.S. 41 (1987); *Metropolitan Life Ins. Co. v. Massachusetts*, 471 U.S. 724 (1985)]

Q.5:45   What is the deemer clause?

The deemer clause provides that a state may not deem a self-funded employee benefit plan to be an insurance company for the purpose of enforcing state insurance laws. Otherwise stated, self-funded ERISA plans are exempt from state insurance laws [29 U.S.C. § 1144(b)(2)(B)]. Thus, a state law that regulates insurance may be saved by the savings clause, but it will not apply to self-funded ERISA plans due to the deemer clause [*FMC Corp. v. Holliday*, 498 U.S. 52 (1990)].

Q.5:46   What state statutes have courts examined under ERISA pre-emption analysis?

- state initiatives to finance health care
- any willing provider laws
- third party administrator laws

Q.5:47   What happens if a state statute is pre-empted?

A state statute that is pre-empted by ERISA cannot be enforced against ERISA plans.

Q.5:48   Can state initiatives to finance health care coverage be ERISA pre-empted?

Yes, although federal courts have not yet clearly established whether ERISA pre-empts these laws. For example, one federal circuit has held that surcharges or taxes on hospital care to finance health services for needy state residents are permissible because the surcharges do not restrict the decision making of ERISA plans or impair their ability to function in other states. The court viewed the state law as similar to any other law that "increases the cost of goods or services that hospitals consume and pass on in hospital costs" [*United Wire, Metal and Mach. Health and Welfare Fund v. Morristown Memorial Hosp.*, 995 F.2d 1179 (3d Cir. 1993), *cert. denied*, 114 S. Ct. 382 (1993)].

A federal trial court in another circuit specifically refused to follow that decision, however, and ruled that ERISA pre-empts state legislation imposing a surcharge on hospital bills to fund the state's uncompensated care pool. The court rejected the view that the statute operates without regard to ERISA plans, noting that although the statute does not single out ERISA plans for special treatment, it relies heavily on such plans to be effective. The pre-emption provision in ERISA is broad and applies to any state law that has a connection with or reference to an ERISA plan, the court noted, concluding that the connection between the state statute and ERISA plans supports pre-emption [*New England Health Care Employees Union Dist. v. Mt. Sinai Hosp.*, 846 F. Supp. 190 (D. Conn. 1994)].

Q.5:49   Does ERISA pre-empt any willing provider laws?

The courts are split as to whether any willing provider (AWP) statutes, which require MCOs to contract with any provider willing to meet the terms and conditions of the network, are pre-empted by ERISA.

Q.5:50   For what reasons have courts held that ERISA does not pre-empt any willing provider laws?

Courts holding that ERISA does not pre-empt state AWP laws have focused on ERISA's savings clause. (See **Question 5:44** for an introduction to this provision.) In a 1993 case, for example, a hospital challenged an insurer's decision not to include the hospital in its preferred hospital provider network, claiming that the insurer was in violation of Virginia's PPO law, which contains an AWP provision. The Fourth Circuit ruled that ERISA does not pre-empt the AWP provision, because it falls within the ERISA savings clause. Deciding that the AWP provision regulates insurance, the court reasoned that (1) it spreads a policyholder's risk, (2) the practice is an integral part of the policy relationship between the insurer and the insured, and (3) the practice is limited to entities within the insurance industry. The court therefore concluded that the statute regulates insurance contracts, albeit indirectly through the structure of PPOs, and is therefore saved from pre-emption [*Stuart Circle Hosp. Corp. v. Aetna Health Management*, 995 F.2d 500 (4th Cir. 1993), *cert. denied*, 114 S. Ct. 579 (1993)]. (For an introduction to the savings clause, see **Question 5:44**.)

In a second case, the highest court in Virginia ruled that ERISA does not pre-empt a state law prohibiting PPOs from unreasonably discriminating against health care providers who apply for preferred provider status. The provision is rescued by the savings clause, the court held, because it regulates insurance within the meaning of the ERISA pre-emption clause. The court emphasized that the provision was part of the insurance code and that the purposes of a PPO are to achieve lower costs and maximize the choice of providers for insureds [*Blue Cross and Blue Shield of Virginia v. St. Mary's Hosp.*, 426 S.E.2d 117 (Va. 1993)].

Q.5:51   For what reasons have courts held that ERISA does pre-empt any willing provider laws?

Courts concluding that ERISA pre-empts AWP laws have ruled that these laws relate to ERISA plans, stressing the effects that AWP laws have on ERISA plan administration. For example, a federal trial court in Georgia held that an AWP law concerning pharmacies was pre-empted by ERISA. The law required all pharmacies that were willing and able to meet the terms of inclusion to be entitled to become participating pharmacies. The court ruled that the law related to employee benefit plans because it imposed an administrative scheme on plan administrators and regulated the discount features provided to plan beneficiaries [*General Motors Corp. v. Caldwell*, 647 F. Supp. 585 (N.D. Ga. 1986)].

A more recent case also ruled that an AWP law relates to an ERISA plan. Clinical laboratories excluded from a laboratory network may not rely on a state law requiring PPOs to give interested providers an opportunity to apply for participation because ERISA pre-empts the statute, according to a Michigan appeals court. Requiring a health insurer administering a preferred provider program to admit additional laboratories in accordance with the state law would alter the plan's administration, the court found, by requiring reimbursement to a larger number of providers, weakening the plan's leverage to negotiate lower fees and impairing the plan's interstate operations. The law is not rescued from pre-emption by the savings clause, the court continued, as it does not regulate the business of insurance because the provider network challenged in this case serves only a single self-funded employee benefit plan [*BPS Clinical Lab. v. Blue Cross & Blue Shield*, 522 N.W.2d 902 (Mich. Ct. App. 1994)].

Q.5:52   Does ERISA pre-empt state laws directed at third party administrators?

There is no clear rule on this issue. One federal court has ruled that ERISA did pre-empt the state third party administrator (TPA) law, holding that the law related to employee benefit plans governed by ERISA because the law regulated the activities of TPAs that provided services for self-insured employee plans [*Self-Insurance Inst. of America v. Gallagher*, TCA No. 86-7308-WS (N.D. Fla. June 2,1989), *aff'd*, 909 F.2d 1491 (11th Cir. 1990)].

In another case, however, a court came to the opposite conclusion, finding that because the state law regulated all TPAs, regardless of whether or not they provided services to ERISA plans, the law was not pre-empted [*Benefax Corp. v. Wright*, 757 F. Supp. 800 (W.D. Ky. 1990)].

6

Liability

INTRODUCTION

Q.6:1 On what grounds can subscribers sue MCOs?

There are several potential bases for liability that a managed care organization (MCO) must be aware of and seek to limit. An MCO may be held liable for the medical malpractice of participating physicians, for example. If the physicians are actually employees, the MCO could be liable for their negligent conduct under the legal doctrine of vicarious liability. Even if the physicians are not employees, however, the MCO may be found liable under agency principles.

An MCO may also be found liable on the basis of its own corporate functions. An MCO could be liable for negligently credentialing or negligently monitoring providers, for example. Similarly, MCOs that rely on outside utilization review organizations could be liable for selecting the organizations without exercising reasonable care to protect subscribers.

In addition, lawsuits against MCOs may be based on the ground that coverage or claims were improperly denied through the utilization review process. Subscribers who are injured because a claim was denied may argue that the claim was negligently denied, that the denial constituted a breach of contract, or that the claim was denied in bad faith.

MEDICAL MALPRACTICE OF HEALTH CARE PROVIDERS

Q.6:2 Can a subscriber sue an MCO based on the negligence of a health care provider if the MCO is not at fault?

A legal doctrine known as vicarious liability or *respondeat superior* holds employers responsible for the negligent acts of employees, even if the employer is otherwise without fault. When there is a bona fide employer—employee relationship between a managed care organization and a physician, the MCO may be held vicariously liable for the physician's negligent acts occurring within the scope of employment. The rationale for this rule is that an employer has the right to control the conduct of an employee, and therefore should be liable for the employee's negligent conduct (see **Questions 6:3–6:6** for a detailed discussion of vicarious liability).

Further, MCOs can be held liable for the negligence of nonemployee physicians under the doctrine of ostensible or apparent agency. Under this legal theory, an MCO that holds itself out to the public as a full service health care provider may be liable if health care services are negligently provided, regardless of whether an independent contractor is responsible. In the health care industry, this doctrine has been most commonly applied to hospitals with regard to the negligence of emergency room physicians. The rationale for this doctrine is that patients who seek health care do so on the basis of the hospital's reputation, not realizing that physicians are independent contractors. Thus, the courts have reasoned, it would be unfair to prevent a patient who has been injured from suing the hospital. (See **Questions 6:7–6:10** for a discussion of apparent agency.)

Q.6:3   What must a subscriber show to recover from an MCO for an injury caused by a health care provider based on vicarious liability?

A subscriber must prove the following elements to recover under the doctrine of vicarious liability:

- the negligent actor was the MCO's employee,
- the employee who committed the negligent act was acting within the scope of employment,
- the employee was negligent, that is, the employee owed the subscriber a duty of care, but failed to exercise reasonable care, and
- the employee's negligence caused the subscriber's injury.

Q.6:4   What will a court consider when determining whether a provider may be characterized as an employee of an MCO?

Although the question, *Who is an employee?* may seem straightforward, it is not always easy to answer. The key is the degree of control that the MCO exerts over the physician. The courts will not simply rely on the language in the contract between the MCO and physician, even if the language specifies that the physician is an independent contractor. Rather, courts will look at the totality of the circumstances to determine the employer's control.

Q.6:5   What are some examples of cases in which courts ruled that a physician was an MCO's employee?

Although each case presents unique circumstances, courts have considered similar factors to hold MCOs liable for the negligence of participating physicians on the basis of *respondeat superior*. For example, an Indiana appeals court held that a physician was employed by an HMO such that it could be held vicariously liable. The court based its determination on the existence of an employment contract between the negligent physician and the HMO, the fact that the physician was paid an annual salary, and the fact that the physician received fringe benefits such as sick leave; life, health, and malpractice insurance; vacation pay; and professional leave [*Sloan v. Metropolitan Health Council of Indianapolis, Inc.*, 516 N.E.2d 1104 (Ind. Ct. App. 1987)].

A New Jersey court also held that an HMO was vicariously liable for a participating physician's actions because the physician was the HMO's employee. The physician was a specialist and a member of a group that had contracted with the HMO. The court considered several factors in drawing its conclusion, including the contract between the HMO and the group, which specified that the physicians' group would abide by the HMO's policies and procedures, indicated the number of hours the physicians would spend at the HMO, and indicated that each physician would spend one day per week at the HMO. The HMO controlled the number of patients seen, and maintained all patient charts and records, including the specialists' records, at the HMO. The physicians agreed that they would not let their private practice interfere with their contractual obligations in order to ensure the timeliness and continuity of HMO patient care. The HMO had control over the lab facilities and outside consulting services available to the specialists; specialists were required to use in-house medical services available at the HMO unless a procedure was not available; and specialists could not order outside tests unless the primary care physician approved the tests. HMO clerks and staff physicians scheduled outside testing, handled the paperwork, and arranged billings. The HMO arranged all patient appointments and had a 24-hour-a-day switchboard to take direct calls from patients to the specialists. The patient literature listed the specialist physicians, representing that they were affiliated with the HMO. Patients were not informed of the independent status of the specialists affiliated with the HMO and patients were not permitted to make independent selections of the consultants or specialists they were to see. These circumstances, the court ruled, could properly lead a jury to find that the HMO employed the physician [*Dunn v. Praiss*, 606 A.2d 862 (N.J. Super. Ct. App. Div. 1992), *considered on other grounds*, 638 A.2d 875 (N.J. Super. Ct. App. Div. 1994)].

Q.6:6 What is *scope of employment*?

Scope of employment is the test that courts apply to determine whether an employee was on the job at the time of the negligent act, such that the employer should be vicariously liable. Typically, courts will hold that an employee was within the scope of employment if the employee was acting in furtherance of the employer's business interests. For example, a nurse who assists a patient from a waiting room to an examining room is acting within the scope of employment, even if the nurse acts negligently.

Courts presented with an employee who committed an intentional injury such as assault or battery will often find that the employee did not act within the scope of employment. There are some circumstances under which even intentional injuries will be held within the scope of employment, however. For example, an Oklahoma court held a nursing home liable for the conduct of an intoxicated nurse's aide who slapped a nursing home resident with Alzheimer's disease while bathing him. The nursing home argued that it was not liable because the employee was not acting within the scope of his employment. The court nonetheless upheld a $1.2 million award against the nursing home, finding that bathing the resident was part of the aide's work duties, Alzheimer's patients are known to be combative, and there was no documentation that the aide had been trained not to slap patients [*Rodebush v. Oklahoma Nursing Homes*, 867 P.2d 1241 (Okla. 1993)].

Q.6:7 Can an MCO be liable for the negligence of a physician who is not an employee of the MCO?

A patient may sue an MCO based on the negligence of independent contractors or nonemployee physicians by invoking the doctrine of ostensible agency, also known as apparent agency. (See **Question 6:2** for an introduction to the concept of apparent agency.)

Q.6:8   What must a patient show to recover from an MCO based on the negligence of a nonemployee provider?

A patient must prove the following two elements to recover under apparent agency:

1. the patient reasonably viewed the MCO, rather than the individual physician, as the source of health care, and
2. the MCO engaged in conduct that caused the patient to reasonably believe that the MCO was the source of health care or that the MCO employed the negligent physician.

Q.6:9   What are some cases in which courts found that MCOs could be liable under the apparent agency doctrine?

In a Pennsylvania case, the family of a woman who died while under the care of an HMO physician sued, claiming that the HMO was liable for the physician's conduct despite the fact that he was an independent contractor. An appeals court held that the following facts were sufficient to raise the issue of apparent agency: the patient paid his fees to the HMO and not to the physician of his choice, the patient selected his primary care physician from a list provided by the HMO, and the patient could not see a specialist without the primary physician's referral. In addition, although the entity was an IPA model HMO, it advertised itself in a brochure as a "total care program," which not only insures its subscribers, but provides medical care, guarantees the quality of the care and controls the costs of health care services. The brochure also stated that the HMO was "an entire health care system," that it "provides the physicians, hospitals, and other health care professionals needed to maintain good health," and "assumes the responsibility for quality and accessibility." The court considered this a representation from which a patient could reasonably conclude that the physicians within the HMO's health care delivery system were its employees [*Boyd v. Albert Einstein Med. Center*, 547 A.2d. 1229 (Pa. Super. 1988)]. In another Pennsylvania case, which also permitted a suit against an HMO to go forward on the basis of apparent agency, one important factor was that the HMO represented that "each and every primary care physician provided by [the HMO] satisfied criteria for participation as a qualified physician after passing vigorous screening criteria . . ." and that "their primary care physicians had to undergo vigorous screening and meet certain criteria to be qualified as a primary care physician for [the HMO]" [*McClellan v. Health Maintenance Organization of Pennsylvania*, 604 A.2d 1053 (Pa. Super. Ct. 1992)].

Q.6:10   Are there any cases in which courts found no MCO liability under the apparent agency doctrine?

Some courts that have applied the apparent agency theory have found HMOs not responsible for physicians' negligence. In an Illinios case, a patient argued that an HMO was liable for the negligence of physicians with whom it contracted by virtue of the HMO's quality assessment and utilization review guidelines. The court ruled, however, that the HMO's quality assurance compliance program is not the type of control from which agency arises. The HMO required documentation that the physicians were following procedures to assure quality health care, but the HMO did not review the contents of the documentation to assess the accuracy of the medical diagnoses, nor did it assume responsibility for determining the correctness or appropriateness of the medical services provided. Instead, the HMO played only an administrative role in overseeing the process of health care delivery. In addition, the court found no evidence that the HMO advertised or held itself out as exerting control over its physicians so that one could reasonably conclude that they were HMO employees. The HMO's requirement that the patient choose her physician from a limited list should not be a dispositive factor on the question of apparent agency, the court ruled, because all HMOs operate in such a manner [*Raglin v. HMO Illinois, Inc.*, 595 N.E.2d 153 (Ill. App. Ct. 1992)].

Similarly, a Massachusetts court found no liability when an HMO contracted with an IPA that contracted with a group that employed physicians. The court found no evidence that the HMO controlled or had the right to control the professional activities of the allegedly negligent physician [*Chase v. Independent Practice Ass'n*, 583 N.E.2d 251 (Mass. Ct. App. 1991)].

Q.6:11   Can patients sue MCOs based on the negligence of nonmember providers?

Yes. In addition to liability for the medical malpractice of physicians with whom it contracts, a managed care entity could be held liable for the medical malpractice of providers to whom it refers patients, even if it has no contractual relationship with those providers. Courts have based such liability on both vicarious liability and ostensible agency grounds.

A court in the District of Columbia, for example, held that an HMO was vicariously liable for the negligence of a physician brought in as a consultant by an HMO primary care physician [*Schleier v. Kaiser Foundation Health Plan*, 876 F.2d 174 (D.C. Cir. 1989)]. One of the factors in this case was that the HMO had at least an indirect ability to control the consultant's behavior because he answered to the HMO's primary care physician. The court also found that it was reasonable for the patient to believe that the physician was the HMO's agent.

In a Michigan case, a court held an IPA-type HMO liable on ostensible agency grounds for the negligence of a specialist who was not a member physician. The court based its ruling on ostensible agency principles, finding that, because HMOs charge subscribers a fee based on the representation that the plans will provide comprehensive health care, it would not be proper to allow HMOs to escape liability for difficult cases by referring them to a nonparticipating physician. The court concluded that the circumstances of each case will determine whether an HMO is liable for the conduct of nonparticipating providers [*Decker v. Saini*, No. 88-361768 NH (Mich. Cir. Ct. Sept. 17, 1991)].

Q.6:12   How might an MCO defend itself in a suit based on an injury caused by a health care provider?

MCOs sued based on an injury caused by a health care provider should attempt to avoid vicarious liability by arguing that the provider is not an employee, and that the provider acted outside the scope of employment. An MCO defending a claim based on ostensible agency should argue that it did not present itself to the public as a direct provider of health care or as a provider of comprehensive health care services. In both vicarious liability and ostensible agency cases, the MCO might also join the provider in arguing that the provider was not negligent and did not cause the subscriber's injury. In addition, MCOs can also argue that a suit based on the malpractice of a health care provider is pre-empted by the Employee Retirement Income Security Act (ERISA). Refer to **Chapter 5** for a detailed discussion of pre-emption.

CORPORATE NEGLIGENCE

Q.6:13   What is corporate negligence?

Corporate negligence is a term that encompasses the legal grounds for MCO liability based on the corporate activities of the MCO itself, rather than on the care-related activities of participating health care professionals. Negligent credentialing and negligent supervision are examples of corporate negligence.

The independent legal duties of health care entities were first recognized in the health care context in *Darling v. Charleston Community Memorial*

Hospital [211 N.E.2d 253 (Ill. 1965), *cert. denied*, 383 U.S. 946 (1966)]. In that case, the Illinois Supreme Court held that the hospital owed an independent duty of care to the patient, separate and apart from the private physician's duty, which the hospital breached by failing to: require examination by a qualified member of the staff, review the treatment the patient received, and require the use of consultants as necessary to ensure the proper care and recovery of the patient. *Darling* is a landmark case because it recognizes the hospital's obligation to provide overall surveillance of the quality of patient care services.

Q.6:14 What is negligent credentialing?

Credentialing is the process of investigating and evaluating physician applicants who want to obtain or renew MCO participation status or hospital medical membership or privileges. MCOs have a legal duty to exercise care in selecting those to be included in the MCO's panel of providers. Thus, an MCO that fails to exercise reasonable care and selects a provider who negligently injures a subscriber can be liable. MCOs should be aware that the term "negligent credentialing" can also apply to the decision to extend or renew a provider's participation status. The term negligent selection, sometimes used in the managed care context, is synonymous with negligent credentialing. Refer to **Chapter 8** for a detailed discussion of negligent credentialing lawsuits.

Q.6:15 Can the negligent credentialing doctrine be applied to make MCOs liable for the selection of a utilization review organization?

Yes. A managed care organization that contracts with a utilization review organization (URO) for utilization review services may be liable for negligently selecting the URO if it does not adequately investigate the quality of the services provided by the URO. Refer to **Chapter 4** for a more detailed discussion of negligent selection of UROs.

DENIALS OF CLAIMS

Q.6:16 On what legal theories can a subscriber sue an MCO or insurer for denying a claim?

When an MCO denies a claim or coverage for a particular course of treatment, the subscriber may have legal recourse against the MCO. Cases in this area may be difficult for MCOs to win, especially if the court is asked to determine in advance whether a subscriber may receive a potentially life-saving treatment. Subscribers suing for wrongful denial of a claim most commonly argue that the MCO is liable based on the legal theories of negligence, breach of contract, or bad faith. Refer to **Chapter 4** for a detailed discussion of lawsuits in this area.

SUITS BY PROVIDERS

Q.6:17 On what grounds can providers sue MCOs?

A provider who is denied employment or participation, or whose employment or participation in an MCO is terminated, may base a lawsuit against the MCO on antitrust principles, alleging that the MCO's rejection of the provider constituted anticompetitive action. Refer to **Chapter 3** for a detailed discussion of the requirements for recovery under federal antitrust laws.

A provider may also sue an MCO based on breach of an employment or participation contract. To avoid liability, MCOs should carefully draft employment and participation contracts to eliminate ambiguities that could result in litigation. MCO administrators should be closely familiar with employment and participation contracts so that they may avoid inadvertent failures to comply with the contracts that could lead to lawsuits by providers. Refer to **Chapter 7** for detailed information on drafting these contracts.

7

Contracting

INTRODUCTION

Q.7:1   Why is contracting so crucial to managed care?

Managed care plans combine aspects of the financing and delivery of health care services into a single organization. In most cases, the mechanism for combining both the financing and delivery of services is through contractual agreements between the managed care plan and providers of health services. These agreements must be negotiated and renegotiated, often on an annual basis. The terms of a managed care plan's agreements with its providers can largely determine whether the plan can compete successfully in the marketplace. A managed care plan that fails to obtain participation agreements from a sufficient number of providers or that fails to negotiate favorable reimbursement arrangements with its providers will find it very difficult to attain its financial and market objectives. This chapter will deal with contracting from the perspective of a hospital contracting with a managed care organization (MCO).

Q.7:2   What issues must a hospital consider when entering into a managed care contract?

When entering into a managed care contract, a hospital must carefully evaluate:

- whether all of the elements of the managed care system are in place,
- what the identities and financial stability of the contracting parties are, and
- how the risks and responsibilities will be distributed.

Q.7:3   In performing a due diligence investigation of a managed care organization, what should the hospital investigate?

After making the initial decision that it is in the best interest of the hospital to contract with a managed care organization, the institution should investigate the MCO under consideration. Specifically, the hospital should raise the following questions:

- Does the MCO have the proper legal structure and authority to enter into the contract?
- Is the MCO financially stable?
- Are all the elements (payer, providers, facilities, administration) in place?
- What is the MCO's reputation in the community and with other providers?
- Can the MCO produce the volume of patients necessary to make the plan profitable?
- Is the anticipated reimbursement method acceptable to the hospital?
- What is the MCO's reputation for timely payment of claims?
- Does the MCO have strong utilization management and quality assessment programs that function efficiently and fairly?

NEGOTIATING THE CONTRACT

Q.7:4   What are the main features of the negotiating process in the context of managed care agreements?

The negotiating process can be said to have the following general characteristics:

- a give and take between two parties,
- a friction or level of discomfort between the parties resulting from the constraints and motivations of the parties,
- an important issue that the parties wish to resolve, and
- a conflict between the positions of the parties to the negotiations.

In the context of negotiating managed care provider agreements, parties approaching the bargaining table have only one factor in common—the desire to provide health care services to a particular population. This common need is the factor that spurs negotiations. Overall, the parties are in conflict over most of the details concerning the provision of those services. The managed care plan seeks to spend as little as possible for this obligation, while the providers seek to maximize their reimbursements. The myriad terms and conditions that constitute a provider agreement place many obstacles in the path of the parties who are attempting to forge an agreement.

Levels of reimbursement, timing of payments, exclusivity provisions, and patient volumes are aspects of potential agreements that heighten friction between the parties and are capable of scuttling once-promising negotiations. Given these predictable sources of conflict, managed care agreements can be reached by accommodation of the parties. Truly successful negotiations result in the parties believing that they fared as well as they could expect considering their relative constraints.

Q.7:5   What are some of the different negotiating styles?

A variety of styles and tactics are used by negotiators, and the type of negotiating style employed can have a significant influence on the outcome. Negotiators tend to use one of two broad types of style: *confrontational* or *collegial*.

Many negotiators believe that an aggressive and confrontational approach is appropriate. These negotiators tend to focus on the real or perceived differences between the parties at the bargaining table. Negotiators may be particularly aggressive when the party they represent is perceived by both sides to be dominant.

In adopting a confrontational style, negotiators can overlook the fact that the parties are attempting to reach an agreement that will govern their relationship over a period of time. A confrontational and overly aggressive approach can poison the relationship between the plan and its providers from the outset and lead to long-term distrust between the parties.

The second negotiating style seeks a collegial relationship in which the negotiators attempt to build a consensus between the parties through the give and take of negotiations. This style is well suited to the concept that the outcome of the negotiations (i.e., the agreement) represents the beginning of the relationship between the managed care plan and its providers.

A collegial style does not imply that negotiators are weak or that they give up important positions while obtaining a valid quid pro quo. It does mean that the dominant party refrains from unilaterally imposing its position on its opponent. It also means that the negotiating sessions themselves are conducted in a cordial fashion and that the negotiators try not to allow personality conflicts to influence the outcome of negotiations.

Some successful negotiators have advocated what they view as a completely different style of negotiations, premised on the belief that negotiations should be principled and should take place on the merits of the issues. The principled method of negotiation involves separating the people from the problem, focusing on the interests of the parties and not on their positions, generating a variety of possibilities for solutions before agreeing on a particular solution, and agreeing to apply an objective standard for selecting the appropriate solution.

One benefit of the principled method of negotiation is that it eliminates the problem of confrontational versus collegial styles of negotiating. Both parties are attempting to reach a common goal of attaining the best possible solution. This method can also foster the sense that agreement between the parties represents the beginning of a relationship and not the end of a disagreement.

One example of an objective standard that can be used in the context of a managed care contract between an HMO and a hospital is the agreement that the hospital is entitled to a fair level of return, or contribution margin, from its HMO patients and that the HMO is entitled to reimbursement rates that are no less favorable than are offered to other, similarly situated payers. The fair level of return could be defined as the hospital's average contribution margin per patient day for all classes of patients. Once these objective standards are agreed upon, the HMO and the hospital can determine whether various combinations of reimbursement rates and exclusivity provisions would satisfy the standards. The focus on these standards can help both parties to understand one another's concerns.

Q.7:6   When should the team approach be used in negotiation?

Negotiating style also encompasses the issue of the number of people who should participate in the negotiation sessions. Some negotiators believe that they should bring a team to the negotiating table. There are definite advantages to a team approach, including a division of labor and the ability to add special expertise to the negotiating process. A team of two people is ideal for many negotiations. One person can direct the negotiations and serve as the spokesperson for the team while the other person can take good notes of the discussion and agreements reached during meetings. Care must be taken in forming the team to make it clear that only the chief negotiator can articulate the team's positions to the other party.

The team approach generally should not be used if the other party is represented by one individual. The danger of using a team approach against a single negotiator is that the other party may feel as though the team is attempting to gain dominance through numbers. These feelings can create an adversarial atmosphere. On the other hand, the team approach works very successfully if both parties agree at the outset to use this approach.

Q.7:7   What is involved in the preparation for negotiations?

Preparations for negotiation are usually the key factor in determining success, and fortunately this factor is within the control of negotiators. Preparation for negotiations should include developing an understanding of the organization's goals and objectives, understanding the other party's goals and objectives, drafting a proposal, and preparing the negotiating team.

Q.7:8   What issues should be considered in acquiring an understanding of the organization's goals and objectives?

Even if the negotiator is a high-level executive within the organization and is already familiar with its goals and objectives, he or she should formally clarify those goals and objectives before entering into direct negotiations. The following issues should be considered to develop such an understanding.

- What does the organization hope to accomplish through the negotiations? A complete list of the items the organization hopes to gain from the negotiations should be prepared, and the value of each item should be assessed. This wish list will serve as a guide during the give and take of negotiations. Motivating factors in managed care negotiations include:
  1. a physician who has recently moved into a community may want to attract patients covered by HMOs or PPOs in the area to help build the practice;
  2. a hospital may want to obtain a participation agreement with a managed care plan to preclude its competitor from negotiating an exclusive agreement; or
  3. a PPO may want to obtain the participation of a specific hospital because certain employer groups have told the PPO that they will not offer it as a benefit option if the hospital is not included on the provider panel.

- What are the organization's strengths and weaknesses, and how will they affect negotiations? Organizations almost always view themselves favorably and convey this positive impression to their outside negotiators. This can leave their negotiators unprepared to confront the organization's weaknesses, as they are presented by the other party. The negotiator must understand both the strengths and the weaknesses of the organization because the other party will have uncovered many of the weaknesses during its preparations. An understanding of the weaknesses can also help place the emphasis on offsetting strengths during discussions with the other party.

- What is the corporate culture of the organization and how will it affect its relationship with the other party? Is the organization perceived as trustworthy by its employees and outsiders or as overly aggressive and always seeking to achieve its own advantage, regardless of the impact on other parties? Does the organization give meaningful authority to its line managers or is all power centralized with a few top executives? These factors will influence how negotiations are conducted, how the other party reacts to proposals, and whether the negotiator is perceived as credible by the other party.

- What is the organization's bottom line for negotiations and how much is it willing to give up to obtain an agreement? This issue must be discussed before commencing negotiations so that management is not forced to address the issue during the heat of the negotiations. The negotiator must be given a clear picture of how much the organization is willing to give up and what it wants in return.

Q.7:9   Are there any alternatives to determing an organization's bottom line with respect to its goals and objectives?

Yes. An alternative to determining the bottom line is to understand the organization's best alternative to a negotiated agreement (BATNA). Instead of focusing on an artificially defined bottom line, the BATNA addresses the issue of what the organization's options are if agreement is not reached. For example, a managed care plan might see the alternative to failing to negotiate an exclusive agreement with one hospital in a community at favorable rates is to obtain agreements with several other hospitals at slightly higher rates. The inclusion of these other hospitals may allow the plan to be marketed more successfully, generate higher enrollment, and provide higher margins. These issues should be considered by the plan in defining its BATNA.

Q.7:10 What issues should be considered in acquiring an understanding of the other party's goals and objectives?

Gaining an understanding of the other party's goals and objectives can be accomplished through review of publicly available information about the other party. In this regard, the issues described for understanding the negotiator's organization should also be evaluated for the other party. (See **Question 7:9.**)

One important issue to consider is the other party's strengths and weaknesses and how they may affect the relationship. A more effective proposal can be prepared if it specifically includes solutions to offset the other party's weaknesses.

For example, a PPO may be attempting to offer its services to employers through a metropolitan area. Employers may be reluctant to offer the PPO option because its panel of providers does not include a well-regarded hospital within the geographic area in which many of their employees reside. A well-regarded hospital within that area would have an opportunity to offset a major shortcoming of the PPO by offering its participation. In return, the hospital could demand higher payment rates than other hospitals within the metropolitan area.

Q.7:11 What should a provider consider in selecting the members of its negotiating team?

The identification and preparation of the negotiating team is an important success factor. The first step in this process is to identify who will be members of the negotiating team.

Because contracting with a managed care plan is largely a financial issue and negotiations tend to focus on financial issues, most providers should plan to include their chief financial officer on their negotiating team. In addition, if the provider has a vice president for managed care, that person should clearly be included in the negotiating team.

If a provider has little experience with negotiating third party agreements, it would be both valuable and cost effective to include outside consultants and lawyers who specialize in managed care. Such outside advisors can bring broad experience to bear on negotiating the few managed care agreements required by the provider.

Larger institutional providers may find it useful to include internal legal counsel to help other members of the team understand the legal issues surrounding potential agreements. In addition, counsel can often provide an objective overview of proposals put forward by the other side.

Managed care plans typically include their provider relations personnel on the negotiating team because they are expected to understand the local marketplace and the concerns of the provider community. Many plans also include at least one financial staff member because of the impact that reimbursement rates have on premium rates and financial results. Some managed care plans include their chief executive officer on the negotiating team, at least at some meetings, to demonstrate the importance of the agreement to the plan.

Q.7:12   What should the negotiating team do to prepare for negotiations?

The negotiating team's preparation should include thorough review of the parameters of the proposal, acceptable trade-offs, and an understanding of the alternatives available to the other party. If discussions are being held to renegotiate a current agreement, the team should review all aspects of the existing agreement to determine problems caused by the current arrangement, changes that should be made, and changes that are likely to be requested by the other party.

During preparations, the negotiating team must clearly define the agenda for the negotiations for both the team as a whole and for individual members. The role of each member of the team should be specified. Weak negotiating positions can result if team members decide to "play it by ear" during the negotiating sessions.

Limits of authority should be established to define the extent to which each member of the team is allowed to set the organization's positions, make counteroffers, or critique the other party's proposals. The team must try to avoid the complications that arise when one member of the team becomes a "loose cannon" who makes overly generous offers or unsupported statements. The process of defining the role and authority of each team member during negotiations helps make the team members aware of the organization's expectations for performance. Members of the team will perform better when they understand their performance expectations.

While preparing, members of the team should familiarize themselves with the characteristics of the other party's negotiators. The team members can research the positions and roles of the other party's negotiators, their educational and professional backgrounds and training, and their philosophical approaches. Some of this information may be available through professional directories, while other information can be obtained by talking with colleagues who have dealt with the other party's team members. Books, articles, and presentations by members of the other party's negotiating team may also provide insights into their styles or philosophies.

Q.7:13   Is the location of the negotiations important to their outcome?

Although the site for negotiations can be important, it usually will not be the decisive factor in success or failure. The selection of an appropriate site can provide one side or the other with a slight advantage, however.

In most cases, it is preferable to have a home-field advantage. Team members are typically more comfortable in familiar surroundings, and this increased comfort level can provide a small edge in conducting the negotiations. It would be a mistake, however, to fight a protracted battle to have negotiations conducted at a favored location. A fight over location will distract both parties from the primary reason for their discussions and could poison the atmosphere for the substantive negotiations.

Q.7:14   Why is it important to assess the limits of the other team's authority to bind the organization it represents?

It is very important to probe the limits of the other team's authority early during negotiations. Some parties to negotiations believe that they should not allow their representatives to bind them to agreements, requiring them to clear all agreements with a higher authority before the agreements are binding. This technique is intended to provide a safety valve for rejecting agreements after they are examined more closely. Some negotiators only reveal that they must appeal to a higher authority after they have obtained significant concessions from the other party, thereby giving themselves a second chance.

Unfortunately, most negotiators expect that the other party will be able to conduct a give-and-take exchange without checking each point with an outside authority. Otherwise, negotiations could be conducted more easily by an exchange of letters. Both parties will probably make final agreement subject to corporate approval, but approval should be based on the entire package, not on every individual point covered during the negotiations.

Q.7:15   What information should the notes of the negotiations contain?

Each negotiating team should keep accurate records of the discussions, and should designate one member to take notes. The notes should reflect the following information:

- dates and locations of all the negotiating sessions,

- names and titles of all participants and observers,
- salient terms of all proposals that are made by either party, including who made the proposal,
- key points made during discussions of proposals, including who made the points,
- agreements made by the parties, including conditions and contingencies related to the agreements, and
- areas of disagreement between the parties.

The notes taken during negotiating sessions should be as factual as possible and should not express opinions that could be damaging or embarrassing if they were released in public. Accuracy is important because the notes serve to draft the documents that will implement the agreement. In addition, the documents may be useful if the parties become involved in litigation concerning the agreements or negotiations. In this context, the records may be subject to discovery and released in open court or made available to the public. Therefore, a neutral account of the discussions is recommended.

Q.7:16 Should negotiators prepare a written outline to be distributed at the initial negotiating session?

It is often helpful to prepare a written proposal for distribution at the initial negotiating session. A written outline establishes a framework and baseline for future negotiations; future offers and counteroffers are made in the context of the initial proposal. The outline can set the tone for the balance of negotiations. The proposal should outline the organization's position on all issues subject to negotiations.

Q.7:17 What are the major objectives of a typical managed care plan involved in contract negotiations with a provider?

The typical managed care plan has four major objectives for its negotiations with providers. They are:

1. an acceptable provider panel
2. reasonable reimbursement
3. a framework for future relationships
4. favorable contractual terms

Q.7:18   What constitutes an acceptable provider panel?

What constitutes an acceptable provider panel varies with the type of managed care plan involved and the type of product offered. For example, an acceptable provider panel will be very different for a network model HMO versus a nongatekeeper model PPO. The PPO will probably seek to include many more physicians and hospitals in its network than the HMO because choice of providers will be more important to its product. The most important factors include:

- *Availability.* Are all services covered by the plan available through its panel of participating providers? This factor may limit the ability of some providers to demand exclusivity if they are unable to provide all covered services under their exclusive arrangement.
- *Accessibility.* Are the services offered by participating providers accessible to the plan's covered beneficiaries? The plan's view of what constitutes accessibility varies depending on the type of plan. In general, however, routine services would not be considered accessible if patients were required to travel more than 30 minutes to a provider. This factor may also limit the ability of providers to demand exclusive arrangements with managed care plans.
- *Specialty coverage.* Most managed care plans attempt to negotiate participation agreements with physicians representing all major specialties and subspecialties.
- *Perceived quality.* Despite the difficulties inherent in measuring quality, managed care plans attempt to align themselves with providers who enjoy good reputations. Conversely, significant price concessions may not be sufficient to entice a managed care plan to align itself with a provider that is perceived to deliver a lower quality of care. The bottom line is that the perceived level of provider quality may influence the reimbursement levels offered by a plan.

Q.7:19   What is considered reasonable reimbursement?

The definition of reasonable reimbursement largely depends on whether it is being viewed from the perspective of the managed care plan or the provider. From the managed care plan's vantage point, reasonable reimbursement generally has two qualities: (1) reimbursement rates should be set as low as possible and (2) they should be predictable.

There are definite trade-offs between predictability and rates. For example, a plan might project that its members will use 350 days per year of inpatient hospital care per 1,000 members. If a hospital offers to provide care for a $750 per diem reimbursement, the plan would expect inpatient hospital costs of $21.88 per member per month. Under this system, the plan would be at risk if the actual number of days of care exceeded the expected number of days.

Because of this risk, the plan might decide to accept a capitated proposal from the same hospital of $22.50 per member per month. Although the expected value of the capitated arrangement would exceed the expected value of the per diem arrangement, the capitated arrangement results in more predictable costs for the plan. In this case, the plan would do better under capitation if actual patient days exceeded the expected number of days by ten days per 1,000 members (a variance of less than three percent). Any reimbursement proposal must also be evaluated by the plan in the context of its premium rates.

Q.7:20   Why is it important for a managed care plan to establish a framework for a long-term relationship with providers?

Most managed care plans hope to establish long-term relationships with providers when they negotiate participation agreements. Renegotiating all the salient points of provider agreements requires personnel and produces friction. Annual changes of reimbursement rates and service terms may mean climbing and unpredictable costs for the plan. Plan members and their employers resent interruptions in the doctor–patient relationship that result from changes in the provider panel. As a result, most plan managers would prefer to establish longer term relationships with their providers.

Q.7:21   What do managed care plans consider favorable contract terms?

Managed care plans usually propose terms where the providers must agree to the following:

- abide by and cooperate with the plan's utilization management and quality assurance protocols,
- look solely to the managed care plan for the payment of claims, even in the event of plan insolvency (the provider "hold harmless" clause); this provision is often required by state regulations,
- submit claims in a format that is acceptable to the plan,

* continue serving the plan's members after termination until the anniversary date of the member's group agreement,
* refrain from encouraging the plan's beneficiaries to change coverage to another plan,
* refrain from derogatory speech and publicity concerning the plan and its sponsors, and
* use binding arbitration to resolve disputes between the provider and patients or the plan.

This list is representative but not exhaustive of some of the terms managed care plans will seek to obtain during negotiations.

Q.7:22   What are some of the negotiating styles adopted by managed care plans?

Managed care plans tend to adopt one of two opposite styles in conducting their negotiations. The first style can be characterized as confrontational. The second style can be characterized as either friendly or neutral.

In adopting a confrontational style, plans behave as if the providers will be devastated if they fail to obtain an agreement with the plan. In many cases, these plans try to influence the provider's negotiating position by emphasizing the number of individuals for whom they provide coverage and may threaten the provider with a loss of these patients. These plans tend to overstate the extent of their market clout.

The neutral approach, which is compatible with the collegial approach described earlier, has been adopted by many plans for their negotiations with providers. The neutral approach is consistent with the plan's objective of establishing longer term relationships with its providers. The basis for such relationships is mutual trust and respect, not intimidation and antagonism.

Q.7:23   What are some negotiating tactics adopted by managed care plans during their negotiations with providers?

Regardless of the negotiating style, there are a variety of tactics used by managed care plans to negotiate favorable agreements. These include the following:

* *Threat of competing proposals.* The managed care plan may indicate either explicitly or implicitly that competing proposals on the table offer more advantages to the plan. Sometimes such proposals exist, but

often this threat is a bluff intended to obtain more favorable pricing terms.

- *Threat of lost market share and reduced income.* Plans may threaten to move their covered patients to other providers if the parties fail to reach agreement. It is important for providers to understand the implications of this threat prior to entering negotiations by assessing the number of patients covered by the plan, what those patients contributed to the provider, and whether the plan can actually move the patients to other providers. Unrealistic threats can then be deflected at the bargaining table.

- *Whipsawing providers.* Some managed care plans play hospitals and physicians against one another in an attempt to get one or the other to participate despite their reluctance. Plans have recruited key physicians from a hospital's medical staff and then forced the hospital's participation at reduced reimbursement rates. This tactic can be avoided when hospitals and physicians work closely together on their managed care relationships.

- *Last chance offers.* Managed care plans sometimes indicate to providers during negotiations that this will be their last chance to participate with the plan. Even though the plan currently may not have many covered individuals, the plan implies that if the provider fails to participate immediately at favorable rates, then the provider cannot participate when the plan becomes successful.

- *Use of information.* Some managed care plans prepare detailed analyses of provider cost and/or charge information for their market areas before they commence negotiations. For example, one large insurance company prepared for each market area briefing books that contained charge information by diagnosis-related group (DRG) and payer for each hospital in the area. Their analysis projected the number of their patients who would fall into each DRG category, and what their total costs of care would be, based on the use of different hospitals in the market area. This sophisticated information allowed them to evaluate any counterproposals by hospitals that had been accepted by other, similarly sized payers.

Q.7:24   What are some of the main objectives providers usually have for their negotiations with managed care plans?

Providers usually have one or more of the following objectives for their negotiations with managed care plans:

- market share
- competition among managed care plans
- satisfaction of other provider needs
- favorable reimbursement
- framework for future relationships
- favorable contractual terms

Q.7:25   How is market share important to providers?

Many providers view participation with managed care plans as a mechanism to protect or expand market share and the income associated with managed care patients. These providers fear that if they fail to participate with certain plans, they will lose some of their patient base. Other providers view managed care plans as a way of attracting new patients and expanding their market share. Generally, these providers insist on some measure of exclusivity as a way of guaranteeing that they will receive incremental patient volume (i.e., patients who otherwise would not have used their services). For a more detailed discussion of how market share raises antitrust considerations, see **Question 3:25.**

Q.7:26   Why is competition among managed care plans important to providers?

Some providers believe that they should participate with as many managed care plans as possible to prevent any single plan from becoming a dominant player in their market area, such as Blue Cross has been in many markets.

Q.7:27   Why is satisfaction of other provider needs important to providers?

Hospitals sometimes participate with managed care plans because their physicians have joined and need to admit their patients to participating hospitals. This objective is related to preventing loss of market share; the hospitals that participate to satisfy their physicians' needs do so to protect their own loss of market share if their physicians were to move their practices to other facilities.

Q.7:28   What does a provider consider favorable reimbursement in the context of a managed care agreement?

From the provider's perspective, favorable reimbursement means maximizing rates and enhancing predictability. In contrast to the managed care plan's perspective, predictability to the provider implies a fee-for-service-based reimbursement approach with prompt payment.

Q.7:29   Why is establishing a framework for future relationships important to providers?

Providers would prefer to consider their relationships with managed care plans on a long-term basis. Assuming that other aspects of a provider's relationship with a plan are satisfactory, it is desirable not to have to frequently renegotiate agreements and fight over terms and conditions. As a result, an important objective is to provide a satisfactory framework for the future relationship between the provider and the plan.

Q.7:30   What do providers consider favorable contract terms?

Like managed care plans, providers also seek to obtain contractual terms that favor their particular situation. These include agreements by the managed care plan to:

- work within the provider's established policies and procedures for implementing utilization management and quality assurance activities,
- pay undisputed claims within 30 days or less,
- obtain consent of the provider before using the provider's name in marketing material,
- minimize the involvement of hospital personnel in implementing the managed care plan's procedures,
- eliminate the managed care plan's ability to retroactively deny legitimate claims, and
- provide adequate protection for the provider in the event of plan insolvency.

Q.7:31   What are the different negotiating styles used by providers?

The negotiating styles used by providers for their relationships with managed care plans fall into three broad categories: emotional, objective, and nonexistent.

Some providers react to proposals by managed care plans in an emotional fashion. They view requests for discounts and imposition of utilization management and quality assurance programs as affronts to their expertise and honesty. In some cases, these providers hold firm on their positions out of a sense of righteousness. Increasingly, however, providers are learning that this type of demand is typical of managed care plans and that they must deal with them in today's health care environment.

The objective negotiating style corresponds to the collegial approach advocated by many successful negotiators. It requires the negotiators to separate themselves from the issues and to evaluate the proposals based on their merits. Providers who adopt an objective style of negotiation typically evaluate participation proposals from many managed care plans. Each proposal is assessed based on its relative benefits and is accepted if it offers business advantages to the provider.

Some providers, however, do not adopt any specific negotiating style, signing virtually all managed care participation agreements that are offered. In many cases, these providers believe they do not have sufficient market clout to force legitimate negotiation on issues of importance to them. Providers who fail to negotiate before signing may be giving up important concessions that they could retain. Most managed care plans are willing to bargain about some aspects of their participation agreements, even with providers holding little power. The provider's failure to negotiate may send the message that plans can take advantage of the provider, and this in the long run will place the provider in an even weaker position.

Q.7:32   What are some of the different tactics used by providers in negotiating with managed care plans?

Providers adopt many different tactics in their attempts to gain negotiating advantages. The following negotiating tactics are among those used by providers:

- *Joint physician–hospital negotiations.* Some hospitals have formed joint ventures with their medical staffs for the purpose of participating with managed care plans. These provider groups, which may be medical staff–hospital organizations, physician–hospital organizations (PHOs), combined provider units, or local provider units, are intended to blunt the ability of managed care plans to whipsaw providers through separate negotiations with hospitals and physicians. The combined provider unit evaluates and negotiates participation arrangements for both the hospital and the affiliated physicians concurrently.

- *Use of information.* Some providers prepare their own analyses of the alternatives available to the managed care plan in an attempt to predict the offers that will be made by competing providers. For example, a hospital negotiating with a PPO sponsored by a large insurance company prepared an extensive analysis of charges and utilization by DRG for itself and for competing hospitals. This hospital was able to prepare a proposal that met the needs of the PPO and could demonstrate, using actual utilization data and the proposed rates, that its proposal was superior to other offers.

- *Threats not to participate.* Some providers have sufficient market clout that their lack of participation can place a managed care plan at a competitive disadvantage in the market. These providers use the threat of not participating as a means of obtaining concessions from the plan.

- *Analysis of the managed care plan.* Some providers use analysis of the managed care plan to their advantage during negotiations. One example of this technique is the analysis of financial statements and premium rate requests filed by HMOs with state regulators. Among the items that can be estimated from these reports is the average amount paid by an HMO to hospital providers for inpatient care. Hospitals have used this information to their advantage during negotiations when, for example, representatives of an HMO claimed that their average hospital payments were below the hospital's proposal. The hospital was able to respond by showing that the HMO's own reports indicated that the amounts were much higher. The use of this information allowed some hospitals to obtain higher reimbursement rates, which more than offset the cost of obtaining and analyzing the regulatory reports.

CONTENTS AND ORGANIZATION OF A MANAGED CARE AGREEMENT

Q.7:33   How is a managed care agreement generally organized?

Many managed health care plan contracts follow fairly similar formats. The contract begins with a title describing the instrument, for example, "Primary Care Physician Agreement." After this is the caption identifying the names of the parties and the legal action taken, along with the transition, which contain words signifying that the parties have entered into an agreement. Then the contract includes the recitals, which are best explained as the *whereas* clauses. These clauses are not intended to have legal significance, but may become relevant to resolve inconsistencies in the body of the contract or if the drafter inappropriately includes substantive provisions in them. The use of the word *whereas* is merely tradition and has no legal significance.

The next section of the contract is the definitions section, which includes definitions of all key contract terms. The definitions section precedes the operative language, including the substantive health-related provisions that define the responsibilities and obligations of each of the parties, representations and warranties, and declarations. The last section of the contract, the closing or testimonium, reflects the assent of the parties through their signatures. Sometimes the drafters of a provider contract decide to have the signature page as the first page for administrative simplicity.

Contracts also frequently incorporate by reference other documents, some of which will be appended to the agreement as attachments or exhibits. Managed health care plans frequently reserve the right to amend some of these referenced documents unilaterally. Exhibits and appendixes are frequently used by managed health care plans to promote efficiency in administering many provider contracts. The managed health care plan, to the extent possible, could design many of its provider contracts, or groups of provider contracts, around a core set of common requirements. Exhibits may be used to identify the terms that may vary, such as payment rates and provider responsibilities.

Q.7:34 What purposes does a contract's structure serve?

A contract's structure is intended to accomplish three purposes: (1) to simplify a reader's use and understanding of the agreement, (2) to facilitate amendment revision of the contract where the contract form has been used for many providers, and (3) to streamline the administrative process necessary to submit and obtain regulatory approvals.

Q.7:35 What are the different types of provisions that are frequently included in managed care agreements?

Managed care agreements frequently include provisions relating to:

- definitions of provider services
- reimbursement issues

- hold harmless agreements
- appeal
- term and termination
- indemnification and insurance
- utilization management
- quality assurance program
- quality review and credentialing
- medical records
- administrative and financial records
- marketing and promotion
- dispute resolution

Q.7:36   What are some of the provider services that should be defined in a managed care contract?

Because the hospital is assuming the contractual obligation to provide covered services to enrollees, it is essential that the contract define what is encompassed within the term *covered services*. This can be accomplished through an exhibit appended to the contract. The hospital should ensure that it has the capability of providing all of the services included in this definition.

The hospital will be reimbursed only for *medically necessary* care. The definition of this term, therefore, is also vital and should be spelled out as clearly as possible. This should reflect the definition of medical necessity used in the utilization review program.

Another term that should be defined is *emergency care*. The hospital is not required to receive pre-authorization for emergency care. If there is a disagreement as to what constitutes emergency care, reimbursement disputes will arise later. Therefore the term should be defined as clearly as possible.

Experimental procedures is an often disputed term. The contract must indicate whether experimental procedures will be included in covered services and if so, what procedures will be included within that definition.

Q.7:37   What are the different reimbursement variations that are frequently included in managed care contracts?

There are several possible reimbursement variations that may be applicable to managed care contracts. The most common are:

- *Discounted charges.* The parties negotiate a percentage discount from the hospital's usual charges, and the hospital accepts this as payment in full.
- *Per diem payment.* Under this variation, the hospital receives a specified amount per patient per day during a hospitalization, regardless of actual costs incurred. There may be different per diem charges for different types of services.
- *Per case payment.* The hospital receives a flat rate for each hospitalization. There usually are different rates for different services. The rate can be set according to DRGs, CPT-4 codes, or any other agreed-upon method.
- *Capitation payment.* The hospital receives a fixed amount per patient per month. The hospital is obligated to provide all covered services necessary at no additional charge.
- *Percentage of premium payment.* The hospital receives an agreed-upon percentage of the plan's monthly premiums, and in return must provide all covered services to enrollees.

Q.7:38 What is a carve out?

A contract may specify the usual payment method to be made under the contract but exceptions can be made for various services or particular circumstances. For example, a hospital that is under a capitation reimbursement scheme may want to carve out particular high-cost services and negotiate a different reimbursement scheme for those particular services.

Q.7:39 What is a stop-loss provision?

A provider may want to include a stop-loss provision to protect itself from an unanticipated volume of patients or unanticipated intensity of services. Such a provision sets a threshold, beyond which the payment method shifts from per diem, per case, or a capitated amount (whichever method is applicable) to standard or discounted charges.

Q.7:40 What is an annual adjustment provision?

A provider may want the right to negotiate adjustment of the payment structure on an annual basis. That will protect it from changes in patient volume or mix. The provider may also need to reassess the reimbursement level in light of its own business decisions that might introduce operational changes that affect reimbursement.

Q.7:41 What is a timely payment provision?

The contract may provide that the MCO's failure to pay a clean claim (which should be defined) within a specified time period will trigger a penalty requiring payment of full charges rather than payment of the negotiated rate. This will probably be difficult to negotiate, especially if the hospital is signing an all payer agreement.

Q.7:42 What is a noncovered services provision?

A managed care organization is responsible for paying the hospital only for covered services. The hospital must accept the contracted reimbursement as payment in full, except for copayments and deductibles, if those are included in the plan. The contract should indicate clearly, however, the hospital's right to collect payment from plan enrollees for noncovered services, deductibles, and copayments.

Q.7:43 What is a claims procedure provision?

A contract should specify the process for submitting claims. It generally will require the submission of claims within a certain number of days. There should be a provision addressing how contested claims will be handled. The contract also should address claims for which the MCO is the secondary payer. It may indicate a specific time period for collection from the primary carrier. If the MCO cannot resolve disputes with the primary carrier within that time, the MCO should reimburse the provider pending final resolution of the dispute.

Q.7:44 What should a copayment provision stipulate?

The contract should indicate whether the patient's copayment is based on full or discounted charges. It should also specify who will collect the copayments.

Q.7:45 What should a contract provide with respect to reimbursement of screening for emergency services?

Because the federal patient antidumping law (and in many instances state law) requires emergency department screening of patients prior to inquiry about insurance, hospitals may require that an MCO reimburse the hospital for that screening, even if a determination is made later that there was no emergency. The MCO will likely respond, however, that it will only pay for covered services under the benefit contract. MCOs will argue that this is a hospital concern and that the hospital has a duty to provide these services, even if there is no MCO involved.

Q.7:46 What is a reconciliation of accounts provision?

A contract should provide for the reconciliation of accounts by including a provision that addresses reconciling overpayments or underpayments. The contract may limit the adjustment period to a specific time period (for example, six months). It may also specify that there will be no reconciliation for amounts below a certain level.

Q.7:47 What should a contract provide with respect to the payment for inpatients upon termination of the contract?

When the contract is terminated, there may be enrollees of the plan who are inpatients in need of further treatment. The contract should clarify payment for continuing services to such enrollees, and may require transfer to another facility when appropriate.

Q.7:48 What should a contract provide with respect to retroactive denial?

The hospital's position with respect to retroactive denial is that if it receives preauthorization to provide a particular service, an MCO should not be allowed to retroactively deny payment for that service. The hospital will argue that the MCO should bear the cost of such errors if it is discovered later, for example, that the enrollee no longer was eligible under the plan. The MCO will argue strenuously against this, however, asserting that an MCO agrees to pay only covered claims and that prior authorization is not a guarantee of payment.

Q.7:49   What is a hold-harmless provision?

Managed care contracts typically contain a hold-harmless provision that specifies that the hospital cannot sue or assert any claims against enrollees for covered services, even if the MCO becomes insolvent. Some state laws require such a contract provision to protect plan beneficiaries.

Q.7:50   What should an appeals provision contain?

The contract should provide for a fair appeals mechanism that the hospital can pursue in instances of claims denials. The appeals process should be spelled out clearly and specify the delays for completing each stage of the process.

Q.7:51   What issues should a term and termination clause address?

A term and termination clause should address the following issues:

- term
- renewal
- termination for cause
- opportunity to cure
- dispute resolution
- termination without cause
- post-termination obligations

Q.7:52   What factors are considered in establishing the term of a contract?

It is generally a business decision on the part of the contracting parties as to whether the contract should be short term or long term. The decision will be influenced by such factors as the managed care environment in the area, the degree of commitment to the arrangement, the level of confidence in the MCO, etc. These factors must be weighed when deciding on the proper term of the contract.

Q.7:53   What should a renewal provision address?

A contract should address whether renewal of the contract is automatic or must be renegotiated. The term of the renewal should be specified. There can also be a notification provision requiring the MCO to provide advance notice of the approach of the end of the contract term.

Q.7:54 Under what circumstances should a contract permit termination for cause?

The contract should allow the parties to terminate the agreement for cause under a number of circumstances, including:

- loss of licensure, certification, or accreditation
- financial instability, based on the MCO's financial statements or other information indicating that the entity shortly will be unable to meet its obligations under the contract
- cancellation of insurance or re-insurance
- changes in the law or the reimbursement system that significantly affect the contract
- failure to make timely payments
- sale of assets, merger, or change of control
- assignment of the contract

The hospital may have negotiated prior approval or notification of changes in certain of the MCO's policies and procedures, such as changes in the utilization review process, billing system, or grievance procedures. Failure to receive notification or to give approval may be stated as grounds for termination of the contract.

Q.7:55 What is an opportunity to cure clause?

The contract may provide for an opportunity to cure breaches of the contract in certain situations, for example, a 30-day opportunity to cure a failure to make timely payment. However, the hospital should protect itself against the possibility of abuse of such a provision. In addition, the hospital should be aware that frequent failure to make timely payments may be an indication of the financial instability of the MCO.

Q.7:56 What should a contract provide with respect to dispute resolution?

The contract should indicate how such disagreements between the parties will be resolved. Arbitration and mediation are good choices because they are usually faster and less costly than litigation. The dispute resolution process can be structured in any way the parties agree. The contract should set out the details of how the process will work, including such items as how the arbitrator or mediator will be chosen, what rules will govern the process (such as, for example, the procedures of the American Arbitration Association), and specific time frames within which the procedures will take place.

Q.7:57   What is a termination without cause provision?

Contracts may contain termination without cause provisions, which allow parties to terminate the agreement if they provide sufficient notice to the other party. The notification period for this is generally substantial (for example 90 to 120 days) because of the impact of termination on the obligations of the MCO and the disruption of the provider network.

Q.7:58   What should a contract provide with respect to post-termination obligations?

A provider should ensure that post-termination obligations are addressed in the contract. In particular, the MCO's responsibility for payment for services rendered and for care initiated before termination should be clarified. Payment for enrollees who are inpatients at the time of the termination should be addressed. Some state laws require providers to continue services for a specific period of time after the contract is terminated.

Q.7:59   What issues should indemnification and insurance provisions address?

Managed care contracts often contain broad indemnification provisions whereby the parties seek to shift risk to another party. The hospital should ensure that each party carries responsibility only for its own actions. If the MCO is responsible for physician selection and credentialing, the hospital should not indemnify the MCO for its decisions. The MCO also should be held responsible for its participation in utilization management decisions. The courts have begun to realize that the MCO does play a role in medical decisions and should be held liable to some extent. (See **Chapter 4** for a more extensive discussion of this subject.) Therefore, the hospital should not assume this potential liability through a broad indemnification clause. Professional liability carriers often will not pay for claims that arise under indemnification clauses because of exclusions from coverage for contractual claims. The contract should also indicate necessary insurance limits and may require notification of cancellation or significant changes to the policy.

Q.7:60 What issues should a utilization management provision address?

Because providers will be obligated to comply with the MCO's utilization management (UM) program, that program should be made part of the contract. The UM program is a vital part of a plan, and hospitals should require advance approval or at least advance notice of significant changes in it.

The contract should also indicate who will make the utilization review (UR) decisions. Although the initial review may be performed by a nurse, if the recommendation is to deny the claim, the claim should be reviewed by a physician, and the attending physician should be contacted to obtain further information before the claim is denied. See **Chapter 6** for information on liability issues arising out of the UR process.

Utilization review determines the medical necessity of the recommended care. The definition of medical necessity used for UR decisions should be clear and should comply with the definition of medical necessity used in describing services the hospital is obligated to provide.

As part of the UM program, preauthorization generally is required before nonemergency care is rendered. The contract should indicate how the provider is to verify the eligibility of enrollees. This often is done through enrollees' identification cards. The contract should clearly spell out the process for obtaining preauthorization for treatment. With respect to emergency care, which does not require preauthorization, the MCO usually requires notification of treatment within a set time period after care is rendered. This time frame should be stipulated in the contract, and the provider should ensure that it is reasonable.

The contract should also address the MCO's right of access to enrollees' medical records to perform utilization review. This stipulation can include parameters to ensure that the times of access are reasonable and that the UR representatives of the MCO do not unnecessarily disrupt the medical records department or patient care.

Finally, the hospital should have the right to appeal denial of a claim based on retrospective review. If there are stringent reauthorization and concurrent review requirements, the hospital may want to limit retrospective review to emergency care and certain specific other services.

Q.7:61   What does the quality assurance program provision address?

A managed care contract will require a hospital to comply with the quality assurance program, which should be distinct from the UM program. The contract should clearly indicate what is required of the provider as well as the consequences of noncompliance.

Q.7:62   What should a contract provide with respect to credentialing?

The parties to a managed care contract must clarify who is responsible for the credentialing process for physician participation in the plan. Although the hospital must credential physicians before granting them medical staff membership or clinical privileges at the facility, it may or may not take on the responsibility (and increased liability exposure) for credentialing physicians for participation in the MCO.

The hospital should be aware that although state peer review laws may protect the confidentiality of the credentialing process for medical staff membership and clinical privileges, the statutory immunity in many cases does not apply to credentialing physicians for plan participation. Immunity will depend on the language of the statute.

Another factor to consider is that only health care entities that provide health care services and engage in professional review activity have access to and reporting requirements for the National Practitioners Data Bank. Although hospitals and HMOs are specifically included within this definition, it is ambiguous as to whether other entities are subsumed in it. In fact, it is the position of the U.S. Department of Health and Human Services that a physician group practice or a PPO that either does not provide health care services or does not have a formal peer review system will not meet the Title IV definition of a health care entity, and therefore is ineligible to report to or query the Data Bank [U.S. Department of Health and Human Services, *National Practitioner Data Bank Guidebook* (Supplement, 1992)].

No matter which party does the credentialing, the hospital should clarify that physicians participating in the MCO will be considered for hospital staff membership and privileges on the same basis as nonparticipating physicians.

With respect to disciplinary procedures, the MCO will have its own procedures that may be based on administrative matters, noncompliance with UR standards, or lack of cost efficiency. The hospital will maintain its own disciplinary procedures, which apply to all physicians who have medical staff membership.

Q.7:63 What should a contract provide with respect to medical records?

The contract should indicate that the MCO has the right to review and copy enrollee medical records after reasonable notice and during normal business hours. It should indicate which party will bear the cost of copying records. The contract should indicate that the MCO has the responsibility of obtaining enrollee consent to access the medical records. State law may give payers limited right of access. Access to records should continue beyond the termination of the contract.

There should also be a contract provision requiring all parties to maintain the confidentiality of patient medical records. There are special confidentiality concerns regarding medical records of minors, persons with communicable diseases, incompetents, and those being treated for alcohol or substance abuse. State and federal law impose specific requirements regarding such records.

Q.7:64 What should a contract provide with respect to administrative and financial records?

The contract should indicate that each party to the contract is entitled to inspect, review, and perhaps copy certain administrative and financial records of the other party. Again, there can be reasonable time limits established, and the issue of payment for copies must be resolved. The parties must agree to keep all such information confidential except as required by law.

8

Credentialing and Peer Review

Q.8:1   What is credentialing?

Credentialing is the process of obtaining information, verifying the information, and evaluating applicants who want to obtain or renew medical staff membership and/or obtain, renew, or revise clinical privileges at health care facilities. Managed care organizations (MCOs) credential physicians who seek to become MCO participating providers. Large group practices, independent practice associations (IPAs), and some medical societies also perform credentialing.

Q.8:2   What is peer review?

An essential part of ongoing evaluation in the credentialing process is peer review, which involves the review of a practitioner's clinical skills and professional conduct by a committee composed of the practitioner's peers.

Q.8:3   Who must be credentialed?

The credentialing process applies to all physicians and other independent practitioners (those permitted by law and by the individual hospital or MCO to provide patient care without direction or supervision, such as dentists and podiatrists).

Allied health practitioners, such as physicians' assistants and nurse practitioners, who cannot practice independently, are subject to a separate credentialing process.

Q.8:4   Why must credentialing be performed?

The first and foremost reason for performing credentialing is to ensure that patients receive quality medical care from qualified practitioners. The vast majority of practitioners do not have credentialing problems. When there are problems, however, and they are not detected and appropriately addressed by the credentialing entity, the consequences with respect to patient harm can be devastating.

The courts and legislatures have recognized that hospitals have a duty to the public to properly credential their medical staffs. Therefore, to minimize legal liability to patients for physician performance, and to ensure compliance with state, federal, and local law, hospitals must ensure that credentialing procedures are properly carried out.

MCOs share with hospitals the goals of providing high quality services and of reducing organizational liability. Careful and thorough credentialing is an important element in reaching those goals. The MCO, no matter what the organizational structure, seeks to include only those providers who will render good medical care. The credentialing process will help the MCO determine which providers are suitable to become participating providers in the plan. Contracting with providers who meet all of the credentialing standards is one method of reducing potential liability for the conduct of a participating provider. If there is a solid credentialing program that is integrated effectively with an ongoing quality assessment program, it will assist the MCO to identify and screen out incompetent physicians and help shield the MCO from liability for their negligence. A strong, consistently applied credentialing program will also provide a record of fairness and objectivity to counter provider challenges that they have been denied participation unfairly.

In addition to those concerns and responsibilities, MCOs are under economic pressure to perform credentialing. Payers expect MCOs to have cost-effective, good quality provider panels or networks. From a contracting standpoint, an MCO is better able to position itself to win a contract if it can demonstrate effective provider performance. Although there are many elements necessary to do this, including physician profiling, effective quality assurance (QA) and utilization review (UR) programs, etc., the credentialing process is also one of the pivotal elements in demonstrating and maintaining good quality participating providers.

Q.8:5   Are MCOs legally responsible for credentialing and peer review?

For many MCOs, such as physician–hospital organizations (PHOs) and preferred provider organizations (PPOs), credentialing is not (yet) required by statute or regulation. HMOs, on the other hand, may be required by state HMO law to perform some level of credentialing.

Several states also have any willing provider laws that apply to managed care organizations. Such laws specify that MCOs cannot categorically exclude a particular class of providers, such as psychologists, podiatrists, or nurse midwives. The MCO therefore must consider such providers as potential participants in the MCO and evaluate each provider fairly. All candidates for participation, however, must be professionally qualified and meet other established criteria for participation before they will be accepted as MCO providers.

Beginning with the *Darling* case in 1965 [211 N.E.2d 253 (1965), *cert. denied*, 383 U.S. 946 (1966)], the courts have established clearly that hospitals have a direct responsibility for the quality of care provided by independent staff members. Failure to meet this responsibility is referred to as corporate negligence. To fulfill its corporate duty, a hospital must carefully select the physicians it permits to practice medicine there and must monitor the care they provide.

The doctrine of corporate negligence is applicable to managed care entities as well. An essential element of managed care is selecting for participation in the managed care system only those who will provide cost-effective, appropriate patient care. If the MCO is making choices among providers (a choice generally left up to the patient in an indemnity insurance environment) and requiring or strongly encouraging enrollees to see only those providers, the MCO has a duty to select those providers carefully and to monitor their performance. Whatever type of MCO is involved, the more that MCO limits covered persons' choice of providers, the greater the risk of liability for negligent credentialing.

The doctrine of *respondeat superior* clearly applies to staff model HMOs in which the HMO employs the physicians and provides the facility within which they offer care. The situation is directly analogous to that of an acute care hospital. When considering PPOs and IPA model HMOs, the circumstances are somewhat different because the patient is not physically on the premises of the entity and the IPA model HMO or the PPO probably does not employ the physician. The corporate negligence doctrine nonetheless may be applied to those models because of the HMO's or PPO's role in selecting the providers who will participate in the plan and in restricting the patient's choice.

Q.8:6 What have the courts held regarding MCOs' legal responsibility for credentialing and peer review?

In a Missouri case, a court considered application of the corporate negligence doctrine to an HMO [*Harrell v. Total Health Care, Inc.*, 1989 WL

153066 (Mo. Ct. App.), *aff'd*, 781 S.W.2d 58 (Mo. 1989)]. The appeals court recognized that the HMO had no direct involvement in patient care, but nonetheless found that it had breached its corporate duty through negligent credentialing. Because the HMO limited members' choice to the physicians it had selected, there was an unreasonable risk of harm to those enrollees if the HMO selected unqualified or incompetent physicians, the court reasoned. The court concluded that the HMO had a duty to conduct a reasonable investigation of the physicians' credentials and community reputation.

Similarly, a Pennsylvania court ruled that an IPA model HMO had a nondelegable duty to select and retain only competent primary care physicians [*McClellan v. Health Maintenance Organization of Pa.*, 604 A.2d 1053 (Pa. Super. *appeal denied*, 616 A.2d 985 (Pa. 1992)]. A patient chose a primary care physician from the list of participating providers and went to him for the removal of a mole on her back. Although the patient had informed the physician that the mole recently had undergone a marked change in size and color, the physician removed the mole, but discarded the specimen without obtaining a biopsy or other histological exam. As a result, the patient's malignant melanoma was not diagnosed or treated in a timely manner, and subsequently, she died. Her family sued the HMO on several grounds, including negligent selection of the physician.

The court held that the HMO had a duty to select and monitor physicians properly, but it did not base this conclusion on a theory of corporate negligence. Instead, it relied on common law principles that impose liability if one undertakes to render services to another and injures that person through failure to exercise reasonable care. Liability will attach if the failure to exercise reasonable care increases the risk of harm, or if the harm is suffered because of the other's reliance on the undertaking.

According to the court, in a case against an IPA model HMO on this basis, the injured party must show that:

- The HMO has undertaken to provide services to the subscriber that the HMO should recognize as necessary for the protection of the member.
- The HMO failed to use reasonable care in selecting, retaining, and/or evaluating the primary care physician.
- The risk of harm to the subscriber was increased as a result of the HMO's failure to use reasonable care.

Typically, state laws governing preferred provider arrangements do not establish credentialing requirements. Although HMO statutes and regulations may require the HMO to maintain such a system, they usually are not prescriptive as to its contents.

Q.8:7   What are the National Committee for Quality Assurance (NCQA) credentialing requirements?

The market trend is to require NCQA or other accreditation of the MCO as a stamp of approval/indicia of quality. Increasingly, employee benefits consultants are including accreditation questions in requests for proposals for large employers.

NCQA standards require:

- maintenance of written policies and procedures for the credentialing and recredentialing of physicians and dentists every two years according to the policies and procedures adopted by the MCO's governing body and implemented through a designated credentialing committee
- formal review and approval of the credentialing policies and procedures
- designation of a credentialing committee or other peer review body to make recommendations regarding credentialing decisions
- conducting credentialing of, at a minimum, all physicians and other licensed independent practitioners listed in the MCO's member literature
- obtaining, at a minimum, information from primary sources verifying:
    1. applicant's license
    2. Drug Enforcement Agency (DEA) or controlled dangerous substances (CDS) certificate where applicable
    3. graduation from medical school, residency training, board certification, as applicable
    4. professional work history
    5. adequate malpractice insurance
    6. professional liability claims history
    7. good standing at the hospital designated as the primary admitting facility
- obtaining a statement by the applicant as to disciplinary activity, physical and mental status, license history, criminal record, lack of impairment, and the correctness and completeness of the application
- requesting information from the National Practitioner Data Bank and the state Board of Medical Examiners as well as requesting information regarding Medicare and Medicaid sanctions
- using an appraisal process, including member complaints, quality review results, utilization management records, and member satisfaction surveys

- visiting each primary care physician's office to review the site and the physician's recordkeeping
- maintaining written policies and procedures for the initial quality assessment of health delivery organizations with which it intends to contract
- establishing a process for periodic verification of credentials
- maintaining a written description of delegated activities and the delegate's accountability
- maintaining a mechanism for suspension, reduction, or termination of participation of providers, including a reporting mechanism and appellate process

Q.8:8   Does the Joint Commission accredit MCOs?

The Joint Commission on Accreditation of Healthcare Organizations has developed accreditation standards for health care networks. These standards contain requirements for credentialing. According to the Joint Commission, there must be written credentialing criteria that are uniformly applied to licensed independent practitioners requesting membership on the provider panel of the network. The standards state that credentialing criteria must be approved by the leaders in the network and that appointment actions must be recommended to network leaders for final action. Appointments and reappointments are for a period of two years. The standards set out the information that each applicant must provide and indicate which information must be verified from the primary source.

One of the more controversial requirements is that the network conduct an assessment of the content of clinical records and office practices of each site where primary or specialty care is rendered by each practitioner being considered for appointment to the provider panel. This requirement applies when such sites are not under the auspices of a Joint Commission-accredited organization or are not accredited through a process recognized by the Joint Commission. This requirement could entail great expense for the network.

The Joint Commission's standards also require a written process for discontinuing the appointment of licensed independent practitioners and an appeals process.

Q.8:9   Do MCOs do their own credentialing?

MCOs are moving toward performing their own credentialing functions, although there is still a lot of delegation of that duty. HMOs may delegate credentialing responsibility to a medical group or an IPA or may rely on hospital credentialing of their providers. Self-funded employers may delegate credentialing of the panels to which it steers its employees to the broker of the provider network, which could be a provider-sponsored entity, an insurer, an HMO, or some other independent entity. If the MCO has delegated certain credentialing functions to the hospital, the MCO will be involved in creating credentialing criteria.

According to the American Accreditation Program, Inc. (AAPI), if a PPO relies on hospital credentialing, it will be downgraded in the AAPI accreditation report. The NCQA standards require a written description of the delegated activities and the delegate's accountability for these activities. The MCO must retain the right to approve new providers and sites and to terminate or suspend individual providers. In addition, the MCO must monitor the effectiveness of the delegate's credentialing and reappointment or recertification processes at least annually [NCQA Standard CR 15.0].

Reasons not to rely on hospital credentialing include:

- Checking with several hospitals where the provider has privileges may result in inconsistent reports.
- A hospital may not have disciplined a physician simply because of the time and money it would take to do so, but the physician may not be a provider who should be included in the MCO.
- The MCO will still be liable for the credentialing decision even if it relies on a hospital's credentialing.
- If a hospital reveals credentialing information, it may lose its status as privileged information. However, many state laws can be interpreted to permit communication between protected peer review entities. In addition, NCQA requires that the delegator assess this information in its audits of the delegatee's performance.

Q.8:10 If an MCO decides to delegate its credentialing responsibility, what should it consider in its contract with the credentialing entity?

An MCO may want to consider contract provisions:

- retaining the right to approve new providers or sites and to terminate or suspend individual providers

- requiring indemnification from the credentialing entity for losses attributable to negligence in the credentialing process
- ensuring that the credentialing entity carries insurance coverage that extends to errors or omissions in credentialing
- requiring the MCO to be named as an additional insured

Q.8:11   Who approves the credentialing policies and procedures?

The governing body or the group or individual to whom the governing body had delegated the credentialing function approves the credentialing policies and procedures. The function may be delegated to the quality assessment committee or a credentialing committee, or to the CEO or chief medical officer.

Q.8:12   What are the credentialing criteria for a managed care organization?

Many of the criteria that apply in the hospital setting are also applicable to MCOs. These include clinical competence, ability to work with others, and board certification. Because practitioners in many MCOs operate from private office locations, the MCO may have very specific criteria relating to evaluation of the physician's office practice. To adhere to its credentialing criteria, an MCO may physically inspect a physician's office to determine whether it provides adequate facilities (i.e., accessibility standards of The Americans with Disability Act are adhered to, office equipment is well maintained, office operates efficiently and has adequate hours of coverage, recordkeeping, and technicians as needed).

Alan Bloom, Senior Vice President and General Counsel of Maxicare Health Plans, Inc., indicates that MCOs must have criteria that ensure that health care professionals provide services that are available, accessible, and acceptable. According to Bloom, staffing patterns of contracting medical groups and the services available should be monitored [Alan Bloom, *Physician Credentialing in Managed Care*, ANNALS OF HEALTH LAW, Vol. I (1992)].

The criteria of efficient practice patterns is, if anything, even more vital in an MCO setting. The MCO may have specific criteria related to patient average length of stay and cost per case. If the MCO is going to make participation decisions based on economic criteria, it must have the data to back up its decisions. This is necessary to ensure fairness and prevent allegations of anticompetitive motives for exclusion decisions.

Q.8:13 How is credentialing done in integrated delivery systems?

Because integrated delivery systems are fairly new in the health care arena and are still evolving, credentialing is still done largely on a facility-by-facility basis. There is recognition in the industry, however, that centralization and integration of credentialing and peer review in integrated delivery systems is a desirable goal. [*See, e.g.,* Lowell C. Brown, *New "Mental Models" for Credentialing and Peer Review,* HEALTH SYSTEMS REVIEW (May/June 1994).] According to Brown, centralization of these activities will reduce or eliminate duplication in both credentialing and medical staff discipline. Instead of applying for separate privileges at several facilities in the same system or network, under a centralized system a practitioner would apply to all of them at once. In the present decentralized system, if a practitioner's privileges are reduced at one facility, that practitioner still retains similar privileges at another facility in the same network, necessitating numerous hearings, as required by the bylaws of each facility. A centralized model would require only one disciplinary hearing.

Q.8:14 What is economic credentialing and why is it particularly pertinent in a managed care environment?

Economic credentialing is the use of economic criteria in making credentialing decisions. The goal of MCOs is to provide quality health care cost effectively. A provider who consistently overutilizes or underutilizes resources is endangering both aspects of that goal. A provider who consistently overutilizes resources may not be providing quality care because that provider may be rendering unnecessary care (e.g., unnecessary surgery or laboratory tests), or care delivered at an inappropriate level (e.g., inpatient rather than outpatient). In addition, the provider who overutilizes resources is endangering the cost-effective operation of the MCO. A provider who consistently underutilizes resources also may be providing less than quality care. Although such conduct initially may seem more cost effective, it is a false economy. A provider who is not rendering medically necessary care eventually will be sued for malpractice. The MCO may share in that liability.

Q.8:15   Have there been any cases that address economic credentialing?

There have been a few cases that directly address economic factors. *Rosenblum v. Tallahassee Memorial Regional Medical Center, Inc.*, is considered to be the first pure economic credentialing case. In that case, a thoracic surgeon sued a hospital that denied him open-heart surgery privileges. The physician was the director of the open-heart surgery program at a competing hospital and was publicly supportive of that program. The court held that the hospital that denied him privileges could properly consider economic factors as well as medical factors in making a determination on granting clinical privileges. It cautioned, however, that although economic considerations are valid, they must not be arbitrary. The court noted that the physician was very highly qualified in a rare specialty that is used infrequently. It concluded that the hospital's decision to deny privileges was reasonable because it otherwise would have incurred substantial cost to establish and equip a department in which the physician could exercise those privileges [*Rosenblum v. Tallahassee Memorial Regional Medical Center, Inc.*, No. 91-589 (Fla. Cir. Ct., June 22, 1992)].

The *Rosenblum* case was based largely on a Florida statute that establishes factors a medical staff must take into consideration in making credentialing recommendations to the governing board and sets out the criteria for eligibility for staff membership that the governing board must use [Fla. Stat. § 395.011(5)]. That law lists the various criteria, then adds, "and by such other elements as may be determined by the governing board." The court ruled that this provision embraces the concept of economic credentialing.

In another managed care case, a federal court upheld the termination of two allergists who had failed to practice in a cost-effective manner. The court explicitly approved the use of participation decisions based on utilization patterns [*Hassan v. Independent Practice Associates*, 698 F. Supp. 679 (E.D. Mich. 1988)].

Q.8:16   How is the peer review process documented in a managed care organization?

The peer review process is documented in the quality assurance plan and the credentialing plan. In nonstaff model managed care organizations, providers generally are bound by contractual obligations rather than by medical staff bylaws. A participating provider that signs a contract with an MCO agrees to be bound by the MCO's policies, including the peer review procedures delineated in the quality assurance plan and the credentialing plan. Passing and maintaining credentialing status routinely is a condition precedent to obtaining and maintaining the contractual relationship.

Q.8:17 What kind of committees are there in an MCO?

The types of committees vary from state to state and from MCO to MCO. There are fewer committees in MCOs than in hospitals. HMOs generally have a separate credentials plan, a separate QA plan, and a separate UR plan. This is generally the case because of the requirements of state regulators and the preferences of payers and employers who may contract with the MCO. There may be a separate committee related to each of these areas. Some HMOs, however, have an umbrella committee that has oversight over all of these areas.

Many times MCO committees will be analogous to hospital committees in function, but will have a different name. For example, the committee that performs the QA function may be called the medical management committee, and the committee performing the credentialing function may be called the provider committee.

Q.8:18 What is the advantage of having an umbrella committee?

This may be desirable from a risk management perspective. When the committees are functioning independently, it is possible for a provider to be under review in one area and passed over in another. With an umbrella committee that performs or oversees all of the functions, this would not happen. There is general oversight and knowledge of the whole picture with regard to particular providers.

Q.8:19 Who is on MCO committees?

Committees are generally composed of community participating physicians as well as members of the MCO management.

Q.8:20 How do complaints about a provider come to the attention of an MCO?

Complaints about providers may come from many different sources. For example, a referral can be made to QA as a result of a member complaint. A complaint can come from an employer, a broker, another provider, an MCO employee—almost anyone can make a complaint that could result in a referral to an MCO QA committee. The appropriate committee must then decide whether to formally investigate the complaint.

Q.8:21   Are the due process requirements the same in MCOs as in hospitals when participation rights are affected?

In the MCO context, physicians generally do not have the same procedural rights as are afforded by hospitals in making credentialing decisions. In a 1994 case, however, a California court held that dentists participating in an HMO have a common law right to fair procedure. The court held that private entities cannot arbitrarily exclude or expel providers if important economic interests are at stake [*Delta Dental Plan of California v. Banasky*, 33 Cal. Rptr. 2d 381 (Ct. App. 1994)].

Whether or not the state courts have addressed the issue of due process rights in MCOs, by establishing a basic fair process scheme, an MCO will:

- provide objective standards as criteria for making credentialing decisions

- satisfy physicians' expectations of fair process created by their hospital experiences

- establish a record of fair treatment should an excluded or disciplined physician contest a decision in court

Basic fair process includes notice and an opportunity to be heard, which need not be elaborate procedures in the MCO context. Some health law attorneys maintain that an opportunity to be heard need not mean a hearing, but could be met by establishing a process whereby the excluded provider can correct the record in writing. If there is a hearing, it need not include the full spectrum of constitutional safeguards, such as a right to counsel. The final credentialing decision, however, should not be made by the applicant's direct economic competitors. [*See* Doug Hastings, "Physician–Hospital Organizations: Structures and Legal Issues," National Health Lawyers Association Annual Meeting, 1994.]

If the MCO wants to avail itself of the protections available under the Health Care Quality Improvement Act of 1986 (the HCQIA), however, it will have to afford practitioners the due process measures mandated by that law. As suggested by Hastings (see preceding citation), an MCO may want to have two separate fair process procedures. When the issue involves a matter of competence or professional conduct, the practitioner would be entitled to the procedures outlined in HCQIA, thereby bringing the MCO within that law's immunity provisions. When the credentialing decision does not pertain to professional competence or conduct, and the HCQIA immunities are therefore not available, the procedure may involve simply notice and an opportunity to be heard.

Once an MCO decides to incorporate fair process into its credentialing program, that process should be spelled out clearly and followed consistently.

Q.8:22   What is the HCQIA?

The HCQIA is a federal law that grants immunity to peer review activity and seeks to improve the quality of health care through reporting requirements [P.L. 99-660]. The HCQIA provides immunity under federal and state law for any individual or entity that participates in the peer review process, including witnesses and providers of information.

Q.8:23   How does the Health Care Quality Improvement Act affect credentialing?

The HCQIA contains both reporting requirements and immunity provisions that affect credentialing. The law requires health care entities to report certain adverse actions taken against health care practitioners. Information must be requested from the National Practitioner Data Bank (NPDB) when practitioners apply for a position on the medical staff, for clinical privileges at the hospital, or for participation status in an HMO. Information also must be requested every two years at the time of reappointment of such individuals.

The immunity provisions provide persons giving information to professional review bodies and those assisting in review activities limited immunity from damages that may arise as a result of adverse decisions that affect a physician's medical staff privileges. The immunity provisions apply only if certain procedural safeguards are satisfied.

If the procedural and reporting requirements of the HCQIA are met, members of a professional review body will not be liable in damages under any law, except the Civil Rights Act or the Clayton Act, which is an antitrust law.

Q.8:24   Do the HCQIA reporting requirements apply to MCOs?

Health care entities, as defined in the HCQIA, must report adverse actions against privileges. *Health care entity* is defined as an entity that "provides health care services and that follows a formal peer review process for the purpose of furthering quality health care" [42 U.S.C. § 11151(4)(A)(ii)]. If an MCO falls within this definition, it has reporting responsibilities.

HMOs are considered health care entities under the HCQIA and therefore have reporting requirements. PPOs, on the other hand, generally are seen as arranging health care services rather than providing health care services. Under this perception, a PPO would not have reporting responsibilities. The perception would apply to PHOs as well. Although the same argument might be made for certain models, there is no distinction made in the statute.

Q.8:25   Are MCOs required to query the NPDB?

HMOs are required to query the NPDB, which is a database mandated by the HCQIA that contains information regarding physician disciplinary actions and malpractice payments. Other types of MCOs are not required to do so. State law may impose such a requirement. Accreditation standards that require NPDB inquiries may eventually be used to set a standard of care in the future.

Q.8:26   Do HCQIA immunities apply to MCOs?

If an MCO is engaged in professional review action, as defined in the HCQIA, it will be entitled to that law's protection from liability as long as it meets the procedural requirements outlined in the law. A professional review action must be based on the "competence or professional conduct of an individual physician . . ." [42 U.S.C. § 11151(a)].

Q.8:27   Is peer review in an MCO the same as peer review in a hospital?

It is very difficult to make generalizations about peer review in MCOs because there are so many different types of MCOs. An MCO that is based on IPA agreements or network agreements may operate very differently than either an open access, fee-for-service HMO that has individual provider agreements or a staff model HMO.

How peer review is conducted in any particular MCO may be determined by a number of factors, including the requirements and immunities of the state peer review law, the market conditions and geographical area, and the leverage of the MCO. An MCO usually develops its quality assessment plan (QA plan), which contains the peer review process. It will do so by taking into consideration whether the state peer review law will afford it some protections if various elements are included. It will also take into consideration the immunities under the HCQIA if certain procedures are followed.

When an MCO negotiates contracts with providers, complying with the QA plan is part of the provider's obligation under the contract. Although many aspects of the contract may be negotiable, the QA plan is not. It would be unmanageable to have different procedures available to different providers. In addition, in the case of HMOs, many state HMO laws require that the QA plan be approved by the state regulator. Once it is approved, it cannot be arbitrarily altered.

Market conditions and provider culture differ in various geographic areas. Although an MCO in one area might be able to have a peer review process that does not contain a hearing requirement, that might be totally unacceptable to providers in another area, and the MCO would not be able to attract or retain providers without including a right to a hearing. The amount of leverage an MCO has in a particular geographic area might also dictate how the peer review process is structured. If participation in an MCO is considered very desirable by providers in a certain area, the MCO may have more latitude in structuring its peer review process.

Q.8:28 How does an investigation begin and proceed?

Generally, the QA committee (or the committee performing that function) determines when a complaint is legitimate and should trigger an investigation. The MCO administrative staff then gathers the necessary materials and information. This may involve obtaining records from the provider's office. Provider agreements often contain provisions that require the provider to cooperate with and participate in all credentialing, quality assurance, and utilization review programs.

If the investigation reveals a problem, the QA committee will assign it a severity level. These vary from plan to plan. As an example, severity level one might be a problem that does not indicate the possibility of patient injury. Severity level three may be a problem that indicates a high possibility of patient injury. The severity level will guide the committee in determining what action it will pursue.

The severity level, as well as the possible disciplinary action for each severity level, should be spelled out in the QA plan. MCOs attempt to provide the QA committee with as much flexibility as possible as far as what kind of discipline can be imposed for each level of severity. The level of creativity available to the committee will depend on the wording of the QA plan. Many times provider discipline consists of education or counseling, but can consist of various measures, including expulsion of the provider from the plan.

If the QA plan indicates that the right to a hearing is triggered, the provider should receive notice of the charges and should be given an opportunity to respond. Depending on how the MCO has structured the provider appeal process, the committee may appoint a hearing officer, who may be an independent attorney familiar with MCO matters. The MCO may also refer the matter to a separate appeals committee.

Q.8:29   Do all disciplinary actions have to go through the credentials committee?

That varies with each MCO. Having all disciplinary actions go through the credentials committee could become cumbersome. For example, the QA committee may be investigating a particular matter and may determine what it considers to be an appropriate corrective action. That committee is composed of various community physicians. If the matter must then be shifted to the credentials committee, another group of community physicians would be reviewing the same information and making the decision. The MCO may want to empower the QA committee to go forward with the disciplinary action and have the credentials committee become involved only on appeal, or have the QA committee refer the matter directly to a broader oversight committee for appellate action. How these procedures are structured will vary with the needs of each MCO and what works well in a given area.

Q.8:30   Are providers in MCOs entitled to appeal a corrective action plan decision?

Whether practitioners in MCOs are entitled to appeal a corrective action plan depends on what is stated in the QA plan. In some plans, an appeal is at the discretion of the MCO, while other plans routinely provide an appeals process. The NCQA standards require that there be an appeals process for instances in which the MCO chooses to reduce, suspend, or terminate a practitioner's privileges [CR 14.2].

Some contracts contain provisions requiring the exhaustion of internal administrative remedies, and most MCO contracts contain binding arbitration clauses. Therefore, if a provider is subjected to corrective action to which he or she objects and there is an appeals mechanism, the provider must appeal. If the provider is dissatisfied with the outcome of the appeal, he or she must submit the dispute to binding arbitration.

Q.8:31 Can an MCO terminate a physician under an employment contract without a hearing?

If an MCO has a quality of care issue with a provider, the MCO is better off addressing that problem directly through the established fair hearing process in the QA plan. This is true for several reasons.

- If contract termination is used as an out in most situations, this will become apparent to practitioners, payers, employers, and regulators. The MCO will then lose credibility.
- Subsequently, if a terminated practitioner sues, charging that the termination was in violation of the antitrust laws, the MCO may have to admit the real reason for termination. At that point, it has lost the protection of the HCQIA because it has not granted a fair hearing.
- If an MCO is aware of quality of care problems but simply terminates without cause, a patient who is subsequently injured by the practitioner may sue the MCO for failing to carry out a corporate duty.
- Whether the quality problem was reportable will depend on the circumstances. If it was reportable and the MCO failed to do so, it may be subject to civil monetary penalties.

Q.8:32 Are there any special considerations in a staff model HMO setting?

The physician contract should be coordinated with the fair hearing plan. If a provider is terminated, that provider should be entitled to only one hearing. The bylaws should state that medical staff privileges are terminated if the provider is excluded from the HMO. There should not be a hearing regarding termination from the HMO, and then another hearing in order to revoke medical staff privileges.

Q.8:33 Who approves the exclusion or participation of practitioners in the MCO?

The MCO committee performing the credentialing function makes its recommendations to the board or to a committee of the board charged with this responsibility. The board will approve contract status, decline to contract, or return the matter to the credentials committee for further clarification.

Q.8:34   Are there antitrust implications in excluding physicians from an MCO?

Providers who are not accepted as participating providers in an MCO may allege that the exclusion constituted a group boycott in violation of the antitrust laws. To establish a group boycott, there must be more than one actor, anticompetitive intent or the absence of legitimate reasons for the conduct, and a certain degree of market power.

Control is an important issue in this context. If the plan is provider controlled, that raises the question of whether the decision to exclude actually was made by a group of competitors, not by the MCO. In one case, for example, a court found that several competing hospitals controlled the board of a Blue Cross Association, and were the parties actually making the exclusionary decisions. That constituted an illegal group boycott. In a nonprovider-controlled plan, there is less risk that competitors will be making such decisions, and therefore less likelihood of a successful group boycott charge [*St. Bernard General Hospital, Inc., v. Hospital Services Association*, 712 F.2d 978 (5th Cir. 1983), *cert. denied*, 466 U.S. 970 (1984)].

Even if there is an agreement among competitors to exclude a provider, however, the actors must have significant market power before the conduct will be considered per se illegal. If the actors do not have significant market power, the conduct will be analyzed under the rule of reason to establish whether the conduct constituted an illegal restraint of trade. That will be determined by balancing the competitive and anticompetitive effects of the conduct. In one case a court held that an HMO that refused to allow a radiology group to participate in the HMO did not violate the antitrust laws because the conduct had no anticompetitive effect. It held that even if there had been a conspiracy to exclude the group, there was no antitrust violation because the IPA and HMO had insufficient market power to restrain trade [*Capital Imaging Associates v. Mohawk Valley Medical Associates, Inc.*, 791 F. Supp. 956 (N.D. N.Y. 1992), *aff'd*, 996 F.2d 537 (2d Cir.), *cert. denied*, 114 S. Ct. 388 (1983)].

9

Fraud and Abuse

INTRODUCTION

Q.9:1   What are the legislative sources of fraud and abuse prohibitions in the health care industry?

The last two decades have witnessed an explosive growth in the reach of Medicaid and Medicare fraud and abuse legislation. Under the Medicare statute as originally enacted, the only provision relating to fraud and abuse was a general prohibition in the Social Security Act against the making of false statements in applications for benefits [P.L. 89-87, § 1872]. Prompted by reports that health care providers were grossly abusing Medicare and Medicaid programs, Congress enacted the Medicare/Medicaid Antifraud and Abuse Amendments to the Social Security Act [P.L. 92-603, § 242] in 1977, to upgrade criminal offenses under the statute to felonies and substantially expand the definition of prohibited kickbacks. Under the amendments, *fraud* is defined as knowing and willful deception or misrepresentation, or a reckless disregard of the facts, with the intent to receive an unauthorized benefit; *abuse* is a manner of operation that results in excessive or unreasonable costs to Medicare or Medicaid.

Medicare/Medicaid fraud and abuse legislation was further toughened in 1981 by the inclusion of a provision that allows the administrative imposition of civil monetary penalties on health care providers who submit false or improper claims for Medicare and Medicaid reimbursement [P.L. 97-35, § 2105(a)]. In 1987, the Medicare and Medicaid Patient and Program Protection Act broadened the grounds for excluding health care providers from participation in Medicare/Medicaid, including any violation of the antikickback statute [P.L. 99-509, P.L. 100-203].

In addition to the Medicare and Medicaid antikickback statute, federal law also regulates patient referrals between a physician and an entity in which the physician (or an immediate family member) has a financial interest. The Ethics in Patient Referrals Act, commonly referred to as Stark I, was enacted as part of the Omnibus Budget Reconciliation Act of 1989 [42 U.S.C. § 1395nn] and became effective January 1, 1992. The legislation was adopted in response to concerns about conflicts of interest that could arise when a physician has a financial relationship with a clinical laboratory and refers patients to that facility for care, and about the inadequacy of existing antifraud and abuse legislation in eliminating the ethical problems associated with patient referrals. In August 1993, as part of the Omnibus Budget Reconciliation Act, Congress amended the Stark law prohibition to apply to referrals for a much expanded list of health care services, in an enactment commonly referred to as Stark II.

Q.9:2   What types of activities are governed by federal law on health care fraud?

Federal health care fraud enforcement activities under the legislation discussed in **Question 9:1** primarily focus on the following practices in the health care industry:

- false claims and other fraudulent billing practices,
- illegal referrals under the Medicare/Medicaid antikickback statute, and
- physician self-referral practices proscribed by the Stark legislation.

Q.9:3   In the context of managed care arrangements, where are fraud and abuse violations most likely to occur?

Because many managed care arrangements involve agreements between different types of providers, the restrictions that both the antikickback statute and the Stark laws place on referrals are of particular importance to these types of organizations. In analyzing any arrangement that directs the flow of health care to any specific provider, the ability of any one of the parties to exercise undue influence over a patient's health care decision is a key issue.

SCOPE OF REFERRAL RESTRICTIONS UNDER THE ANTIKICKBACK STATUTE

Q.9:4   What is the scope of the prohibition on referral payments under the antikickback statute?

The antikickback statute forbids any knowing and willful conduct involving the solicitation, receipt, offer, or payment of any kind of remuneration in return for referring an individual or for recommending or arranging the purchase, lease, or ordering of an item or service that may be wholly or partly paid for through the Medicare/Medicaid program.

Remuneration is defined broadly to include any payment in cash or in kind, made either directly or indirectly, overtly or covertly. However, remuneration does not include a discount or price reduction if the amount is disclosed properly and is reflected in the cost claimed as reimbursement or in charges. Remuneration also does not include any amount paid by an employer to an employee for work performed in providing covered items for services. Both the Health Care Financing Administration (HCFA) and the Office of the Inspector General (OIG) at the Department of Health and Human Services have indicated that the term remuneration refers to any economic benefit, which can be conferred in a variety of ways, including reduced rent, compensation guarantees, equipment loans, administrative and billing services, and participation in ventures offering the opportunity to generate fees.

Judicial interpretation has also endorsed a broad definition of the term *remuneration*. In 1985, the Third Circuit examined the issue of whether payments to a physician were a kickback for patient referrals or could be justified by services rendered. In *United States v. Greber* [760 F.2d 68 (3d Cir. 1985), *cert. denied*, 474 U.S. 988 (1988)], a physician owned a cardiac monitoring company that paid other physicians interpretation or consultation fees for each patient they referred to the service. The evidence showed that the interpretation fees for each patient were paid for physicians' initial consultation services, as well as for explaining test results to patients. In some instances, however, the interpretations and consultations were not actually provided, and in other instances, the referring physicians merely duplicated the services performed by the service itself. In addition, the amounts paid to the referring physicians were more than Medicare would allow for such services, but without those fees, physicians would not use the service. The appeals court upheld the physician's criminal conviction under the antikickback statute, finding that if any portion of the payments was intended to induce the physician to use the monitoring services, the statute would be violated.

Other courts have endorsed the ruling in the *Greber* case, agreeing that if even only one purpose of the payment is to induce referrals, the antikickback statute is implicated. For example, the Ninth Circuit ruled that an arrangement between a clinic, in which a physician had a 25 percent ownership interest, and a laboratory violated the antikickback statute [*United States v. Kats*, 871 F.2d 105 (9th Cir. 1989)]. The clinic submitted specimens to the laboratory, which billed the clinic for the testing services. The clinic then submitted claims to the MediCal and Medicare programs, but according to the court's findings, 50 percent of the payments received were in fact "kicked back" to the clinic. The court ruled that the providers could not escape conviction under the antikickback statute by proving that the payments were not wholly attributable to the referral of services.

Q.9:5   What types of arrangements among health care providers are likely to implicate the antikickback statute?

The types of arrangements prohibited under the antikickback statute far exceed the original ban on acts that constituted kickbacks, bribes, or rebates, and now impact on a broad number of ordinary business transactions. In the context of managed care organizations, joint ventures, physician recruitment and retention arrangements, and purchases of physician practices in particular should be scrutinized for compliance with the antikickback statute.

Q.9:6   How do the prohibitions in the antikickback statute apply to health care joint ventures?

The proliferation of health care joint ventures in the 1980s raised concerns that these arrangements were created primarily as a vehicle to induce physicians to refer patients and enhance revenues, rather than as a means to provide new needed service.

The OIG responded to these concerns by issuing a Special Fraud Alert on Joint Venture Arrangements, which described suspect features of joint ventures and encouraged providers independently to disband many of those arrangements [Department of Health and Human Services (HHS), OIG-89-04 (April 1989)]. According to the Fraud Alert, the OIG will consider an arrangement to be a suspect joint venture under the antikickback statute if:

- investors are potential referral sources,
- physicians who are likely to be a significant referral source are provided the opportunity to purchase a larger share in the entity,
- physicians are encouraged to refer to the entity or to divest interest if referrals fall below an acceptable level,
- the entity tracks and distributes information regarding referral sources,
- physicians are required to divest their interest upon retirement or any other change in status that makes them unable to refer, or
- an investment interest is nontransferable.

Q.9:7   Has the OIG ever imposed administrative exclusions from the Medicare/Medicaid program on a health care provider based on its participation in a joint venture?

Yes. In 1989, the OIG brought its first action to impose administrative exclusions from Medicare/Medicaid in a case involving three joint venture, limited partnership clinical laboratories. The clinical laboratory joint ventures were formed by the Hanlester network's general partners and physician limited partners. An arrangement between Hanlester and SmithKline-Beecham Laboratory put the latter in the position of lab manager for each joint venture clinical lab. Separate management contracts with each clinical lab made SmithKline the provider of almost all lab services, with SmithKline assuming all the financial risk of profit and loss. The physician limited partners received a share of the overall profits, based on the number of units of the limited partnership they owned. The physicians were told that the success of the limited partnership depended on the number of referrals they made to the laboratory, although they were not required to make referrals. In fact, the clinical labs performed few tests themselves, and the physicians performed no services for the labs. The labs billed Medicare, paid SmithKline 76 percent of the amount collected and retained 24 percent for themselves. According to the OIG, the arrangement violated the antikickback statute, because the labs essentially were shell structures designed to funnel business from physician investors to SmithKline in exchange for payments to the physicians.

According to the Department of Appeals Board's (DAB) final decision, the inducement to refer in this case was illegal [*Inspector General v. Hanlester*

Network, No. C-448, HHS Department of Appeals Board, Appellate Div., July 24, 1992, *aff'd, Hanlester Network v. Sullivan,* No. CV-92-4552-LHM (C.D. Cal. Feb. 10, 1993)]. A violation of the antikickback statute occurs whenever an individual or entity knowingly and willfully offers to pay or pays any remuneration, in any manner or form, to induce the referral of program-related business. An offer or payment may violate the law even if it is not conditioned on an agreement to refer. If the sum of the benefits received by a party is excessive compared with the legitimate benefits conferred, it is reasonable to infer that the excess benefits were received in return for referrals.

In this particular case, the DAB considered the following factors:

- The physician partners received extremely high rates of return based on expected, rather than actual, receipts.

- The profit distributions were related indirectly to the volume of referrals made by the physician limited partners because profits would grow with increased referrals.

- The profit distributions permitted physicians to benefit financially from their Medicare referrals, although reimbursement restrictions prohibited them from marking up and billing Medicare for such services.

- Laboratory usage by physician investors was monitored carefully by the partnership, which also notified physicians when business was slow.

- The physicians performed no services for any of the labs but simply referred work to those facilities.

The DAB's final decision also addressed the benefits the partnership received from SmithKline, including the company's assumption of operating risks and management responsibilities, its payment of operation receipts in advance, and the use of its name. Moreover, the labs received 24 percent of the receipts collected by SmithKline in exchange for nothing more than providing a referral course. The DAB concluded that those benefits far exceeded the value of what the partnership provided to SmithKline, other than referrals, finding therein the illegality of the transaction.

Q.9:8   How does the referral payment ban in the antikickback statute apply to hospital–physician relationships?

The referral payment ban can be implicated in both hospital to physician referrals and in physician to hospital referrals. Financial arrangements between hospitals and hospital-based physicians can violate the antikickback statute if the arrangements require physicians to pay more than fair market value for services. The OIG has indicated that hospitals are in a position to direct referrals to hospital-based physicians, defined to include anesthesiologists, pathologists, and radiologists. The antikickback statute would be implicated in such referrals if payment for those services from hospital-based physicians were made through Medicare/Medicaid. Suspect agreements include those that require physicians to pay more than fair market value for services provided by the hospitals and that compensate physicians for less than the fair market value of the goods and services they provide to hospitals. The OIG has recommended that contracts between hospitals and hospital-based physicians be based on the fair market value of services, unrelated to physician billings and limited to goods and services necessary for the provision of medical services by the hospital-based physicians [*Management Advisory Report, Financial Arrangements Between Hospitals and Hospital-Based Physicians,* Office of Inspector General, Department of Health and Human Services (October, 1991)].

Physician to hospital referrals, and in particular, hospital recruitment and retention programs that are intended to influence a physician's hospital referral decisions, also implicate the antikickback statute. In this regard, the OIG has issued a Special Fraud Alert [*OIG Special Fraud Alert— Hospital Incentives to Physicians,* Department of Health and Human Services (May 7, 1992)] listing some suspect incentive arrangements, including payment of an incentive for each referral, free or significantly discounted office space, equipment, or staff services, compensation guarantees, low interest or interest-free loans that are subject to forgiveness based on referral patterns, payment of a physician's travel expenses or continuing education courses, inappropriately low-cost coverage on a hospital's insurance plans, and payments for services that exceed their fair market value.

Q.9:9   How have the courts analyzed physician–hospital agreements under the antikickback statute?

Reflecting the OIG's view on this type of arrangement, a federal trial court in Texas struck down a physician–hospital agreement under the antikickback statute [*Polk County Memorial Hospital v. Peters,* 800 F.Supp. 1451 (E.D. Tex. 1992)]. Under a recruitment agreement with a physician, the hospital was obligated to provide the physician with an office for three months at no cost, provide a capped amount of free utilities for the physician's office, reimburse the physician's moving expenses, and guarantee the physician gross cash receipts of $8,500 per month during the first 12 months of practice. Although the contract required the physician to repay those amounts, the hospital made no effort to collect until several years after the due date when it became involved in other litigation with the physician. The agreement required the physician to practice medicine as a general surgeon in the community for at least 12 months. It also stipulated that the physician should utilize the hospital for his patients who required hospitalization unless the use of another facility was necessary to provide appropriate treatment to a patient.

The court found that the contract violated the antikickback statute. It said that the hospital in effect had provided the physician with remuneration in the form of an interest-free loan, as well as free office space, rent, utilities, subsidies, and reimbursement for medical malpractice insurance. Those remunerations clearly were subject to the physician's referral of patients to the hospital, the court held. Accordingly, the court concluded that the agreement violated the antikickback statute.

More recently, a hospital successfully sued to void the leases of several physician-tenants in the hospital's medical office building based on the illegality of the lease under this legislation [*Vana v. Vista Hosp. Systems, Inc.*, No. 233623 (Cal. Super. Ct., Riverside County, Oct. 25, 1993)]. The hospital's attorneys discovered that approximately 50 leases were significantly below market rental rates. The hospital subsequently attempted to renegotiate the leases at prevailing market rates and succeeded with respect to all but ten leases. The hospital then sued to void the contracts under state and federal antikickback law, but the physicians argued that the leases were valid because there was no referral agreement, explicit or implied, underlying the leases. In ruling for the hospital, the court said the hospital's motive to induce referrals was sufficient to make the leases illegal, even without any implied agreement by the physicians to refer patients. The contracts constituted a sufficient inducement to refer, the court concluded, because they went "beyond mere encouragement."

Q.9:10   How does the referral ban in the antikickback statute apply to hospital purchases of physician practices?

In response to health care reform initiatives, many hospitals are extending their operations into managed care arrangements and integrated delivery systems. This process frequently has involved a hospital's acquisition of physician group practices. The OIG has expressed concern about such types of acquisitions, however, because the payments to the selling physicians can constitute illegal remuneration for patient referrals. [See December 22, 1992 letter from Mac Thornton to T.J. Sullivan, Office of the Associate Chief Counsel at the IRS.]

According to the OIG, two issues are crucial to determining whether a physician practice acquisition violates the antikickback statute. The first concerns the amount of compensation paid to the physician and the types of items for which the physician receives payment. Any amount paid for assets that relate to the continuing treatment of the physicians' patients could be considered as payment for referrals, including payment for good will, noncompete covenants, exclusive dealing agreements, patient lists, and patient records. It may be necessary to exclude those intangibles from the fair market value assessment of a physician practice for purposes of antikickback analysis.

The second issue involves the amount and manner in which the hospital compensates the physician whose practice is sold for providing services to the hospital. The OIG has questioned the legitimacy of subsequent payments to physicians, even if they become hospital employees. Although the statute exempts any amount paid by an employer to an employee who has a bona fide employment relationship with the employer for employment in the provision of covered items or services, the OIG has suggested that the exemption does not permit a hospital to pay a physician employee for patient referrals.

Q.9:11 Are there any specific payment practices that are protected from the application of the antikickback statute?

Yes. The Medicare and Medicaid Patient and Program Protection Act specifically directed the Secretary of the Department of Health and Human Services (HHS), in consultation with the Attorney General, to publish regulations specifying payment practices that would not be treated as criminal offenses under the antikickback provisions [P.L. 100-93]. The statute provides that once those rules have been promulgated, any payment practice specified in such regulation will not be considered illegal. Failure to fall squarely within a safe harbor, however, does not necessarily mean that the practice is illegal; it simply indicates that it is not automatically safe. Regulations establishing 11 safe harbors were published on July 9, 1991, and became effective on that date [56 Fed. Reg. 35,952, codified at 42 C.F.R. § 1001.951-953].

Q.9:12   What are the 11 safe harbors protecting certain payment practices from sanction under the antikickback statute that went into effect on July 9, 1991?

On July 9, 1991, the Department of Health and Human Services finalized 11 safe harbors under the antikickback statute as follows:

1. investments in large publicly traded entities,
2. investments in smaller ventures,
3. specific types of lease arrangements relating to space and equipment,
4. personal services and management contracts that meet specific standards,
5. the sale of a practitioner practice under specific circumstances,
6. referral services,
7. warranties,
8. discounts,
9. payments made by an employer to an employee for providing covered items or services,
10. payments by a vendor of goods or services to a group purchasing organization, and
11. waivers of beneficiary coinsurance and deductibles.

Specific requirements apply to each of the above safe harbors, and the arrangement must meet these regulatory standards to benefit from safe harbor protection.

Q.9:13   Are there any safe harbors that apply to managed care plans?

Yes. Two additional safe harbors for managed care plans were published in the *Federal Register* as interim final rules [57 Fed. Reg. 57,723, Nov. 5, 1992]. The safe harbors are intended to protect certain business and payment relationships between health care plans, providers, and enrollees that allow them to compete in the marketplace for managed care. The two managed care safe harbors apply to (1) coverage, cost-sharing, or premiums offered to enrollees and (2) price reductions providers offer to health plans.

In addition, the rules creating the managed care safe harbors amended one of the safe harbors discussed in **Question 9:12** relating to waivers of inpatient coinsurance and deductible amounts under Medicare. The amendment permits certain hospital waivers of inpatient insurance and deductible amounts under a pilot project, Medicare SELECT.

Q.9:14   What is an enrollee under the managed care safe harbors?

For the purpose of applying the safe harbors listed in the preceding questions, an enrollee is an individual who has entered into a contractual relationship with a health plan (or on whose behalf an employer, or other private or governmental entity, has entered into such a relationship) under which the individual is entitled to receive specified health care items and services, or insurance coverage for such items and services in return for payment of a premium.

Q.9:15   What is a contract health care provider under the managed care safe harbors?

A contract health care provider under the managed care safe harbors is an individual or an entity under contract with a health plan to furnish items or services to enrollees who are covered by the health plan, Medicare, or a state health care program.

Q.9:16   What is a health plan under the managed care safe harbors?

A health plan under the managed care safe harbors is an entity that either furnishes or arranges under agreement with contract health care providers to furnish items or services to enrollees or furnishes insurance coverage for the provision of such items and services in exchange for a premium. To qualify as a health plan under the proposed regulations, such entity must either (1) operate in accordance with a contract or statutory authority approved by HCFA or a state health care program or (2) have its premium structure regulated under a state insurance statute or a state enabling statute governing HMOs or PPOs. The definition does not appear to cover employer self-insurance plans and includes ordinary HMOs and PPOs only if the state has oversight that includes state regulation of the premiums charged to subscribers.

Q.9:17   What standards must a managed care plan comply with to qualify for protection under the coverage, cost sharing, or premiums offered to enrollees safe harbor?

Under this safe harbor, managed care plans may offer incentives to beneficiaries, including additional coverage of any item or service to an enrollee, reduction of some or all of the enrollee's obligations to pay the health plan or a contract health care provider for cost-sharing amounts (such as coinsurance, deductible, or copayment amounts), or reduction of the premium amounts attributable to items or services covered by the health plan, Medicare, or a state health plan. Although the antikickback statute is not implicated when a health care plan provides an insurance package to either a state health care program or Medicare beneficiary, it could be involved when discounts on those premiums or other incentives are offered to enroll in the plan. To qualify for protection under this safe harbor, a health plan must comply with all of the standards in one of the following two categories of health plans.

1. If the health plan is a risk-based HMO, competitive medical plan (CMP), prepaid health plan, or other health plan under contract with HCFA or a state health care program, it must offer the same increased coverage or reduced cost sharing or premiums amounts to all enrollees unless otherwise approved by HCFA or by a state health care plan.

2. If the health plan is an HMO, CMP, prepaid health plan, or other health plan that has executed a contract or agreement with HCFA or with a state health program to receive payment for enrollees on a reaonable-cost or similar basis, it must:

   (a) offer the same increased coverage or reduced cost sharing or premium amounts to all enrollees unless otherwise approved by HCFA or by a state health plan, and

   (b) not claim the costs of the increased coverage or the reduced cost sharing or premium amounts as bad debt or otherwise shift the burden of the increased coverage or reduced cost sharing or premium amounts onto Medicare, a state health care program, other payers, or individuals.

Q.9:18   What standards must a managed care plan comply with to qualify for protection under the safe harbor governing price reductions offered by providers to health plans?

This safe harbor protects certain price-reduction agreements between health care plans and health care providers. The antikickback statute can be implicated in this type of arrangement because providers typically will agree to discount items and services to enrollees of health plans in return for obtaining a large volume of patients from the health plan. The agreements must be in writing and must relate only to the price of items or services that are covered by Medicare/Medicaid. Contract health care providers may offer a reduction in price to health plans as long as both the health plan and contract health care provider comply with all of the applicable standards within one of the following three categories of health plans.

1. If the health plan is an HMO, CMP, or prepaid health plan under contract with HCFA or a state agency, the contract health provider must not claim payment in any form from HHS or the state agency for items or services furnished in accordance with the agreement except as approved by HCFA or the state health care program, or otherwise shift the burden of such an agreement onto Medicare, a state health care program, other payers, or individuals.
2. If the health plan has executed a contract or agreement with HCFA or a state health care program to receive payment for enrollees on a reasonable-cost or similar basis, the health plan and contract health provider must comply with all of the following four standards.
    (a) The term of the agreement between the health plan and the contract health care provider must be for not less than one year.
    (b) The agreement between the health plan and the contract health care provider must specify in advance the covered items and services to be furnished to enrollees and the methodology for computing the plan's payment to the contract health care provider.
    (c) The health plan must fully and accurately report, on the applicable cost report or other claim form filed with HHS or the state health care program, the amount it has paid the contract health care provider under the agreement for the covered services furnished to enrollees.
    (d) The contract health care provider must not claim payment in any form from HHS or the state health care program for items or services furnished in accordance with the agreement (except as approved by HFCA or the state health care program), nor may it otherwise shift the burden of such an agreement onto Medicare, a state health care provider, other payers, or individuals.
3. If a health plan does not fit into either of the preceding two categories, both the health plan and contract health care provider must comply with all of the following six standards:
    (a) The term of the agreement between the health plan and the contract health care provider must be for not less than one year.
    (b) The agreement between the health plan and the contract health care provider must specify in advance the covered items and

services to be furnished to enrollees, which party is to file claims or requests for payment with Medicare or the state health care program for such items and services, and the schedule of fees the contract thealth provider will charge for furnishing such items and services to enrollees.

(c) The fee schedule in the agreement between the health plan and the contract health care provider must remain in effect throughout the term of the agreement unless a fee increase results directly from a payment update authorized by Medicare or the state health care program.

(d) The party submitting claims or requests for payment from Medicare or the state health program for items and services furnished in accordance with the agreement must not claim or request payment for amounts in excess of the fee schedule.

(e) The contract health care provider and the health plan must fully and accurately report on any cost report filed with Medicare or a state health care program the fee schedule amounts charged in accordance with the agreement.

(f) The party to the agreement that does not have the responsibility under the agreement for filing claims or requests for payment must not claim or request payment in any form from HHS or the state health care program for items or services furnished in accordance with the agreement, or otherwise shift the burden of such an agreement onto Medicare, a state health care program, other payers, or individuals.

Q.9:19   What sanctions can be imposed for violations of the antikickback statute?

Antikickback violations can result in significant criminal sanctions, including fines and imprisonment as well as exclusions from the Medicare program. The statutory language for the criminal penalties is as follows:

(1) Whoever knowingly and willfully solicits or receives any remuneration (including any kickback, bribe, or rebate) directly or indirectly, overtly or covertly, in cash or in kind:

    (A) in return for referring an individual to a person for the furnishing or arranging for the furnishing of any item or service for which payment may be made in whole or in part under title XVII, or a State health care program, or

    (B) in return for purchasing, leasing, ordering or arranging for or recommending purchasing, leasing or ordering any good, facility, service or item for which payment may be made in whole or in part under title XVII, or a State health care program,

shall be guilty of a felony and upon conviction thereof, shall be fined not more than $25,000 or imprisoned for not more than five years, or both.

(2) Whoever knowingly and willfully offers or pays any remuneration (including any kickback, bribe, or rebate) directly or indirectly, overtly or covertly, in cash or in kind, to induce such person—

(A) to refer an individual to a person for the furnishing of any item or service for which payment may be made in whole or in part under title XVIII, or a State health care program, or

(B) to purchase, lease, order, or arrange for or recommend purchasing, leasing, or ordering any good, facility, service, or item for which payment may be made, in whole or in part under title XVIII, or a State health care program,

shall be guilty of a felony and upon conviction thereof, shall be fined not more than $25,000 or imprisoned for not more than five years or both [42 U.S.C. § 1320a-7(b)].

In addition to the criminal sanctions mentioned here, the antikickback statute also provides that violations can result in exclusion from Medicare, Medicaid, and other state health care programs [42 U.S.C. § 1320a-7(b)], if the Secretary of the Department of Health and Human Services (acting through the OIG) finds that such a violation has occurred. Under this provision, the OIG does not have to wait for a criminal conviction to impose an exclusion.

SCOPE OF REFERRAL RESTRICTIONS UNDER STARK LEGISLATION

Q.9:20 **What is the Stark legislation governing physician self-referral?**

In addition to the Medicare and Medicaid Fraud and Abuse statute, federal law also regulates patient referrals between a physician and an entity in which the physician (or an immediate family member) has a financial interest. The Ethics in Patient Referrals Act, commonly referred to as Stark I, was enacted as part of the Omnibus Budget Reconciliation Act of 1989 [42 U.S.C. § 1395nn]. The legislation was adopted in response to concerns about conflicts of interest that could arise when a physician has a financial relationship with a facility and refers patients to that facility for care, and about the inadequacy of existing antifraud and abuse legislation in eliminating the ethical problems associated with patient referrals.

Stark I prohibited a physician investor or a physician having a financial relationship with an entity from making a referral to that entity for clinical laboratory services. In August 1993, as part of the Omnibus Budget Reconciliation Act, Congress amended the Stark law prohibition to apply to referrals for a much expanded list of health care services, in an enactment commonly referred to as Stark II. The self-referral legislation, as it now stands, generally states that if a physician has a relationship with an entity, (1) the physician may not make a referral for any designated health care service that is reimbursable by Medicare or Medicaid and (2) the entity that provides the services may not present a bill to Medicare or Medicaid for services provided as a result of a prohibited referral. The legislation provides penalties for illegal referrals, including the denial of payment, civil monetary penalties, and program exclusion penalties [42 U.S.C. § 1395nn(g)]. Stark II became effective January 1, 1995, although the Department of Health and Human Services has yet to finalize regulations it proposed under Stark I [57 Fed. Reg. 8588 (Mar. 11, 1994)] and to propose regulations under Stark II.

Q.9:21   What is the scope of the ban on referrals contained in the Stark legislation?

Several key definitions establish the scope of the referral prohibition in the Stark legislation. First, the notion of *referral*, as it is defined in the statute, determines when a physician, in the course of caring for a patient, actually refers the patient to other entities. The second definition, *designated health services*, enumerates the types of health care services to which the prohibition applies. The third definition, *financial relationship*, establishes the type of financial interest that must exist between a referring physician (or an immediate family member of that physician) and the provider of the designated health service for the prohibition to apply. In analyzing physician referral activity under the Stark legislation, therefore, it is necessary to determine whether (1) the referral of a Medicare or Medicaid patient is for the provision of a designated health service and (2) there is a financial relationship between the referring physician and the entity that will provide the health care service. If the answer to both of these questions is affirmative, then the referral is prohibited, unless one of the exceptions discussed in the following questions applies.

Q.9:22 What is a referral under the Stark legislation?

The notion of referral under the Stark legislation is broad. It includes the request by a physician for any Part B item or service, including the request by a physician for a consultation with another physician, and any test or procedure ordered by or to be performed by or under the supervision of the other physician [42 U.S.C. § 1395nn(h)(5)(A)]. Accordingly, a physician's request for consultation from another physician is considered a referral, and any tests or services ordered by the consulting physician will be considered to have been ordered by the referring physician. In addition, the request or establishment of a plan of care by a physician that includes the provision of any of the designated health services constitutes a referral under the law. Therefore, a physician makes a referral whenever an item or service is ordered, even if the service or item will be provided within that same physician's practice. The definition of referral does not apply, however, to requests by a pathologist for clinical laboratory tests and pathological examination services; a radiologist for diagnostic radiology services; and a radiation oncologist for radiation therapy, if the services are furnished by or under the supervision of such pathologist, radiologist, or radiation oncologist pursuant to a consultation requested by another physician [42 U.S.C. § 1395nn(h)(5)(c)].

Q.9:23 What is a designated health service?

The Stark legislation bans referral of Medicare or Medicaid patients for any of the following items or services:

- clinical laboratory services,
- physical therapy services,
- occupational therapy services,
- radiology services including magnetic resonance imaging, computerized axial tomography scans, and ultrasound services,
- radiation therapy services,
- durable medical equipment,

- parenteral and enteral nutrients, equipment, and supplies,
- prosthetics, orthotics, and prosthetic devices,
- home health services,
- outpatient prescription drugs, and
- inpatient and outpatient hospital services [42 U.S.C. § 1395nn(h)(6)].

Q.9:24 What is a financial relationship under the Stark legislation?

Financial relationship refers to either an ownership or investment interest in the entity or a compensation arrangement between the physician (or an immediate family member of the physician) and the entity [42 U.S.C. § 1395nn(h)(6)].

An ownership or investment interest may exist through equity, debt, or other means. A financial relationship exists if the physician has an interest in an entity that holds an ownership or investment interest in the entity providing the designated health service. The ownership or investment interest therefore includes related entities. For example, a physician owning an interest in a hospital that in turn owns an investment interest in a home health agency would fall within the scope of the Stark II prohibition.

Compensation arrangement is broadly defined to include any remuneration, direct or indirect, overt or covert, and in cash or in kind, between a physician (or an immediate family member of the physician) and an entity providing designated services [42 U.S.C. § 1395nn(h)(1)]. The Stark I statute did not clearly indicate whether compensation arrangement included any arrangement regardless of which way the money flowed. In Stark II, however, certain arrangements in which physicians pay an entity for services are specifically included in an exception to the self-referral prohibition. The statute implicitly indicates that the definition includes arrangements in which the physician pays the entity some form of remuneration. The law also illustrates other forms of remuneration, including the forgiveness of amounts owed for inaccurate test results or the correction of minor billing errors [42 U.S.C. § 1395nn(h)(1)(C)(i)].

Q.9:25 What are the exceptions to the general prohibition on physician referral contained in the Stark legislation?

The statutory exceptions to the general prohibition are numerous and complex. The exceptions can be divided into three different categories: (1) exceptions that apply to ownership or investment financial relationships, (2) those that apply to compensation arrangements, and (3) general exceptions that apply to all types of financial relationships.

Q.9:26   What are the general exceptions to both ownership/investment and compensation arrangement prohibitions?

The exceptions that apply to both the ownership/investment and compensation arrangement prohibitions relate to physician services, in-office ancillary services, and prepaid plans.

Q.9:27   What is the physician services exception?

An exception to the Stark legislation prohibition on referrals applies when services are provided personally (or under the personal supervision of) the referring physician or by another physician in the same group practice [*group practice* is defined at 42 U.S.C. § 1395nn(h)(4) and is discussed in **Question 9:30**] as the referring physician [42 U.S.C. § 1395nn(b)(1)].

Q.9:28   What is the in-office ancillary services exception?

Certain ancillary services provided in the same group practice (see **Question 9:30**) are exempted from the self-referral prohibition, as long as the services satisfy the conditions set out in the statute. First, the service must be provided either personally by the referring physician, personally by a physician who is a member of the same group practice as the referring physician, or personally by individuals who are directly supervised by the referring physician or another physician member of the group practice. The statute also imposes a location requirement, stipulating that the service must be provided either (1) in a building in which the referring physician (or another physician who is a member of the same group practice) furnishes physician services unrelated to the furnishing of designated health services or (2) (if the referring physician is a member of a group practice) in another building that is used by the group practice for the provision of some or all of the group's clinical laboratory services, or for the centralized provision of the group's designated health services (other than clinical laboratory service). Finally, to qualify under the in-office ancillary services exception, the services must be billed either by the physician who performs or supervises them, by a group practice of which such physician is a member under a billing number assigned to the group practice, or by an entity that is wholly owned by such physician or such group practice [42 U.S.C. § 1395nn(b)(2)(A)].

The in-office ancillary services exception does not apply to the provision of durable medical equipment, except for infusion pumps, nor does it apply to parenteral and enteral nutrients, equipment, and supplies.

Q.9:29 What is the prepaid plan exception?

The third general exception covers services provided by various prepaid plans. It provides that the physician self-referral ban does not apply to federally qualified HMOs [42 U.S.C. § 300e et seq.] or similar entities recognized by federal law. These entities include those with contracts under Section 1876 of the Social Security Act, plans described in Section 1833(a)(1)(A) of the Social Security Act, plans that receive payments on a prepaid basis under demonstration projects as described in either Section 402(a) of the Social Security Amendments of 1967 or Section 222(a) of the Social Security Amendments of 1972.

Q.9:30 What is a group practice under the Stark legislation?

Satisfying the requirements of the first two general exceptions (relating to physicians' services and in-office ancillary services) depends in large part on whether a group or collection of physicians qualifies as a group practice under the statute. *Group practice* means a group of two or more physicians legally organized as a partnership, professional corporation, foundation, nonprofit corporation, faculty practice plan, or similar association that satisfies the following conditions:

- Each physician who is a member of the group must provide substantially the full range of services that the physician routinely provides (including medical care, consultation, diagnosis, or treatment) through the joint use of shared office space, facilities, equipment and personnel.
- Substantially all of the services of the physicians who are members of the group must be provided through the group and billed under a billing number assigned to the group. Amounts received in this manner must be treated as receipts of the group.
- The overhead expenses of and the income from the practice must be distributed in accordance with methods previously determined.

- No physician who is a member of the group must receive, either directly or indirectly, compensation based on the volume or value of referrals by the physician.
- Members of the group must personally conduct no less than 75 percent of the physician–patient encounters of the group practice [42 U.S.C. § 1395nn(h)(4)(A)].

As indicated earlier, physicians may not be compensated based on the value or volume of referrals by that physician with the exception of two special rules relating to the compensation of physicians in the group practice. A physician in a group practice may be paid a share of overall profits of the group, or a productivity bonus based on services personally performed or services incident to personally performed services, as long as the share or bonus is not determined in any manner that is directly related to the volume or value of referrals by such physician. In addition, in the case of a faculty practice plan associated with a hospital, institution of higher education, or medical school with an approved medical residency training program in which physician members may provide a variety of different specialty services and provide professional services both within and outside the group, as well as perform other tasks such as research, the group practice definition applies only with respect to the services provided within the faculty practice plan [42 U.S.C. § 1395nn(h)(4)(B)].

Q.9:31 What are the exceptions that relate only to the ownership or investment arrangement prohibition?

The exceptions that only apply to the ownership/investment and compensation arrangement prohibitions relate to ownership in publicly traded securities and mutual funds, ownership interest in hospitals, rural providers, and hospitals in Puerto Rico.

Q.9:32 What is the ownership in publicly traded securities and mutual funds exception?

For the purposes of the Stark legislation, ownership of investment securities or shares in a regulated investment company, if certain statutory conditions are met, does not qualify as a financial relationship. Ownership of investment securities (including shares or bonds, debentures, notes, or other debt instruments), which may be purchased on terms generally available to the public, qualifies under this exception if the securities:

- are listed on the New York Stock Exchange, the American Stock Exchange, or any regional exchange in which quotations are published daily, or are foreign securities listed on a recognized foreign, national, or regional exchange in which quotations are published daily, or are traded under an automated interdealer quotation system operated by the National Association of Securities Dealers, and
- are in a corporation that had, at the end of its most recent fiscal year or on average during the previous three fiscal years, stockholder equity exceeding $75 million.

Ownership of shares in a regulated investment company (as defined in Section 851(a) of the Internal Revenue Code) will also qualify under this exception if the company had, at the end of its most recent fiscal year or on average during the previous three fiscal years, total assets exceeding $75 million [42 U.S.C. § 1395nn(c)].

Q.9:33   What is the ownership interest in hospitals exception?

The Stark legislation's ban on self-referral does not apply to designated health services provided by a hospital, if the referring physician is authorized to perform services at the hospital and the physician's ownership or investment interest is in the hospital itself and not simply one of its subdivisions or departments [42 U.S.C. § 1395nn(d)(3)].

Q.9:34   What is the rural provider exception?

The self-referral ban does not apply to designated health services furnished in a rural area [42 U.S.C. § 1395nn(d)(2)(D)] by an entity if substantially all of the designated health services furnished by the entity are furnished to individuals who reside in the rural area. A physician therefore can refer patients to an entity with which he or she has a financial relationship, if the entity is located in a rural area, and primarily serves patients residing in that same area [42 U.S.C. § 1395nn(d)(2)]. The wording of this exception reflects legislative intent to prevent providers from attempting to fall within the exception by moving their locations to the boundary of a rural area while continuing to serve patients in a nonrural area.

Q.9:35   What is the exception relating to hospitals in Puerto Rico?

The Stark legislation prohibition does not apply to designated health services provided by hospitals in Puerto Rico [42 U.S.C. § 1395nn(d)(1)].

Q.9:36   What are the exceptions that relate only to the compensation arrangement prohibition?

Specific compensation arrangements defined in the Stark laws will not be considered financial relationships that trigger the self-referral ban, as long as the arrangements meet the conditions outlined in the statutes. The types of compensation arrangements that fall within this exception are the rental of office space and equipment, bona fide employment relationships, personal service arrangements, remuneration unrelated to the provision of designated health services, physician recruitment, isolated (one-time) transactions, certain group practice arrangements with a hospital, payments by a physician for items and services, and *de minimus* remuneration.

Q.9:37   What is the exception that applies to arrangements for the rental of office space and equipment?

Payments made by a lessee to a lessor for the use of office space or equipment are not included in the self-referral ban if:

- the lease is in writing, is signed by the parties, and indicates the space/equipment covered by the lease;
- the space/equipment rented or leased does not exceed what is reasonable and necessary for the legitimate business purposes of the lease or rental, and is used exclusively by the lessee when being used by the lessee. With respect to office space rentals, however, the lessee may pay for the use of space consisting of common areas, if the payments do not exceed the lessee's pro rata share of expenses for such space based upon the ratio of space used exclusively by the lessee to the total amount of space (other than the common areas) occupied by all persons using such common areas;
- the term of the lease is for at least one year;
- the rental charges over the term of the lease are set in advance, are consistent with fair market value, and are not calculated in any way on

the basis of the volume or value of referrals or other business between the parties;

- the lease would be commercially reasonable even if no referrals were made between the parties; and

- the lease meets any other requirements that the Secretary may impose by regulation in order to protect against program or patient abuse [42 U.S.C. § 1395nn(e)(1)].

Q.9:38 What is the bona fide employment relationships exception?

The self-referral ban does not apply to any amount paid by an employer to a physician (or a member of the physician's immediate family) if the physician (or family member) has a bona fide employment relationship with the employer for the provision of services, as long as:

- the employment is for identifiable services,

- the remuneration is consistent with the fair market value of the services and is not determined in any manner that takes into account the volume or value of any referrals made by the referring physician,

- the remuneration is provided under an agreement that would be commercially reasonable even if no referrals were made to the employer, and

- the employment meets any other requirements the Secretary may impose by regulation as needed to protect against program or patient abuse [42 U.S.C. § 1395nn(e)(2)].

Note that in bona fide employment relationships, the law expressly allows remuneration in the form of a productivity bonus, as long as the bonus is based on services performed personally by the physician (or by an immediate family member of the physician). Unlike the type of compensation permitted in the definition of group practice (see **Question 9:30**), the productivity bonus under this exception cannot be based on services provided under the referring physician's supervision, and it cannot include sharing in the group's profits.

Q.9:39 What is the exception that applies to personal service arrangements?

The ban on self-referral does not apply to remuneration from an entity under an arrangement for the provision of physician services (including remuneration for specific physicians' services furnished to a nonprofit blood center) if:

- the arrangement is in writing signed by the parties and specifies the services it covers,
- the arrangement covers all of the services to be provided by the physician (or an immediate family member of such physician) to the entity,
- the aggregate services contracted for do not exceed those that are reasonable and necessary for the legitimate business purposes of the arrangement,
- the term of the arrangement is for at least one year,
- the compensation to be paid over the term of the arrangement is set in advance, does not exceed fair market value, and except in the case of a physician incentive plan described subsequently, is not determined in any manner that takes into account the volume or value of any referrals or other business generated between the parties,
- the services to be performed under the arrangement do not involve the counseling or promotion or a business arrangement or other activity that violates any state or federal law, and
- the arrangement meets any other requirements the Secretary may impose as needed to protect against program or patient abuse [42 U.S.C. § 1395nn(e)(3)].

The statute creates a special rule with respect to physician incentive plans for this exception. *Physician incentive plans* are defined as any compensation arrangement between an entity and a physician or physician group that may directly or indirectly have the effect of reducing or limiting services provided with respect to individuals enrolled with the entity [42 U.S.C. § 1395nn(e)(B)(ii)]. Under this rule, if a physician incentive plan meets the conditions set out in the statute, then the compensation paid under the terms of a personal services arrangement may be determined in a manner that takes into account, either directly or indirectly, the volume or value of any referrals or other business between the parties. To qualify under this rule, the plan must meet the following requirements:

- No specific payment may be made directly or indirectly under the plan to a physician or a physician group as an inducement to reduce or limit medically necessary services provided to a specific individual enrolled with the entity.
- In the case of a plan that places a physician or a physician group at substantial financial risk as determined by the Secretary under Section

1876(i)(8)(A)(ii), the plan must comply with any requirements the Secretary may impose pursuant to such section.

- Upon request by the Secretary, the entity must provide the Secretary with access to descriptive information regarding the plan, in order to permit the Secretary to determine whether the plan is in compliance with the preceding requirements [42 U.S.C. § 1395nn(e)(B)(i)].

Q.9:40   What exception applies to remuneration unrelated to the provision of designated health services?

An exception to the compensation arrangement prohibition applies to remuneration or payments by a hospital to a physician, if the payment does not relate to the provision of designated services. Such remuneration does not constitute a compensation arrangement to which the ban on self-referral applies [42 U.S.C. § 1395nn(e)(4)].

Q.9:41   What is the physician recruitment exception?

If a hospital provides remuneration to a physician to induce the physician to relocate to the geographic area served by the hospital and join the hospital's medical staff, the Stark prohibition will not apply as long as:

- the physician is not required to refer patients to the hospital,
- the amount of the remuneration is not determined in a manner that takes into account directly or indirectly the volume or value of any referrals by the referring physician, and
- the arrangement meets any other requirements the Secretary may impose by regulation to protect against program or patient abuse [42 U.S.C. § 1395nn(e)(5)].

It is important to note that this exception only protects incentives paid to physicians to relocate their practices to a new service area. It does not cover incentives paid to retain physicians or incentives paid to physicians who do not have existing practices.

Q.9:42   What is the isolated transactions exception?

An exception to the self-referral ban also applies to one-time transactions, such as the one-time sale of a property or practice, if:

- the amount of the remuneration paid under the transaction is consistent with fair market value and is not based, either directly or indirectly, on the volume or value of any referrals by the referring physician,
- the remuneration is provided under an agreement that would be commercially reasonable even if no referrals were made to the entity, and
- the arrangement meets any other requirements the Secretary may impose by regulation in order to protect against program or patient abuse [42 U.S.C. § 1395nn(e)(6)].

Q.9:43 What exception applies to certain group practice arrangements with a hospital?

The self-referral ban does not apply to an arrangement between a hospital and a group practice for designated health services to be provided by the group but billed by the hospital, if:

- for services provided to an inpatient of the hospital, the arrangment is pursuant to the provision of inpatient services under Section 1861(b)(3),
- the arrangement began before December 19, 1989, and has continued uninterrupted since that date,
- substantially all of the designated health services covered by the arrangement that are furnished to hospital patients are furnished by the group under the arrangement,
- the arrangement is pursuant to a written agreement that specifies the services to be provided and the compensation for the services,
- the compensation is provided pursuant to an agreement that would be commercially reasonable even if no referrals were made to the entity, and
- the arrangement between the parties meets any other requirements the Secretary may impose by regulation to protect against program or patient abuse [42 U.S.C. § 1395nn(e)(7)].

Q.9:44 What types of payment by a physician for items and services fall under an exception to the Stark prohibition?

The self-referral ban does not apply to payments made by a physician to a laboratory for the provision of clinical laboratory services, or to an entity as compensation for other items or services, if the price of the items or services are consistent with fair market value [42 U.S.C. § 1395nn(e)(8)]. By not applying the fair market value standard to clinical laboratory services, the statute implicitly recognizes the heavy discounting practices prevalent in this industry.

Q.9:45   What is the *de minimis* remuneration exception?

A final exception to the Stark prohibition can be found in the definition of the term *remuneration* [42 U.S.C. § 1395nn(h)(1)(c)]. The statute provides that the forgiveness of amounts owed for inaccurate tests or procedures, or the correction of minor billing errors, is not considered "remuneration" under the law. In the same manner, the provision of items used solely to collect, transport, process, or store specimens of the entity performing the diagnostic tests or to order or communicate the results of these tests or procedures are not remuneration.

Q.9:46   Are there reporting requirements under the Stark legislation?

Yes. Under regulations adopted under Stark I and finalized by HCFA, entities that are subject to the reporting requirements must submit the required information on a HCFA prescribed form within the time period specified by the servicing carrier or intermediary. All entities will be given at least 30 days from the date of the carrier's or intermediary's request to provide the initial information. All entities must retain documentation sufficient to verify the information provided on the forms and make the information available to HCFA or the OIG upon request. Failure to submit the information in accordance with the regulations can result in fines of up to $10,000 for each day of the period following the deadline for submission of the information until the information is finally submitted [42 C.F.R. § 411.361].

Q.9:47   What sanctions can be imposed for violations of the Stark legislation?

The Stark legislation enumerates the sanctions that may be imposed for referrals made or claims submitted in violation of the self-referral ban. They include:

- denial of payment,
- requiring refunds for certain claims,

- civil monetary penalties, and
- program exclusion [42 U.S.C. § 1395nn(g)].

Q.9:48 What are the differences between the Medicare/Medicaid antikickback statute and the Stark legislation?

Although the Medicare and Medicaid antikickback statute and the Stark legislation both attempt to eliminate what are perceived as unacceptable conflicts of interest that exist when a provider has a financial relationship with an entity to which he or she refers patients, it is important to analyze the statutes separately. Compliance with both statutes is necessary to operate lawfully within the Medicare and Medicaid program. The fact that a relationship falls within an antikickback safe harbor does not determine whether a Stark violation has occurred. Similarly, falling within a Stark exception does not protect against possible antikickback violations. The statutes can be distinguished in several ways.

The Stark laws are not criminal statutes, but the antikickback statute is. Under the antikickback statute, evidence of a corrupt intent is necessary to prove a violation under the law; intent is irrelevant in a Stark legislation analysis. The antikickback law imposes criminal sanctions for specified offenses, including fines and prison sentences, the amount and duration of which vary depending on whether the violation is classified as a misdemeanor or a felony.

The Stark legislation has been described as an exceptions bill, meaning that it establishes a broad prohibition on certain categories of referrals, but permits numerous exceptions. If a particular service or financial relationship is covered by one of the exceptions discussed previously, the referral is not prohibited. If no exception applies, however, the referral is illegal and Medicare/Medicaid will not reimburse the cost of the service. The antikickback statute does not prohibit certain referrals per se. Rather, the statute forbids any knowing and willful conduct involving the solicitation, receipt, offer, or payment of any kind of remuneration in return for referring an individual or for recommending or arranging the purchase, lease, or ordering of an item or service that may be wholly or partly paid for through the Medicare/Medicaid program. The safe harbors under the antikickback statute are not mandatory, in that an arrangement must fall into a safe harbor to comply with the law. Rather, the safe harbors exist to provide absolute immunity to specific arrangements that are free from abuse. If a safe harbor does not apply, however, the activity may or may not constitute a violation of the law depending on the facts and circumstances involved.

10

Special Issues for Tax-Exempt Organizations in Managed Care

TAX EXEMPTION UNDER SECTION 501(c)(3)

Q.10:1 What is tax exemption under the Internal Revenue Code?

Under Section 61 of the Internal Revenue Code, gross income from all sources is subject to taxation except as otherwise provided in the Code. Section 501 of the Code creates an exception to Section 61, by enumerating various classifications that could be recognized as tax exempt. More than 20 different classifications of tax-exempt organizations are described in Section 501(c). In particular, Section 501(c)(3) exempts from federal income tax entities that are organized and operated exclusively for charitable, educational, or scientific purposes. Most nonprofit hospitals fall within the purview of this Section if they qualify for tax-exempt status under the restrictions it contains.

Q.10:2 What are the advantages of obtaining tax-exempt status for a health care organization?

There are several advantages to obtaining tax-exempt status, in addition to the obvious advantage of exemption from federal income taxes. Fund raising for these organizations is facilitated because charitable contributions they receive are deductible by the donor. Charitable contributions to a hospital or medical research organization are deductible by the donor up to 50 percent of the donor's gross income [I.R.C. § 170(b)(2)]. If the organization is not a hospital or a medical research organization within the meaning of Section 170 of the Code, charitable contributions can still be deductible up to 50 percent of an individual's gross income if the entity is an educational one that normally maintains a regular faculty, curriculum, and students or a charitable, scientific, or educational organization as defined in Section 501(c)(3), and receives a substantial part of its support from the general public. Donations to charitable health care institutions that are considered private foundations under Section 509 of the Code (excluding operating foundations under Section 170(b)(1)(E)) are deductible up to the lesser of 30 percent of the donor's adjusted gross income or the excess of 50 percent of the donor's gross income over the amount of deductible contributions permitted for the charitable, scientific, or educational organizations in the preceding sentence.

Exempt organizations also benefit from special postage rates, as well as exemption from other federal statutes, including the Federal Unemployment Tax Act, price discrimination legislation, and the Organized Crime Control Act. In addition, state legislation frequently links tax-exempt status under state law to tax status under federal law. Another significant advantage available to 501(c)(3) organizations is the opportunity to engage in tax-exempt financing. Bondholders who lend money to such an entity can be exempt from tax on the interest on the bonds as long as certain requirements are met. As a result, Section 501(c)(3) organizations usually are eligible for more favorable interest rates when borrowing money.

Q.10:3   How does an organization qualify for tax-exempt status under the Internal Revenue Code?

To qualify for tax-exempt status under Section 501(c)(3), an organization must meet all the requirements specified in that Section. In particular, the statute states that an organization is tax exempt if:

- it is a corporation, community chest, fund, or foundation,
- it is organized and operated exclusively for one of the enumerated exempt purposes,
- no part of its net earnings inures to the benefit of any private shareholder or individual, and
- no substantial part of its activities relates to carrying on propaganda or other lobbying efforts.

Q.10:4   How do exemption requirements under Section 501(c)(3) apply to a health care organization?

The most significant requirement for a health care organization attempting to obtain tax-exempt status under Section 501(c)(3) is that it be structured and operated for one of the exempt purposes listed in that section. By far the most relevant source of tax exemption for health care institutions is the charitable purpose requirement.

Q.10:5   What is the charitable purpose requirement?

According to the Treasury Regulations, the term *charitable* includes relief of the poor, distressed, and underprivileged; advancement of education and science; advancement of religion; erection or maintenance of public buildings, monuments, or works; and the promotion of social welfare designed to accomplish any of those purposes [Treas. Regs. § 1.501(c)(3)-1(d)(2)].

Q.10:6   How is the charitable purpose requirement applied to health care institutions?

Until 1956, there were no specific standards for determining whether hospitals qualified for exemption as charitable organizations. In 1956, Revenue Ruling 56-185 [1956-1C.B. 202] enumerated a number of requirements for health care facilities to qualify for tax exemption, and in particular required that the facility be operated to the extent of its financial ability for those not able to pay for the services provided. These requirements reflected the IRS's position that the provision of health care per se was not charitable, and that to serve a charitable purpose, the services must relieve poverty. Under that standard, if less than five percent of a hospital's patients received free care, the facility generally would not qualify for tax-exempt status. In practice, however, the standard was difficult to apply and, over time, generated concern that hospitals would lose their tax exemption because they were unable to provide sufficient uncompensated care to meet the requirement.

In 1969, the IRS responded to these concerns by eliminating the financial ability standard and substituting for it a new test known as the community benefit standard. The ruling explicitly states that the promotion of health is an established objective under the general law of charity and that it is recognized by the IRS as a charitable purpose within the meaning of that section. Revenue Ruling 69-545 is still a primary source of whether a hospital qualifies for tax-exempt status under Section 501(c)(3).

Q.10:7   What is the community benefit standard enunciated in Revenue Ruling 69-545?

Under the community benefit standard enunciated in Revenue Ruling 69-545, a hospital must promote the health of a class of persons broad enough to benefit the community as a whole and must operate to serve a public rather than a private interest. The standard focuses on a number of factors that would be used to determine whether a hospital operates to benefit the community. In particular, the IRS would consider:

- the operation of an active emergency room
- control of the hospital by a board of trustees composed of independent civic leaders
- maintenance of an open medical staff with privileges available to all qualified physicians
- a policy of leasing available space in the hospital's medical building to members of the active medical staff
- the use of surplus funds from operations to improve the quality of patient care, expand facilities, and advance the hospital's medical training, education, and research programs

Revenue Ruling 69-545 acknowledges that a hospital can satisfy the community benefit standard in many ways and directs that the relevant facts and circumstances be weighed in each case. For tax-exempt purposes, however, the two most significant aspects about the way a hospital operates are (1) the provision of care without regard to the ability to pay and (2) the absence of private inurement or benefit.

Q.10:8   What is the provision of care without regard to the ability to pay?

The provision of care without regard to the ability to pay, or uncompensated care, remains a major factor in the IRS's analysis of whether the facility meets the community benefit standard. Whether charitable care will remain a major factor in defining the community benefit standard if health care reform institutes universal coverage remains to be seen.

The operation of an active and generally accessible (regardless of ability to pay) emergency room has been used to satisfy the community benefit requirement for an organization seeking tax-exempt status. The reasoning behind such a requirement was that many members of the community, particularly indigents, do not have private physicians and rely on hospital emergency rooms as their principal means of access to medical care. The advent of Medicare and Medicaid reimbursement for many individuals who previously were unable to pay forced the IRS to reconsider its position in this regard.

In 1983, Revenue Ruling 83-157 [1983-2 C.B. 94] created a narrow exception to that requirement, granting tax-exempt status to a hospital that met the other restrictions in Revenue Ruling 69-545, but did not operate an emergency room. In that case, the hospital did not have an emergency room solely because a state health planning agency had determined independently that it would unnecessarily duplicate services already provided by other facilities in the community. Although that ruling clarified that there is no absolute requirement that a hospital operate an emergency room or provide a particular level of uncompensated care, those two activities remain the most effective ways to demonstrate community benefit.

In 1992, the IRS published examination guidelines developed for use by its agents in the exempt organizations examination program in which it restated the necessity for hospitals to meet the community benefit standards in Revenue Ruling 69-545. The guidelines reiterate the importance of:

- a governing board composed of prominent civic leaders rather than hospital administrators or physicians, etc.
- corporate separateness as reflected in the minutes of the governing board if the organization is part of a multi-entity hospital system
- a policy of open admission to the medical staff for all qualified physicians in the area, consistent with the size and nature of the facilities
- the operation of a full-time emergency room open to everyone regardless of ability to pay
- the provision of nonemergency care to everyone in the community who is able to pay either privately or through third parties, including Medicare and Medicaid

Q.10:9 What is private inurement?

As stated earlier, an organization will qualify for exemption under Section 501(c)(3) only if no part of its net earnings inures to the benefit of any private shareholder or individual. If any part of the entity's net earnings do so, it will not be deemed to operate exclusively for charitable or public purposes.

Inurement is likely to be found when a tax-exempt organization transfers any part of its financial resources to an individual solely by virtue of that person's relationship with the entity and without regard to achieving its exempt purposes. Inurement is likely to occur if a tax-exempt organization provides goods or services to an insider without demanding fair consideration in return. Because the law seeks to prevent anyone who is in a position to do so from extracting any part of the organization's assets for personal use, the presence of even a minor amount of private inurement may cause the organization to lose its tax-exempt status.

Q.10:10 Who are insiders within the meaning of the private inurement prohibition?

The prohibition against private inurement applies only to insiders, that is, individuals whose relationship with the organization offers them an opportunity to make use of its income or assets for personal gain. The power to influence the organization from the inside does not involve a measured amount of ownership or voting power. Rather, it refers to the opportunity of causing the entity to take the action that gives rise to inurement. Examples of insiders include trustees, board members, officers, managers, and the organization's founders.

The IRS has adopted the position that physicians on a hospital's medical staff, working either as employees or as nonemployees, are insiders subject to the private inurement prohibition. Historically, however, the IRS did not always consider that mere membership on a hospital's medical staff constituted an insider relationship, applying the private inurement prohibition only to cases in which a physician had founded or owned the hospital or otherwise controlled it. In 1986, the IRS classified as insiders physicians who were recruited by a hospital either as employees or as nonemployees having a close professional working association with the facility [GCM 39,498 (Jan. 28, 1986)]. One year later, the IRS adopted the position that all persons performing services for an organization have a personal and private interest and therefore possess the requisite relationship to find private benefit or inurement [GCM 39,770 (Oct. 14, 1987)]. In 1991, in its well-publicized General Counsel Memorandum on physician joint ventures [GCM 39,862 (Nov. 21, 1991)], the IRS reiterated this position. The IRS's *1992 Examination Guidelines* also indicate that physicians are considered insiders and are therefore subject to the inurement prohibition in their dealings with the hospital. The particular application of the private inurement prohibition to hospital–physician relationships, and in particular as it applies to joint ventures, is discussed in greater detail in **Questions 10:22** and **10:23**.

Q.10:11 What is the private benefit prohibition?

Tax-exempt organizations are also subject to the broader private benefit prohibition, which requires that any private benefit obtained by an individual through the activity of an exempt institution be incidental to the accomplishment of the public benefits involved. The IRS applies a qualitative and quantitative balancing test between the activity's tax-exempt purpose and the private benefits derived from such activity. Under the qualitative test, the private benefit obtained by certain individuals as a result of the activity must be necessary to achieve the public benefit the activity seeks to achieve. Under the quantitative test, the private benefit must not be substantial when compared with the overall public benefit of the activity. The activity will be found to jeopardize the organization's tax-exempt status if it yields more than an incidental private benefit or if it does not have a valid exempt purpose.

Q.10:12 What are the differences between private inurement and private benefit?

Although the requirements for a finding of inurement or benefit are similar, the two concepts differ in key respects. First, even a minimal amount of inurement will result in disqualification for exempt status, whereas private benefit must be more qualitatively or quantitatively incidental to have an impact on tax-exempt status. Second, the private inurement prohibition applies only to insiders as defined earlier, whereas private benefit may accrue to anyone.

Q.10:13 How does the private inurement/benefit prohibition affect hospital–physician relationships within an exempt organization?

Different types of physician–hospital arrangements may involve private inurement/benefit and therefore affect an organization's tax-exempt status. These relationships generally relate to compensation arrangements or physician–hospital joint ventures.

Q.10:14 How do compensation arrangements between hospitals and physicians impact on the tax-exempt status of an organization?

There are a number of different compensation arrangements that can exist between physicians and hospitals. These include salaries, income guarantees, and incentive compensation, as well as arrangements relating to office space, support staff, loans, the purchase of equipment, and outright cash assistance. The structure and terms of these arrangements will determine whether the arrangement has an impact on the tax-exempt status of the organization.

Q.10:15 How can salaries create private inurement/benefit in the context of physician–hospital relationships?

A hospital may pay a reasonable salary to physicians, even to those who could be considered insiders, without creating private inurement and jeopardizing its tax-exempt status. The IRS will focus on whether the salaries or other types of remuneration paid to an individual are excessive or unreasonable. Reasonable compensation is the amount that ordinarily would be paid for like services by like enterprises under like circumstances [Treas. Regs. § 1.162-7(b)(3)]. Determining whether compensation is reasonable involves a facts and circumstances test to decide what is being paid for (what has the individual provided of value to the exempt organization?) and how the amount paid compares with the fair market value of the service provided.

Q.10:16 What factors does the IRS consider in determining whether compensation is reasonable?

The IRS has identified several specific factors to be considered in determining the reasonableness of compensation. These include:

- whether the agreed-upon compensation has been the result of arm's length negotiation between the parties,
- whether the party receiving the compensation has control over the exempt organization or the compensation process,
- whether the compensation received is reasonable in terms of the responsibilities and activities assumed under the contract,
- whether the salary would qualify as an expense deduction under Section 162(a) of the Internal Revenue Code,
- whether the payments serve a real and discernible business purpose of the hospital system independent of any purpose to operate the institution for the direct or indirect benefit of the employee,
- whether the compensation is dependent principally upon the incoming revenue of the exempt organization or upon the accomplishment of the object over the compensating contract, and
- whether there is a ceiling or reasonable maximum to avoid the possibility of a windfall benefit.

These factors are not all-inclusive and will be considered and weighed depending on the circumstances of the arrangement.

Q.10:17 Under what circumstances would income guarantees provided by a hospital to a physician jeopardize the facility's tax-exempt status?

Although income guarantees are an extremely popular recruitment tool, the IRS has raised considerable doubts about whether nonprofit hospitals can continue to employ this recruitment strategy without jeopardizing their tax-exempt status. In particular, the IRS has indicated that a hospital's contract with physicians providing a guaranteed minimum annual income for two years with no obligation by the physicians to repay subsidies out of the income earned could justify the revocation of the institution's tax exemption [GCM 39,498 (April 24, 1986)]. The IRS stated that:

> the provision of the revised guaranteed minimum annual income contract as part of the hospital's physician recruitment program may result in the physician's private interests being served other than incidentally and inurement of the hospital's net earnings to individuals having a personal and private interest in the hospital's activities.

In a subsequent GCM [GCM 39,674 (June 17, 1987)], the IRS mitigated the harshness of this finding, stating that it had not intended to create a negative presumption as to whether the compensation provided under any particular plan is reasonable and emphasizing that it could not determine in advance whether compensation is reasonable.

The tax consequences of using income guarantees as a recruitment tool remain uncertain. Although the use of income guarantees with no obligation to repay subsidies after the contract period would be risky, income guarantees that include subsidy caps or requirements for additional physician services could be acceptable. (See IRS 1992 *Examination Guidelines for Hospitals*, § 333.3(7)(a), and **Question 10:20.**)

Q.10:18 Under what circumstances does the IRS consider that incentive compensation results in private inurement/benefit?

The IRS's original position on incentive compensation was that it resulted in per se private inurement and a loss of exemption. [*See, e.g.*, GCM 37,180 (June 30, 1977).] The IRS later began to revise its position, stating in GCM 38,283 (Feb. 15, 1980) that a tax-exempt organization can have an incentive plan for compensating employees if it qualifies as a profit-sharing plan under Section 401(a) of the IRC. The operation of an incentive compensation plan in which profits are a factor in the compensation formula, as long as the plan is adequately limited and safeguarded, will not jeopardize tax exemption.

The IRS has specifically addressed the establishment of a profit-sharing compensation plan for hospital employees. In GCM 39,674 (June 17, 1987) for instance, it stated that:

> the mere establishment of incentive compensation plans to pay a percentage of the "profits" of the hospitals as additional compensation is not inconsistent with exempt status, such as when the compensation transforms the activity into a joint venture or is a mere device to distribute profits to principals. Both [plans] have been established to advance the exempt purpose of the hospital by improving the quality and efficiency of patient care, and appear reasonably designed to accomplish this purpose.

Q.10:19 What other types of compensation arrangements between hospitals and physicians could jeopardize a facility's tax-exempt status?

A hospital could jeopardize its tax-exempt status by charging physicians no rent or below-market rent for space in hospital-owned office buildings. Hospitals frequently provide physicians with the right to use office space within their facilities. According to the 1992 IRS *Examination Guidelines*, office space in a hospital or medical office building for use in a physician's private practice generally must be provided at a reasonable rental rate. It is acceptable for a physician to split activities between duties for the hospital and a private practice, but in this case, the hospital should apportion the use and charge a reasonable rent for the private practice activities.

In some circumstances, however, the provision of below-market rental of office space may not result in a finding of private benefit or inurement. The IRS has held, for example, that a hospital's rental of office space at below-market rates to induce a physician to locate in an isolated rural area did not justify revocation of the facility's exempt status [*Olney v. Commissioner*, 17 T.C.M. 982 (1958)]. More recently, the guidelines elaborated in the IRS settlement with *Hermann Hospital* (see **Question 10:20**) illustrate the IRS's response to recruitment initiatives that involve this type of compensation.

The provision of support staff and management services for recordkeeping, billing, and collection services for physicians is another popular recruiting/retention device that could result in private inurement/benefit. The relevant analysis of this type of benefit is similar to the provision of office space. If physicians use the support staff for their private practice, the hospital must charge a reasonable rate for the services, proportionate to the private practice activities. A physician's right to use a hospital's property or support staff free or at a below-market-value rate would constitute private benefit, which could jeopardize the facility's tax-exempt status if it is not incidental to the institution's public purpose. The problem could be avoided by demonstrating that the benefit is needed to induce physicians to practice in the community and that the overall compensation package is reasonable. Here again, the *Hermann Hospital* settlement is relevant to determining how the IRS might respond to a practical situation involving this type of arrangement. (See **Question 10:20.**)

The provision of loans by an exempt organization to an "insider" at below-market rates or without adequate security will generally constitute impermissible private inurement. If, however, a hospital makes a loan to a physician that is at a market interest rate, is secured adequately, establishes a reasonable term given the size and purpose of the loan, and is made for reasons that primarily benefit the exempt organization, the loan should not have an impact on tax status. The IRS has also acknowledged that below-market interest loans may be necessary to induce physicians to join a hospital's medical staff in certain localities [LTR 80-28-011, 84-18-003], and the guidelines enunciated in the *Hermann Hospital* settlement include loans and lines of credit as permissible incentives if they are at an interest rate that reflects market conditions.

Outright cash assistance in the form of a recruitment or signing bonus may be permissible, according to GCM 39,498, if the amount is determined not by reference to services to be rendered but by reference to the value assigned to recruiting a particular physician to a particular service area. However, the *Hermann Hospital* guidelines provide that signing bonuses or other bonus payments are examples of incentives that are not permissible for that particular hospital under the terms of that settlement.

Another type of compensation arrangement that could generate private inurement/benefit involves the hospital's purchase of equipment for use by a physician to treat hospital patients as well as the physician's private patients. To ensure that such an arrangement does not jeopardize the hospital's exempt status, the institution must demonstrate that the benefit it derives from having the equipment available to treat its patients in addition to the benefit of having the physician available in the community outweighs the private benefit conferred on the physician to treat private patients. To minimize the private benefit, the hospital can retain ownership of the equipment and grant a right of use to the physician or transfer ownership to the physician for only a limited time, with a reversionary interest if the physician leaves the facility's medical staff.

Q.10:20 How does the IRS view these various types of compensation arrangements when they are used to recruit physicians?

In 1994, the IRS released a closing agreement with a tax-exempt hospital, containing a specific number of physician recruitment guidelines that the hospital agreed to adopt and follow as part of its settlement with the IRS [*IRS Closing Agreement with Hermann Hospital*, September 16, 1994]. The hospital voluntarily disclosed to the IRS certain of its physician recruitment and retention arrangements to determine whether they had jeopardized its tax-exempt status by conferring either prohibited inurement or private benefits on the individuals involved. Under the agreement, the hospital agreed to adopt and follow specific guidelines regarding recruitment incentives offered to physicians. Under the guidelines, an incentive offered to a physician recruit is permissible if a community need for the physician has been demonstrated.

Community need can be evidenced in a variety of ways, including:

- a population-to-physician ratio in the community that is deficient in the particular specialty of the physician being recruited,
- demand for a particular medical service in the community coupled with a documented lack of availability of the service or long waiting periods for the service, if the physician is being recruited to increase availability of that service,
- designation of the hospital's service area as a Health Professional Shortage Area by the Department of Health and Human Services,
- a demonstrated reluctance of physicians to relocate to the hospital due to its physical location,
- a reasonably expected reduction in the number of physicians of that specialty in the hospital's service area due to the anticipated retirement within the next three-year period of physicians currently practicing in the community, or
- a documented lack of physicians serving indigent or Medicaid patients in the hospital's service area, if the newly recruited physicians commit to serving a substantial number of Medicaid and charity care patients.

The agreement also provides examples of permissible incentives, including loans, lines of credit, or loan guarantees offered to physicians, as long as they are documented, as evidenced by a promissory note, adequately secured and at an interest rate that reflects market conditions. Reasonable income guarantees for physician recruits can also constitute permissible incentives, as long as specific requirements are respected. Permissible incentives also include payment of actual moving expenses and relocation costs, as long as they are reasonable and subject to a fixed ceiling amount.

The settlement also includes a list of incentives that are not permissible. For example, the payment or provision of malpractice insurance for the current private practice of a nonemployee physician, subsidized parking, telephone allowances, car allowances, health insurance or payment of medical society dues or licensing fees, and signing bonuses or other bonus payments are some of the incentives that are not permissible. Although the IRS has cautioned that the agreement only applies to the facts and circumstances of this case, the settlement illustrates a practical application of IRS policy on physician recruitment.

Q.10:21 What is a hospital–physician joint venture?

Joint ventures of exempt hospitals may take the form of a contract, a partnership, a corporation, or any variation thereof. As indicated in the 1992 IRS *Examination Guidelines*, § 333.4:

> a joint venture . . . may be a contractual agreement between two or more parties to cooperate in providing services or it may involve the creation of a new legal entity by the parties, such as a limited partnership or closely held corporation, to undertake an activity or provide services.

Examples of the items or services provided in these arrangements are clinical diagnostic laboratory services, medical equipment leasing, durable medical equipment, and other outpatient, medical, or diagnostic services.

Q.10:22 How do joint ventures impact the tax-exempt status of a health care organization generally?

Some joint ventures in which tax-exempt health care organizations participate may be consistent with that status depending upon the specific facts and circumstances. Health care networks are frequently established by integrating tax-exempt hospitals with other providers through joint ventures. A tax-exempt hospital may enter into joint ventures with nonexempt entities if it can demonstrate that the venture will further its tax-exempt purpose. In particular, the arrangement must provide community benefit and not result in either private inurement or impermissible private benefit.

The IRS has recently approved a number of affiliations of exempt and for-profit facilities. For example, the IRS has ruled that a nonprofit hospital will not jeopardize its tax-exempt status or generate taxable unrelated business income by participating in a joint venture with a for-profit entity to provide rehabilitation services. The IRS found that the alliance would further the hospital's exempt purposes by providing the community benefit of expanding the current rehabilitation center and providing access to more comprehensive medical rehabilitation services in the community. It further noted that no physicians would have an ownership interest in the partnership and that the hospital would retain control of critical management decisions through its 50 percent participation on a six-member management board [IRS Private Letter Ruling No. 9352030 (Oct. 8, 1993)].

Q.10:23 What is the IRS's position on the impact of hospital–physician joint ventures on the tax-exempt status of the hospital?

The IRS has indicated its intent to closely scrutinize hospital–physician joint ventures because such arrangements have the potential of generating prohibited private inurement/benefit for the physician investors. However, hospital–physician joint ventures are not per se illegal, and to the extent that they can demonstrate community benefit and the absence of prohibited inurement, they will continue to pass muster.

The IRS has ruled, for instance, that a tax exempt hospital may enter into a joint venture with a physician partnership to construct and operate a for-profit ambulatory surgery center without compromising its tax-exempt status. The hospital and physician partnership agreement provided that the hospital would build the center without physician ownership, but that the physician partnership would have the option to purchase half the center once it was operational. The two entities would form a joint venture to own and operate the center only if the IRS confirmed that such an arrangement would not jeopardize the hospital's tax-exempt status.

The IRS observed that the sale of a 50 percent interest in the surgery center to the partnership will be used by the hospital to expand cardiac care services to meet community needs in this area. In addition, financial arrangements between the hospital and the partnership, including the purchase price of the center and rental of the real estate in which the center is located, will be at fair market value. Operating the surgery center through a medical partnership allows the hospital to obtain the capital and expertise necessary to expand its health care resources and ensure efficient management, the IRS noted. Because the hospital's participation in the transaction will improve its capacity to provide needed cardiac services to the community, the IRS concluded that the joint venture furthers the hospital's charitable purposes [IRS Private Letter Ruling, No. 9407022 (Nov. 22, 1993)].

The IRS has, however, taken the position that a specific type of hospital–physician joint venture involving the sale of net revenue streams, will jeopardize a hospital's exempt status [GCM 39,862, (Nov. 21, 1991)]. The IRS has indicated in this GCM that it does not ban all hospital–physician joint ventures, stating that:

> nothing herein should be read to imply that a typical joint venture that involves true shared ownership, risks, responsibilities, and rewards and that demonstrably furthers a charitable purpose should be met automatically with suspicion or disapproved merely because physician-investors have an ownership interest.

Q.10:24 What is a net revenue stream joint venture between a hospital and physicians?

A net revenue stream joint venture between a hospital and physicians, typically members of its medical staff, involves the sale by the hospital of the net revenue stream derived from part of its operations or a specific department to a joint venture between the hospital (or an affiliate) and physician members of its medical staff. The joint venture acquires an interest in the profits of specific hospital operations or a department for a defined period of time, generally in exchange for payment to the hospital of an amount representing the current fair market value of the net revenue stream.

Q.10:25 What is the IRS's position on net revenue stream joint ventures between hospitals and physicians?

GCM 39,862 enunciates the IRS's position that a net revenue stream joint venture jeopardizes a hospital's tax-exempt status for several reasons. First, it causes the hospital's net earnings to inure to the benefit of private individuals (i.e., physicians on its medical staff). Second, the private inurement is not merely incidental to the public benefits achieved through the operation of the joint venture. Finally, hospitals participate in such arrangements as a means of retaining and rewarding members of their medical staffs, to attract admissions and referrals, and to pre-empt physicians from investing in or creating a competing provider. Although the joint venture may further a hospital's competitive position by increasing referrals and utilization, this is not sufficient to prevent a finding of either private inurement or substantial private benefit. The venture must benefit the community, rather than the hospital itself. Such joint ventures jeopardize tax-exempt status, according to the IRS, because they do little to further a hospital's charitable purpose of promoting health in the community.

PHYSICIAN–HOSPITAL ORGANIZATIONS

Q.10:26 What effect does a 501(c)(3) hospital's participation in a physician–hospital organization (PHO) have on its exempt status?

A tax-exempt hospital's participation in a PHO typically involves the hospital's sharing of control of the PHO with either a medical group, an individual practice association, or individual physicians who are affiliated with the hospital. The PHO contracts with payers on behalf of the hospital and physicians and coordinates resources and the delivery of medical treatment. The PHO itself provides no health care services.

The IRS has stated that a hospital's participation in a PHO jeopardizes tax exemption if such participation is a vehicle for the hospital to share its net income with the medical staff. This would occur if the hospital's control or profit share in the PHO is less than its share of the capital contribution, allowing the member physicians to receive benefits that are greater than their risk. A hospital's tax-exempt status would also be jeopardized if the PHO is a vehicle for sharing capitated payments with the physicians, and the physicians receive more than reasonable compensation for their services or the hospital otherwise receives less than a fair portion of income.

Q.10:27 What factors will the IRS consider in determining if a hospital's participation in a PHO jeopardizes its exempt status?

The IRS has indicated that it will rely on factors it enunciated in a GCM on hospital–physician partnerships to determine if a hospital's participation in a PHO adversely affects its exempt status. These factors are:

- a disproportionate allocation of profit or loss in favor of the for-profit partner,
- an insufficient or nominal capital contribution made by the for-profit partner,
- the addition of new equipment or services to the partnership or the current availability of such services or equipment in the area,
- the sale or lease of existing hospital equipment or facilities to the partnership,
- the provision of any service by the hospital at less than fair market value,
- significant influence and control of a for-profit limited partner over the partnership's operations,
- the assumption by the exempt organization of all risk or liability for the partnership's losses, and
- the existence of commercially unreasonable loans to the partnership [GCM 39,732 (May 19, 1988)].

Q.10:28 Has the IRS ever specifically ruled on the issue of whether a tax-exempt hospital can participate in a PHO without jeopardizing its status?

Yes. According to a private letter ruling issued in September 1994, a nonprofit, acute care hospital may become a member of a physician–hospital organization, along with certain health care professionals with medical staff privileges at the facility, without jeopardizing its tax-exempt status under Section 501(c)(3). In this case, the PHO was to be organized as a limited liability company that would provide centralized contracting, credentialing, quality assurance, and education for both the hospital and the physician members. Under the agreement, the hospital will have a 50 percent membership ownership in the PHO, and participating individual physicians will own the remaining 50 percent membership interest. The hospital will contribute 50 percent of the initial capital contributions, and the physicians will contribute the other 50 percent. No more than 20 percent of membership on the PHO's board of directors may be medical staff members. A price negotiating committee will have exclusive authority to manage all the financial aspects of managed care contracts, in addition to fee schedule and reimbursement issues for medical staff members. The IRS emphasized in this private letter ruling that member physicians will not exert control over the PHO's operations and that the hospital's interest in the PHO is proportionate with its share of capital contribution. Member physicians will not receive benefits disproportionately greater than their risk, the IRS commented in this regard, concluding that any private interest served by the PHO would be incidental. Based on this information, the IRS concluded that the hospital's participation in the PHO would not jeopardize the hospital's tax exemption [IRS Private Letter Ruling, no number available (Sept. 29, 1994)].

Q.10:29 Can a PHO be tax exempt under Section 501(c)(3)?

The IRS's view is that a PHO's activities substantially serve the private interests of its member physicians. The IRS compares the operations of a PHO with that of an Independent Practice Association (IPA), noting that an IPA does not qualify for exemption because its primary beneficiaries are its member-physicians rather than the community as a whole. In the case of a PHO, the physician members are considered "private individuals," and may also be insiders, subjecting them to both the private benefit and the private inurement prohibitions. This substantial private benefit would preclude exemption under Section 501(c)(3). [*See, IRS Continuing Education Program, Exempt Organizations, Technical Instruction Program for FY 1995*, p. 154.]

MANAGEMENT SERVICES ORGANIZATIONS (MSOs)

Q.10:30 Will a tax-exempt hospital's participation in a management services organization (MSO) affect its tax-exempt status?

The IRS's position with respect to the effect of a tax-exempt hospital's participation in an MSO is similar to its position regarding participation in a PHO. Specifically, the IRS will examine the arrangement to determine if it meets the requirements for an exempt organization's participation in investments and joint ventures. Regardless of the form that a hospital's participation takes, the MSO must represent a reasonable investment for the hospital. In this regard, the IRS emphasizes that the expenses of the arrangement must be paid by the hospital and the aggregate physician members in proportion to the benefit derived by each. In addition, the arrangement may jeopardize the hospital's exempt status if the hospital's control and financial share of the MSO is disproportionately less than its capital contribution.

Q.10:31 Can an MSO qualify for tax-exempt status under Section 501(c)(3)?

According to the IRS, an MSO generally will not qualify for exemption under Section 501(c)(3), because it is not likely to operate for a charitable purpose. Like a PHO, an MSO operates primarily to serve the private interests of participating physicians, thereby generating more than either incidental private benefit or inurement.

CORPORATE REORGANIZATION AND TAX EXEMPTION

Q.10:32 How does the reorganization of tax-exempt health care facilities into systems affect their exempt status?

In the 1980s, the health care industry witnessed a number of reorganizations of health care facilities into systems, frequently involving the creation of a nonprofit parent organization with both tax-exempt and for-profit subsidiaries. Such reorganizations raise issues regarding the qualification of the parent organization for both tax-exempt status under Section 501(c)(3) and as a supporting organization under Section 509(a)(3), as well as the effect of the reorganization on the tax-exempt status of the related entities.

Q.10:33 What is a supporting organization under Section 509(a)(3)?

Organizations that are tax exempt under Section 501(c)(3) are classified as private foundations unless they qualify as public charities under the terms of Section 509. Some organizations are automatically recognized as public charities under Section 509. Other organizations can qualify for such status if they meet the various conditions enunciated in that Section. Section 509(a)(3) creates a specific category of public charity—the supporting organization. To qualify as a supporting organization, and hence as a public charity, an exempt organization must meet three requirements. It must:

1. be organized and at all times operated exclusively for the benefit of, to perform the function of, or to carry out the purposes of one or more public charities as defined in Sections 509(a)(1) or 509(a)(2) (supported organizations),
2. be operated, supervised, or controlled in connection with one or more of these other public charities, and

3. not be controlled directly or indirectly by one or more disqualified persons (defined in Section 4946 of the Code) other than foundation managers and other than one or more organizations described in Sections 509(a)(1) and 509(a)(2).

Q.10:34 How does a parent organization in a health care system qualify as a supporting organization under Section 509(a)(3)?

In GCM 39,508, the IRS analyzed under what circumstances a parent organization can qualify for status as a Section 509(a)(3) supporting organization, and hence as a public charity. In this GCM, the IRS states that a parent organization will qualify as a supporting organization if its articles of incorporation state that it is organized and operated exclusively to benefit its supported organization subsidiaries and a majority of the parent's board members serve on the boards of each of its supported organization subsidiaries. The IRS must determine whether control or management in the supporting organization is vested in the same persons who control and manage each of the organizations it supports.

Q.10:35 How has the IRS responded to the reorganization of health care facilities into systems that involve the establishment of a tax-exempt parent corporation?

The IRS has recently approved a number of reorganizations of health care facilities involving the creation of a nonprofit parent organization that qualifies as a supporting organization under Section 509(a)(3). In one case, a tax-exempt hospital created an organization to provide financial, management, and advisory support services for the hospital itself and two other related exempt organizations: one that provides nonacute care services and one that performs fund-raising activities for the hospital's benefit [IRS PLR No. 9333046 (May 27, 1993)]. The hospital has a taxable subsidiary, which would operate a multispecialty physicians' clinic and would sell its home health and durable medical equipment assets to the exempt nonacute care organization.

The IRS ruled that the management organization qualified as a supporting organization under Section 509(a)(3) because it was both organized and operated for the benefit of specific publicly supported organizations—the acute care hospital and its related exempt organizations. Five members of the hospital's board of directors will serve on the management organization's board, providing the supported organizations with significant voice in the management organization's policy making. In addition, the management organization will provide overall planning and coordination for the health care system, and generally will perform functions that the hospital and other exempt entities would otherwise have to perform themselves. Because the management organization is an integral part of the system and is operated in connection with one or more supported organizations, it qualifies as a supporting organization under Section 509(a)(3), according to the IRS.

Similarly, the IRS approved the restructuring of a relationship between a tax-exempt hospital, its parent organization, and a newly created supporting organization [IRS PLR No. 9326055 (April 6, 1993)]. In this case, the tax-exempt parent of a multi-entity health care system provided management and fund-raising support to its subsidiaries, including a tax-exempt hospital and a for-profit subsidiary. The for-profit subsidiary operates in turn as the parent holding company for several for-profit corporations. This parent corporation proposed to transfer its management functions and the stock of its for-profit subsidiary to a newly created Section 501(c)(3) corporation that would operate as the parent of the entire health care system. The boards of directors of the hospital, its former parent, a proposed fund-raising affiliate, and its new parent would overlap.

The IRS noted that the new parent corporation will provide overall planning and coordination, and essentially perform the same supervisory functions that the former tax-exempt parent performed prior to the reorganization. In addition, control of the new parent is vested in the same persons who control and manage the publicly supported organizations. The parent's ownership of the stock of the for-profit subsidiary would not jeopardize its tax-exempt status, nor would the transfer of personnel from the former parent to the new one, the IRS stated. The new parent would not engage in the day-to-day management of the for-profit subsidiary, and the transfer of assets between these two entities would only be a redistribution of assets among tax-exempt organizations, to be used for the same charitable purposes. The reorganization has no effect on the tax-exempt status of either the former parent, and the new parent, and both qualify as supporting organizations under Section 509(a)(3).

Q.10:36 Can a parent organization qualify as a supporting organization if it provides support services to both exempt and nonexempt subsidiaries?

The IRS has allowed a parent organization to qualify as a supporting organization under Section 509(a)(3), even if it supports both exempt and nonexempt subsidiaries. The strict legality of these rulings has been queried, however. In particular, technical advice requests from several IRS regional offices to the National Office have suggested that such parent organizations would be more appropriately classified as private foundations under Section 509. As is indicated in **Question 10:34**, to qualify as a supporting organization, and hence as a public charity, an exempt organization must be organized and at all times operated *exclusively* for the benefit of, to perform the function of, or to carry out the purposes of one or more public charities as defined in Sections 509(a)(1) or 509(a)(2) (supported organizations). This would imply that to qualify as a supporting organization, a parent corporation must only support a specific category of tax-exempt organizations. In a typical system, however, 501(c)(3) parent corporations provide strategic planning and management services to both tax-exempt and taxable subsidiaries, frequently offering these services at the same cost to all. The National Office has responded by recommending in its proposals to Congress regarding health care reform that legislation contain a provision that would statutorily classify such parent organizations as non-private foundations. [*CPE Exempt Organizations, Technical Instruction Manual for FY 1995* at p. 146.]

Q.10:37 Can a superparent organization in a health care system qualify for tax-exempt status and supporting organization status under the Internal Revenue Code?

Yes. In 1993, the IRS issued the first ruling of this kind, granting 501(c)(3) status and public charity status as a supporting organization under Section 509(a)(3) to a corporation that is the superparent of an entire system of affiliated health care institutions, including several hospital systems with their own parent corporations [*IRS Private Letter Determination for Northwestern Healthcare Network* (Sept. 1, 1993)]. As part of an affiliation agreement between four health care systems, a nonprofit corporation was established to act as the parent organization of each of the affiliated institutions. Each of the affiliated institutions is tax exempt under Section 501(c)(3), either as the parent organization of a reorganized hospital system or as a single corporate entity that owns and operates hospitals. All of them qualify as public charities under Section 509. Each affiliated organization will appoint seven members to the network parent's council of governors, four of whom must be officers, directors, or physician members on the medical staff of the hospitals controlled or operated by the affiliated organization. Physicians may not comprise any more than 20 percent of the council membership, however. The corporation will have the power to remove institution directors; expel an institution from the network; impose minimum credentialing standards for each hospital's medical staff, as well as quality assurance and utilization review standards; adopt overall budgets and strategic plans; and direct the mergers, acquisitions, or affiliations of the hospitals and institution group members with other entities. In this case, the IRS concluded that the goal of the affiliation and the creation of the superparent corporation is to further the exempt purposes of the affiliated institutions by creating efficiencies of operation and enabling them to provide higher quality, more cost-effective health care services. Accordingly, the IRS ruled that the corporation qualifies for tax-exempt status under Section 501(c)(3) and as a supporting organization under Section 509(a)(3).

INTEGRATED DELIVERY SYSTEMS (IDSs)

Q.10:38 Can an integrated delivery system obtain tax-exempt status under Section 501(c)(3)?

Yes. The IRS has and will likely continue to grant requests for tax-exempt status to integrated delivery systems on a case-by-case basis. The similarities in some of the earlier IRS rulings granting tax-exempt status to integrated delivery systems (in particular, the rulings on the *Friendly Hills* and *Facey* health care systems [IRS Determination Letter, Friendly Hills Healthcare Foundation, Jan. 29, 1993 and IRS Determination Letter to Facey Medical Foundation, March 31, 1993]) provide some general guidance on what the IRS considers significant in determining the tax status of an IDS.

In *Friendly Hills* and *Facey*, the IRS applied standards similar to those enunciated in Revenue Ruling 69-545 (see **Question 10:4**) and has indicated that the community benefit standard defined in this ruling provides the basis for most of its rulings in the health care provider area. Both systems offered emergency care regardless of ability to pay, participated in Medicare and Medicaid programs in a nondiscriminatory manner, had open medical staffs at their own or affiliated hospitals, and conducted health education and medical research programs. In addition, in both cases, the boards had broad community representation and only 20 percent of the membership was composed of members from the physician groups.

Perhaps most significantly, the creation of both systems involved the purchase of one or more existing medical practices for an amount that was represented as less than or equal to the fair market value. The price paid in both instances included an amount for intangible assets (such as trade name, patient files, noncompetition agreements, goodwill, etc.) as well as tangible assets. The IRS conditioned both rulings on the caveat that the arrangement not violate the Medicare and Medicaid antikickback statute, thereby acknowledging the potential fraud and abuse implications when a hospital pays for the intangible assets of a physician practice and the selling physicians continue to serve patients on behalf of the hospital. (See **Question 10:43** for a more detailed discussion of this issue.)

One significant difference between the two systems was that Friendly Hills was to own and operate an acute care hospital, whereas the Facey Foundation did not intend to do so. Rather, the Facey Foundation, through contractual arrangements, relied on hospitals owned by its tax-exempt member to provide inpatient care for its enrollees. The IRS did not require Facey to provide emergency room services directly to the community, apparently satisfied with the role the foundation played in facilitating access to such services and to other types of charity care. This position reflects some flexibility on the part of the IRS in analyzing IDS exemption requests under the standards set out in Revenue Ruling 69-545 and suggests that an IDS may be eligible for tax exemption under Section 501(c)(3) if it facilitates or enhances the delivery of health care as described in Revenue Ruling 69-545.

Q.10:39 How have the IRS criteria for granting tax exemption to an integrated delivery system evolved since its original rulings in *Friendly Hills* and *Facey*?

As was illustrated in the IRS rulings in *Friendly Hills* and *Facey*, an integrated delivery system, like all applicants for tax exemption under Section 501(c)(3), must establish on the basis of all the facts and circumstances, that it is organized and operated exclusively for charitable purposes and that no part of its net earnings inures to the benefit of any private shareholder or individual. In this regard, the agency has continued to apply the community benefit standard as defined in Revenue Ruling 69-545, but as it has the opportunity to analyze other integrated health care systems, it has also focused on some issues that are particularly problematic in the context of tax exemption for integrated delivery systems. Specifically, the arrangements between the IDS and the physician component of the system (i.e., issues relating to the valuation of medical practices that the IDS intends to purchase, and physician recruitment and compensation) are of particular concern to the IRS when analyzing either an application from a newly created IDS or an existing organization.

Q.10:40 How does the purchase of a medical practice affect an integrated delivery system's qualification for tax exemption?

The formation of an integrated delivery system will frequently involve the purchase of a for-profit medical group practice by the system's central organization responsible for integrating both outpatient and inpatient medical services, and administering the entire system. If the central organization in tax-exempt, the purchase of a for-profit medical group practice can jeopardize that status in several ways, in particular by generating either prohibited inurement or more than incidental private benefit for the group itself or its members.

Q.10:41 What private benefit issues arise as a result of the purchase of a medical practice by an IDS?

In the context of an integrated delivery system, the private benefit prohibition applies to all the physicians in the medical practice or group that sells its assets to the organization and that subsequently has its physicians perform services for the organization. The IRS will closely scrutinize the potential private benefit to the physicians involved in the creation of an IDS, although the benefits to a particular medical group will vary depending upon the group's unique situation. Benefits to physicians or the medical group must be both qualitatively incidental (i.e., it would be impossible for the IDS to accomplish its exempt purpose without providing these benefits), as well as quantitatively incidental (i.e., the private benefit must be insubstantial when compared with the overall public benefit conferred by the organization's activity).

The possible benefits of such a transaction to physicians or the medical group include the elimination or facilitation of buyins and buyouts of the medical group. As a result of the purchase, the IDS, and not the physicians, owns all of the medical group's assets and becomes liable for all of its debts. This means that a physician who wishes to buy into the practice will not have to produce cash, and physician-members of the practice will not have to retire debt when a physician withdraws from the group [*IRS CPE Exempt Organizations Technical Instruction Program* (1994), at p. 231].

The IRS will also examine the adequacy of the purchase price to determine if prohibited private benefit has arisen as a result of the transaction. The assets of a medical practice generally include both tangible (real estate, equipment, etc.) and intangible assets (goodwill, patient lists, etc.). The IRS requires that fair market value be paid for all of these assets and includes the following language in all favorable 501(c)(3) exemption rulings: "Applicant represents that all assets acquired will be at or below fair market value and will be the result of independent appraisals and arm's length negotiations."

Q.10:42 What private inurement issues arise as a result of an IDS's purchase of a medical practice?

Private inurement can also occur as a result of an IDS's purchase of a physician practice, thereby jeopardizing the organization's qualifications for tax exemption. To be subject to this prohibition, an individual must be an insider (i.e., someone whose relationship with the organization offers an opportunity to make use of its income or assets for personal gain). In the context of the sale of a medical practice, the IRS recognizes insider status to physicians in a medical group who provide services for the IDS under an exclusive contract. Prohibited private inurement may arise as a result of the purchase of a medical practice if the IDS pays more than fair market value for any of the assets it acquires, or if the valuation of the assets is not based on independent negotiations between unrelated parties and certified appraisals from independent third parties.

Q.10:43 How has the IRS responded to the possible fraud and abuse implications of including the value of intangible assets in the assessment of the fair market value of a medical practice?

As is indicated in the preceding question, the IRS analyzes the purchase price paid for both tangible and intangible assets of the medical group and, under its current rulings, allows the fair market value of an ongoing practice to include the value of intangible assets. The agency states, however, that in determination rulings involving practice acquisitions, it will include a caveat that the ruling is conditioned upon the nonviolation of federal antikickback restrictions. The language is as follows:

> This ruling is conditioned upon your not violating the federal antikickback restrictions contained in Section 1128(b) of the Social Security Act, 42 U.S.C. Section 1320a-7b(b)(1) and (2), which prohibit the payment of remuneration in return for the referral of Medicare or Medicaid patients. We express no opinion as to whether your planned purchase of a private group medical practice or your subsequent purchase of services from that group practice for a percentage of your gross revenues complies with these provisions.

Q.10:44 How do physician recruitment practices affect the tax exemption of an integrated delivery system?

The important role played by primary care physicians as gatekeepers within managed care plans raises concerns that an integrated delivery system will offer these physicians recruitment incentives that are not justified in light of the community benefit that will result from their association with the IDS. The IRS will examine the terms and conditions under which new physicians are recruited. In this regard, the guidelines enunciated in the *Hermann Hospital* settlement (see **Question 10:20**) provide illustrations on what types of arrangements could pass muster under the agency's scrutiny. The IRS will also examine the total compensation to determine whether it is reasonable both in the way it is determined and the actual amount. Recruitment and compensation arrangements can jeopardize the tax exemption of an organization to the extent that they generate either prohibited private inurement or benefit.

Q.10:45 What factors does the IRS consider in evaluating the physician compensation arrangements for a tax-exempt health care provider?

Physician compensation must be reasonable so as not to jeopardize the exempt status of the organization. The reasonableness of compensation is judged under a facts and circumstances test and is determined on a case-by-case basis [*CPE Technical Instruction Manual, IRS* (1995), p.161]. The compensation plan of an exempt organization will not result in prohibited inurement if it:

- is not inconsistent with tax-exempt status,
- is the result of arm's-length bargaining, and
- results in reasonable compensation.

In applying this test, the IRS will focus on the independence of the board of directors that determines the compensation. The IRS will consider the number of financially interested individuals (physicians) who serve on the board and whether those physicians are eligible to vote on the issue of physician compensation. The IRS states in its *1995 CPE Technical Instruction Program* (p. 161) that "if a board contains no financially interested members, or financially interested members refrain from voting, there is a greater presumption that compensation is reasonable." In rulings on health care integrated delivery systems, the IRS has consistently required that no more than 20 percent of board members represent physicians or other interested parties' interests, stating that the private benefit to physicians through significant board participation is a serious threat to an IDS's exemption.

The IRS also determines whether physician compensation is comparable to the compensation levels of physicians in similar specialties. The IRS performs this analysis using regional data if it is available as well as data compiled by national associations, and state and local medical societies. Written evidence of arm's length salary negotiations between physicians and the IDS, such as formal offers between the parties, or other documentation of face-to-face negotiations, can also assist in determining the reasonableness of compensation.

Q.10:46 Can health maintenance organizations (HMOs) qualify for tax exemption under Section 501(c)(3) of the Internal Revenue Code?

Yes. In the case of *Sound Health Association v. Commissioner* (71 T.C. 158) 1978, the Tax Court ruled that a staff model HMO qualified for tax exemption under Section 501(c)(3). The case involved a nonprofit, nonstock membership corporation, which employed physicians and other health care practitioners and also operated facilities as a health care provider. The IRS previously had denied tax exemption to the HMO, stating that although the HMO provided some health services to the general public, it clearly accorded preferential treatment to its member-subscribers. The characteristic was inconsistent with the requirement that an organization serve a public, rather than private, interest to qualify for tax exemption under Section 501(c)(3). In addition, the IRS concluded, the effect of the HMO's prepayment feature was to provide a form of insurance for its member-subscribers and that did not further a public charitable purpose.

Analyzing the HMO under the tests enunciated in Revenue Ruling 69-545, the Tax Court emphasized that the HMO opened its emergency room to all persons requiring emergency care, regardless of their ability to pay or their membership status. The court also emphasized that the HMO had established both research and education programs, had directed its ambulance company to bring emergency patients to the clinic, and had otherwise developed programs and facilities similar to those of tax-exempt hospitals described in Revenue Ruling 69-545. The court also noted that the HMO had an open medical staff and did not have any insider benefit that would disqualify it for tax exemption under Section 501(c)(3).

Q.10:47 What factors does the IRS examine in determining whether a health maintenance organization qualifies for tax exemption?

The IRS recognizes an HMO as tax exempt under Section 501(c)(3) if it meets the tests enunciated in the *Sound Health* decision [*CPE Technical Instruction Manual* (1995), p. 141]. This generally means that 501(c)(3) HMOs will be organized on the staff model (with care provided in a central location by physicians and others working as salaried employees of the HMO) and should also have enough of the characteristics of the *Sound Health* organization to establish that they operate to benefit the community as a whole and not merely their subscribers. The more factors an HMO has in common with the *Sound Health* organization, the more likely the conclusion that it operates primarily for the benefit of the community.

Several rulings in *Geisinger Health Plan v. Commissioner*, No. 20793-90X (U.S. Tax. Ct. Dec. 30, 1991) and No. 92-7251 (3d Cir. Feb. 8, 1993) have served to further clarify the eligibility of HMOs for tax-exempt status under Section 501(c)3). In this case, the IRS denied the HMO tax exemption as a charitable organization, contending that it operates for the benefit of its subscribers and not for the community at large. The Tax Court subsequently ruled, however, that the HMO did qualify for exemption under Section 501(c)(3), but the Third Circuit reversed this decision on appeal.

According to the Third Circuit ruling, no strict multifactor test is appropriate when determining whether an HMO qualifies for tax-exempt status; rather the totality of circumstances must indicate whether the organization benefits the community in addition to its subscribers. The court observed that in the *Sound Health* case, the organization provided health care services itself, offered services to both subscribers and members of the public through an outpatient clinic where it treated all emergency patients regardless of ability to pay, conducted research, and offered educational programs. The HMO in *Geisinger*, on the other hand, benefits no one but its subscribers, the court held, because its requirement of subscribership is a condition precedent to any service. The presence of a subsidized dues program does not sufficiently benefit the community to justify tax-exempt status, the court declared, relying on the fact that only 35 people received subsidies as compared with more than 70,000 paying subscribers. In addition, arranging for the provision of medical services only to members is not necessarily charitable, the court concluded, especially in light of the small number of persons who are subsidized.

In addition, the IRS also holds the position that unless the risk of loss is shifted to providers, either by the use of an employed staff or through capitation, the HMO will be considered to provide commercial-type insurance and will be ineligible for tax exemption under Section 501(m). Section

501(m) provides that organizations described in Sections 501(c)(3) or 501(c)(4) cannot be tax exempt unless no substantial part of their business consists of offering "commercial-type" insurance. Commercial-type insurance, although not defined in the IRC, generally refers to any insurance of a type provided by commercial insurance companies. Because many health maintenance organizations today have moved toward managed care models that allow patients to consult physicians who are unaffiliated with the HMO, it may be difficult for HMOs to qualify for tax-exempt status by arguing that insurance is only incidental to the provision of health care under Section 501(m).

Appendix A

Any Willing Provider, Freedom of Choice, Due Process, and Related Laws ("AWP")

Key to Information Contained in this Survey:

Law: Legal citation, including year enacted, and effective date, if pending.

Contact: Governmental entity responsible for enforcing law; phone number.

Type of Law: Is the law "any willing provider," "freedom of choice," "due process," or a combination?

Providers: What types or classes of providers are affected by the law?

Carriers: To what carriers does the law apply? HMOs, PPOs, all provider networks?

Notes: Other information necessary to understand the law, including recent legislative and regulatory activity.

Unless otherwise noted, we have used the following definitions.

Any Willing Provider (AWP)—Forces a health plan to accept any provider willing to meet the health plan's terms and conditions as a participating provider.

Freedom of Choice (FOC)—Permits plan members to seek care from non-participating providers. May prohibit financial incentives designed to promote use of participating providers.

Due Process (DP)—Places constraints on the process by which provider applications are accepted and considered.

ALABAMA

Law: Ala. Code § 27-45-5 (1988)
Contact: Department of Insurance (205) 269-3550
Type of Law: AWP/FOC
Providers: Pharmacy

Source: Reprinted with permission from *1995 State Managed Care Legislative Resource*, copyright 1994, American Managed Care and Review Association.

Carriers: PPOs
Law: 1994 Ala. Acts 638
Contact: See above
Type of Law: FOC
Providers: All health benefits, including medical, pharmacy, podiatric, chiropractic, optometric, durable medical equipment, and home care services.
Carriers: All
Notes: The law excludes state-administered health benefit plans.

ALASKA

Law: No AWP, FOC, DP or related laws have been enacted.
Contact: Department of Commerce and Economic Development Division of Insurance
                 (907) 349-1230
Notes: An AWP/FOC bill for dentists was defeated during the 1994 legislative session.

ARIZONA

Law: No AWP, FOC, DP or related laws have been enacted.
Contact: Department of Insurance
                 (602) 912-8420
Notes: A chiropractic FOC bill failed in 1994.

ARKANSAS

Law: Ark. Stat. Ann. § 23-79-114(b) (1993)
Contact: Insurance Department Life and Health Division
                 (501) 686-2900
Type of Law: FOC
Providers: Optometrist
Carriers: All, with the exception of federally qualified HMOs
Notes: The legislature did not convene for a regular session in 1994.

Law: Ark. Stat. Ann. § 23-79-143(c)(2) (1991)
Contact: See above
Type of Law: AWP/FOC
Providers: Pharmacy

Carriers: All, with the exception of federally qualified HMOs
Notes: This law is of interest because it was enacted during Bill Clinton's
                   tenure as Arkansas Governor.

CALIFORNIA

Law: Chapter 614, Acts of 1994 (SB 1832)
Contact: Department of Corporations
                   (213) 736-2741
                   Department of Insurance Legal Division
                   (415) 904-5665
Type of Law: FOC (emergency services only)/DP
Providers: All
Carriers: HMOs
Notes: Requires HMOs to reimburse any health care provider for
                   providing emergency care, even if the HMO member was able
                   to obtain care from a participating provider. Requires HMOs to
                   disclose the reasons for terminating a provider's contract if the
                   termination occurs during the contract year.

COLORADO

Law: No AWP, FOC, DP or related laws have been enacted.
Contact: Health Care Policy and Financing Dept.
                   (303) 866-5700
Notes: In 1994, Governor Roy Romer vetoed SB 98, a pharmacy FOC
                   bill. A task force was created to further explore the issue.

CONNECTICUT

Law: 1994 Conn. Acts 235 (Reg. Sess.)
Contact: Insurance Department
                   (203) 297-3800
                   Commission on Hospitals and Health Care
                   (203) 566-3880
Type of Law: DP
Providers: All
Carriers: All
Notes: Networks must file selection criteria with the Commission on
                   Hospitals and Health Care. They must also provide public
                   notice of the formation of a network.
Law: Conn. Gen. Stat. § 38a-471 (1982)
Contact: See above

Type of Law: AWP/DP
Providers: Pharmacy
Carriers: All third party prescription programs

DELAWARE

Law: Del. Code Ann., tit. 18, § 7301 (1994)
Contact: Insurance Department
                (302) 739-4251
Type of Law: AWP
Providers: Pharmacy
Carriers: All, with the exception of staff/group model HMOs.
Notes: Bill sunsets in 1997

Law: Del. Code Ann., tit. 24, § 717 (1993)
Contact: See above
Type of Law: FOC
Providers: Chiropractor
Carriers: All, with the exception of federally qualified HMOs
Notes: Entitles chiropractors to compensation for all services within
                their scope of practice.

DISTRICT OF COLUMBIA

Law: No AWP, FOC, DP or related laws have been enacted.
Contact: Insurance Administration
                (202) 727-8000
Notes: A broad "any willing provider" bill (10-299) is pending in the
                Consumer and Regulatory Affairs Committee.

FLORDIA

Law: Fla. Stat. Ann. § 408.76 (1993)
Contact: Department of Insurance
                (904) 922-3131
Type of Law: AWP (FOC for pharmacy only)
Providers: All
Carriers: All carriers participating as Accountable Health Plans (AHPs)
                in health alliances.
Notes: An AHP must open 60% of its available provider positions to
                providers willing to meet the AHP's terms and conditions.

                AWP was a privotal issue in attempts to pass further health care
                reform laws. Governor Lawton Chiles expressed his staunch

opposition to AWP. No AWP legislation was passed by the legislature in 1994.

GEORGIA

Law:	Ga. Code Ann. § 33-20-16 (1976)
	Ga. Code Ann. § 33-30-25 (1988)
Contact:	Office of the Insurance Commissioner
	(404) 656-2056
Type of Law:	AWP
Providers:	All
Carriers:	Insurer-based PPOs
Notes:	Law allows PPOs to place reasonable limits on the number and classes of participating providers. However, the law further states that all health care providers within a defined service area who are licensed and qualified to provide a covered benefit and who satisfy the standards set forth by an insurer shall be given the opportunity to become a participating provider.

AWP legislation that would have applied to all PPOs and HMOs failed in 1994.

HAWAII

Law:	No AWP, FOC, DP or related laws have been enacted.
Contact:	Health Planning and Development Agency
	(808) 587-0788
Notes:	An AWP bill failed in 1994.

IDAHO

Law:	Id. Code § 41-3937 (1994)
Contact:	Department of Insurance
	(208) 334-4220
Type of Law:	AWP/DP
Providers:	All
Carriers:	HMOs
Notes:	Requires carriers to admit "any willing provider"; requires written notice for provider contract termination; requires provider grievance system.

ILLINOIS

Law:	Ill. Rev. Stat. § 370h (1984)
Contact:	Department of Insurance
	(217) 782-4515

Type of Law: AWP/DP
Providers: All non-institutional providers
Carriers: PPOs (insurers and administrators)
Notes: Insurers and administrators must establish non-discriminatory terms that non-institutional providers must meet.

INDIANA

Law: Ind. Code Ann. § 27-8-11-3(b-c) (as amended by 1994 Ind. Acts 134)
Contact: Department of Insurance
                 (317) 232-2385
Type of Law: AWP/DP
Providers: All
Carriers: PPOs
Notes: Insurers must establish non-discriminatory terms that providers must meet to join the network. However, permits insurers to offer "closed-panel" networks to an employer as long as they also offer an "any willing provider" network.

                 1994 legislation also establishes a "preferred provider plan study committee," consisting of eight members of the General Assembly, to study and report on the impact on the AWP law by November 1, 1997.

IOWA

Law: No AWP, FOC, DP or related laws have been enacted.
Contact: Insurance Division
                 (515) 281-5705
Notes: AWP legislation failed in 1994.

KANSAS

Law: 1994 Kan. Sess. Laws 733
Contact: Insurance Department
                 (913) 296-3071
Type of Law: DP
Providers: Pharmacy
Carriers: All
Notes: Requires notice to Commissioner of the formation of a network. Plans must contract with at least one pharmacist in each county in the plan's service area, or within certain distances. Such

contracting is subject to the same terms and conditions for the plan's other pharmacy contracts.

KENTUCKY

Law: Ky. Rev. Stat. Ann. Ch. 304, Subtitle 17A (1994)
Contact: Department of Insurance
                (502) 564-6090
Type of Law: AWP
Providers: All
Carriers: All
Notes: This provision passed as part of 1994 health reform legislation, and is rather ambiguous. It does not say that health plans shall accept all willing providers, but rather that carriers *shall not discriminate* against providers willing to meet their terms and conditions.

LOUISIANA

Law: La. Rev. Stat. Ann. § 22:1214(15) (1992)
Contact: Department of Insurance
                (504) 342-5900
Type of Law: AWP/FOC
Providers: Pharmacy
Carriers: All
Law: La. Rev. Stat. Ann. § 40:2201 et seq. (1984)
Contact: Department of Insurance
                (504) 342-5900
Type of Law: AWP/FOC
Providers: All licensed providers, other than hospitals
Carriers: PPOs
Notes: The law states that it shall not be construed "to require any hospital to grant any provider or class of providers medical staff membership."

MAINE

Law: No AWP, FOC, DP or related laws have been enacted.
Contact: Bureau of Insurance
                (207) 582-8707
Notes: The legislature did not consider AWP this year.

MARYLAND

Law:	Md. Code Ann., Health-Gen. § 19-713.3 (1993)
Contact:	Insurance Administration
	(410) 333-6300
Type of Law:	DP
Providers:	Pharmacy
Carriers:	HMOs
Notes:	Requires HMOs to notify the Maryland Pharmacists Association of intent to contract for pharmacy services.
	Several broad AWP laws failed in 1994.

Law:	Md. Code Ann., Ins. § 354 (1988)
Contact:	See above
Type of Law:	FOC
Providers:	Pharmacy
Carriers:	Non-profit health service plan (Blue Cross Plans)

MASSACHUSETTS

Law:	1994 Mass. Acts 60, §§ 148, 149, 241
Contact:	Insurance Division
	(617) 521-7794
Type of Law:	AWP
Providers:	Pharmacy
Carriers:	All
Notes:	The AWP requirement was contained in the 1995 budget bill. Governor William Weld line-item vetoed the AWP provision. The legislature overrode his veto. Numerous other AWP bills were pending in 1994.

MICHIGAN

Law:	No AWP, FOC, DP or related laws have been enacted.
Contact:	Insurance Bureau
	(517) 373-9273
Notes:	Pending legislation (SB 590, 592) requires all carriers to have a sixty-day open-enrollment period prior to contracting for pharmacy or durable medical equipment services, during which providers may apply for inclusion in the network. Such open-enrollment must occur at least once every three years. Plans

must establish selection criteria and give providers reason for denial. Plans must assure reasonable levels of access to care.

MINNESOTA

Law:	1994 Minn. Laws 2927
Contact:	Health Department
	(612) 623-5000
Type of Law:	AWP
Providers:	Advanced practice nurse, audiologist, chiropractor, dietician, home health care provider, licensed marriage and family therapist, nurse practitioner, occupational therapist, optician, optometrist, outpatient chemical dependency counselor, pharmacist, physical therapist, podiatrist, licensed psychologist, psychological practitioner, licensed social worker, speech therapist.
Carriers:	All
Notes:	Part of 1994 Minnesota Care legislation.

MISSISSIPPI

Law:	Miss. Code Ann. § 41-83-3 (1994)
Contact:	Insurance Department
	(601) 359-3569
Type of Law:	AWP
Providers:	Pharmacy
Carriers:	All, with the exception of staff/group model HMOs

MISSOURI

Law:	No AWP, FOC, DP or related laws have been enacted.
Contact:	Department of Insurance
	(314) 751-1165
Notes:	AWP legislation failed in 1994.

MONTANA

Law:	Mont. Code Ann. § 33-22-1704, et seq.
Contact:	State Auditor's Office
	Insurance Department
	(406) 444-2006

Type of Law:	DP/FOC
Providers:	All
Carriers:	All
Notes:	Requires carriers to enter into preferred provider contracts using an RFP process, allowing all health providers to submit a bid. Law also addresses incentives for use of participating providers, and limits payment differential for out-of-network service to 25% of the reimbursement for in-network service.

AWP law was permitted to sunset in 1993.

The legislature did not convene for a regular session in 1994.

NEBRASKA

Law:	No AWP, FOC, DP or related laws have been enacted.
Contact:	Department of Insurance
	(402) 471-4610
Notes:	AWP legislation failed in 1994.

NEVADA

Law:	Nev. Rev. Stat. § 695C.176
Contact:	Commissioner of Insurance
	(702) 687-7690
Type of Law:	FOC
Providers:	Chiropractors, marriage/family therapists
Carriers:	HMOs
Notes:	The legislature did not convene for a regular session in 1994.

Law:	Nev. Rev. Stat. § 616.344 (1989)
Contact:	See above
Type of Law:	FOC
Providers:	Chiropractor, hospital, pharmacy, physical therapist, physician.
Carriers:	All insurers except HMOs.
Notes:	Applies only to workers' compensation.

NEW HAMPSHIRE

Law:	N.H. Rev. Stat. Ann. § 420-B:12(V) (1992)
Contact:	Insurance Department
	(603) 271-2261
Type of Law:	AWP
Providers:	Pharmacy

Carriers: HMOs
Notes: In 1994, Governor Stephen Merrill vetoed an "any willing mental health provider" bill (HB 1456). The veto was sustained by the legislature. Additionally, the legislature passed SB 539 (1994 N.H. Acts 164), which establishes a committee to study AWP and report its findings by November 1, 1994.

NEW JERSEY

Law: SB 886/AB 1221 (1994)
Contact: Department of Insurance
                (609) 292-5360
Type of Law: AWP/FOC
Providers: Pharmacy
Carriers: All
Notes: Other AWP/FOC bills are pending in 1994.

NEW MEXICO

Law: No AWP, FOC, DP or related laws have been enacted.
Contact: Department of Insurance
                (505) 827-4647
Notes: HMO Act requires HMOs to contract with at least one of several classes of providers.

NEW YORK

Law: No AWP, FOC, DP or related laws have been enacted.
Contact: Insurance Department
                (518) 474-6600

NORTH CAROLINA

Law: N.C. Gen. Stat. § 58-51-58 (1993)
Contact: Department of Insurance
                (919) 733-7343
Type of Law: AWP/FOC
Providers: Pharmacy

Carriers: All, with the exception of staff/group model HMOs.

NORTH DAKOTA

Law: N.D. Cent. Code § 26.1-36-12.2(1)(c) (1989)
Contact: Insurance Department
                  (701) 224-2440
Type of Law: AWP/FOC
Providers: Pharmacy
Carriers: PPOs
Notes: The legislature did not convene for a regular session in 1994.

OHIO

Law: No AWP, FOC, DP or related laws have been enacted.
Contact: Department of Insurance
                  Life and Health Services, Managed Care
                  (614) 644-2661
Notes: AWP legislation is pending in the state legislature.

OKLAHOMA

Law: Okla. Stat. tit. 36, § 3634 (1994)
Contact: Insurance Department
                  (405) 521-2828
Type of Law: AWP
Providers: All
Carriers: All

Law: Okla. Stat. tit. 36, § 3634 (1993)
Contact: See above
Type of Law: FOC
Providers: Certified clinical social worker, podiatric physician, psychologist
Carriers: All

OREGON

Law: Or. Rev. Stat. § 731 (1993)
Contact: Consumer and Business Services Dept.

	Insurance Division
	(503) 378-4271
Type of Law:	DP
Providers:	Pharmacy
Carriers:	All
Notes:	Requires notification to all pharmacies before the establishment of a network.

The legislature did not convene for a regular session in 1994.

PENNSYLVANIA

Law:	No AWP, FOC, DP or related laws have been enacted.
Contact:	Insurance Department
	(717) 787-5173
Notes:	AWP legislation is pending in 1994.

RHODE ISLAND

Law:	No AWP, FOC, DP or related laws have been enacted.
Contact:	Department of Business Regulation
	Insurance Division
	(401) 277-2223
Notes:	AWP legislation failed in 1994.

SOUTH CAROLINA

Law:	S.C. Code Ann. § 38-71-147 (HB 3631, 1994)
Contact:	Department of Insurance
	(803) 737-6160
Type of Law:	AWP/FOC
Providers:	Pharmacy
Carriers:	All

SOUTH DAKOTA

Law:	S.D. Codified Laws Ann. § 58-17-54 (1993)
Contact:	Division of Insurance
	(605) 773-3563

Type of Law: FOC
Providers: Chiropractor, dentist, independent social worker, nurse anes-
                 thesiologist, optometrist, osteopath, physician, podiatrist, psy-
                 chologist, surgeon
Carriers: All, with the exception of HMOs

Law: SD Code 58-18-37(1) (1990)
Contact: See above
Providers: Pharmacy
Carriers: HMOs/PPOs

TENNESSEE

Law: No AWP, FOC, DP or related laws have been enacted.
Contact: Department of Commerce and Insurance
                 (615) 741-4000
Notes: AWP and FOC legislation failed in 1994.

TEXAS

Law/Regulation: Tex. Admin. Code tit. 28 § 3.3701 et seq.
Contact: Department of Insurance
                 (512) 463-6169
Type of Law: FOC and DP
Providers: All providers are affected by FOC; only physicians are affected
                 by DP.
Carriers: PPOs
Notes: Two memoranda issued by the DOI in 1993 attempted to clarify
                 Texas's statute. They state that "an insurer may require provid-
                 ers to comply with terms and conditions of their contracts that go
                 beyond acceptance of a reduced fee. Such terms and conditions
                 may include "economic, quality and accessibility considerations."
                 These may include network adequacy considerations, i.e., pro-
                 vider vs. patient demographics. However, a provider must be
                 given a "fair, reasonable, and equivalent opportunity to become"
                 a preferred provider. If such designation is withheld relating to a
                 physician, "the insurer shall provide a review mechanism to
                 address the withholding." The memorandum goes on to describe
                 due process for physicians, including disclosure of selection
                 criteria and a review panel composed of at least three physicians.

                 The legislature did not convene for a regular session in 1994. An
                 interim study report on "any willing provider" is due prior to
                 the 1995 session.

Law: Tex. Admin. Code tit. 28 § 11.1402 (1991)
Contact: See above
Type of Law: DP
Providers: All
Carriers: HMOs
Notes: Requires a 20-day period each calendar year during which any provider in the service may apply to become a network provider.

UTAH

Law: Utah Code Ann. § 31A-22-617 (1985)
Contact: Department of Insurance
(801) 538-3802
Type of Law: AWP/DP
Providers: All
Carriers: PPOs
Notes: Insurers may place "reasonable limitations" on the number of participating providers.

Upon written request by a provider, the Insurance Commissioner may hold a hearing to determine if the exclusion of the provider was consistent with the law.

VERMONT

Law: No AWP, FOC, DP or related laws have been enacted.
Contact: Banking, Insurance, and Securities Dept.
(802) 828-3301
Notes: AWP and FOC legislation failed in 1994.

VIRGINIA

Law: Va. Code Ann. § 38.2-4312.1 and .2 (HB 840, 1994)
Contact: State Corporation Commission
Insurance Bureau
(804) 371-9278
Type of Law: FOC
Providers: Pharmacy and ancillary services (those services required to support, facilitate, or otherwise enhance medical care)

Carriers: All
Notes: After initial passage of HB 840, Governor Allen returned the bill
                to the legislature under the "reenactment clause," requiring the
                legislature to re-vote the bill. They voted in favor of the legisla-
                tion once again, and it was signed by Governor Allen.

Law: Va. Code Ann. § 38.2-4209(B-D) (1983)
Contact: See above
Type of Law: AWP
Providers: Audiologist, chiropodist, chiropractor, clinical nurse specialist,
                clinical social worker, hospital, optician, optometrist, physical
                therapist, physician, podiatrist, professional counselor, psy-
                chologist, speech pathologist
Carriers: PPOs

WASHINGTON

Law: 1993 Wash. Laws 492 (SB 5304)
Contact: Office of the Insurance Commissioner
                (206) 753-7300
                Health Services Commission
                (206) 407-4039
Notes: Rules to be established by state health services commission,
                pursuant to 1993 Washington Health Services Act.

WEST VIRGINIA

Law: No AWP, FOC, or DP laws have been enacted.
Contact: Office of the Insurance Commissioner
                (304) 558-3354

WISCONSIN

Law: Wis. Stat. Ann. § 628.36 (1989)
Contact: Office of the Commissioner of Insurance
                (608) 266-3585
Type of Law: AWP
Providers: Pharmacy
Carriers: PPOs/HMOs
Notes: Provides for 30-day annual "open enrollment" period during
                which a pharmacist may elect to participate as a preferred
                provider.

WYOMING

Law: Wyo. Stat. § 26-22-503(a)(1) (1993)
Contact: Insurance Department
(307) 777-7401
Type of Law: AWP/FOC/DP
Providers: All Wyoming providers
Carriers: HMOs/PPOs
Notes: Permits enrollees to select any Wyoming provider, rather than go out of state to receive similar services.

Additionally requires any willing Wyoming provider be admitted to networks. Requires health plans to establish terms for participation in networks. The terms may not discriminate against Wyoming providers.

Appendix B ———————————————

Preferred Provider Arrangements Model Act

TABLE OF CONTENTS

SECTION 1. SHORT TITLE

This act shall be known and may be cited as the Preferred Provider Arrangements Act.

SECTION 2. PURPOSE

The purpose of this Act is to encourage health care cost containment while preserving quality of care by allowing health care insurers to enter into preferred provider arrangements and by establishing minimum standards for preferred provider arrangements and the health benefit plans associated with those arrangements.

Source: Reprinted with permission of The National Association of Insurance Commissioners, copyright 1987, NAIC.

269

Drafting Note: The use of the term "allowing" in this section is not intended to indicate that health care insurers are acting unlawfully in a state which has not enacted a law allowing Preferred Provider Arrangements.

SECTION 3. DEFINITIONS

The following words and phrases when used in this Act shall have the meanings given to them in this section unless the context clearly indicates otherwise:

A. Commissioner—The Insurance Commissioner of the State of _____.

B. Covered Person—Any person on whose behalf the health care insurer is obligated to pay for or provide health care services.

C. Covered Services—Health care services which the health care insurer is obligated to pay for or provide under the Health Benefit Plan.

D. Emergency Care—Covered services delivered to a covered person who has suffered an accidental bodily injury or contracted a medical condition which reasonably requires the beneficiary or insured to seek immediate medical care under circumstances or at locations which reasonably preclude the beneficiary or insured from obtaining needed medical care from a preferred provider.

E. Health Benefit Plan—The health insurance policy or subscriber agreement between the covered person or the policyholder and the health care insurer which defines the covered services and benefit levels available.

F. Health Care Insurer—An insurance company as defined in _____ , a hospital plan corporation as defined in _____ , a health services plan corporation as defined in _____ , a health maintenance organization as defined in _____ , or a fraternal benefit society as defined in _____ .

Drafting Note: This definition may need to be modified to conform to the state's service plan enabling statutes.

G. Health Care Provider—Providers of health care services licensed as required in this State.

H. Health Care Services—Services rendered or products sold by a health care provider within the scope of the provider's license. The term includes, but is not limted to, hospital, medical, surgical, dental, vision, and pharmaceutical services or products.

I. Preferred Provider—A health care provider or group of providers who have contracted to provide specified covered services.

J. Preferred Provider Arrangement—A contract between or on behalf of the health care insurer and a preferred provider which complies with all the requirements of this Act.

SECTION 4. PREFERRED PROVIDER ARRANGEMENTS

Notwithstanding any provisions of law to the contrary, any health care insurer may enter into Preferred Provider Arrangements.

A. Such arrangements shall:

(1) Establish the amount and manner of payment to the preferred provider. Such amount and manner of payment may include capitation payments for preferred providers.

(2) Include mechanisms which are designed to minimize the cost of the health benefit plan. These mechanisms may include among others:

(a) The review or control of utilization of health care services.

(b) A procedure for determining whether health care services rendered are medically necessary.

(3) Assure reasonable access to covered services available under the Preferred Provider Arrangement and an adequate number of preferred providers to render those services.

B. Such arrangements shall not unfairly deny health benefits for medically necessary covered services.

C. If an entity enters into a contract providing covered services with a health care provider, but is not engaged in activities which would require it to be licensed as a health care insurer, such entity shall file with the Insurance Commissioner information describing its activities and a description of the contract or agreement it has entered into with the health care providers. Employers who enter into contracts with health care providers for the exclusive benefit of their employees and dependents are exempt from this requirement.

Drafting Note: Section 4C is an optional section if a state desires to require verification of PPO activity of non-insurance entities.

SECTION 5. HEALTH BENEFIT PLANS

A. Health care insurers may issue health benefit plans which provide for incentives for covered persons to use the health care services or preferred providers. Such policies or subscriber agreements shall contain at least the following provisions:

(1) A provision that if a covered person receives emergency care for services specified in the Preferred Provider Arrangement and cannot reasonably reach a preferred provider that emergency care rendered during the course of the emergency will be reim-

bursed as though the covered person had been treated by a preferred provider; and

(2) A provision which clearly identifies the differentials in benefit levels for health care services of preferred providers and benefit levels for health care services of non-preferred providers.

B. If a health benefit plan provides differences in benefit levels payable to preferred providers compared to other providers, such differences shall not unfairly deny payment for covered services and shall be no greater than necessary to provide a reasonable incentive for covered persons to use the preferred provider.

SECTION 6. PREFERRED PROVIDER PARTICIPATION REQUIREMENTS

Health care insurers may place reasonable limits on the number or classes of preferred providers which satisfy the standards set forth by the health care insurer, provided that there be no discrimination against providers on the basis of religion, race, color, national origin, age, sex or marital status, and further provided that selection of preferred providers is primarily based on, but not limited to, cost and availability of covered services and the quality of services performed by the providers.

Drafting Notes:

Categories of Discrimination—Individual states may wish to add protected classes in accordance with state laws or policies.

Quality of Services—The statement of a quality criterion as used in this section is not intended to create any higher standard of care for delivery of services by a preferred provider than is appropriate for other health care providers.

SECTION 7. GENERAL REQUIREMENTS

Health care insurers complying with this Act shall be subject to and are required to comply with all other applicable laws, rules and regulations of this State.

SECTION 8. REGULATIONS

The Commissioner may promulgate regulations necessary to the enforcement and administration of this Act.

SECTION 9. SEVERABILITY

If any provision of this Act is declared invalid or unenforceable by a court of competent jurisdiction, the remaining provisions which are severable from the invalid provisions shall remain in force and effect.

Drafting Note: If a state elects to permit exclusive provider arrangements, the following section should be added to the Act:

Notwithstanding any other provision of this Act, health care insurers may issue policies or subscriber agreements which provide benefits for health care services only if the services have been rendered by a preferred provider, provided the program has met all standards imposed by the Commissioner for availability and adequacy of covered services.

Legislative History (all references are to the *Proceedings of the NAIC*). 1987 Proc. I (adopted).

Appendix C _____

Health Maintenance Organization Model Act

TABLE OF CONTENTS

Source: Reprinted with permission of The National Association of Insurance Commissioners, copyright 1993, NAIC.

SECTION 1. SHORT TITLE

This Act may be cited as the Health Maintenance Organization Act of [insert year].

Introductory Comment:
Nature of the Health Maintenance Organization

A health maintenance organization may be described as an organization which brings together a comprehensive range of medical services in a single organization to assure a patient of convenient access to health care services. It furnishes needed services for a prepaid fixed fee paid by or on behalf of the enrollees. An HMO can be organized, operated and financed in a variety of ways. For example, an HMO may be organized by physicians, hospitals, community groups, labor unions, government units, insurance companies, etc. Generally speaking, an HMO delivery system is predicated on three principles: (1) It is an organized system for the delivery of health care which brings together health care providers; (2) Such an arrangement makes available basic health care which the enrolled group might reasonably require, including emphasis on the prevention of illness or disability; (3) The payments will be made on a prepayment basis, whether by the individual enrollees, Medicare, Medicaid, or through employer-employee arrangements.

How might the HMO concept contribute to alleviating the difficulties posed by the current health care delivery system?

An HMO can directly address itself to the problems of availability, accessibility and continuity, since it is a health care delivery system. It assumes responsibility for actually furnishing to its enrollees those health care services necessary to meet the obligations it undertakes. Thus the HMO occupies a position through which both the accessibility and continuity of care may be affected.

An HMO, by its very nature, may provide incentives toward lessening costs in delivering health care. It has a limited membership prepaying fixed sums of money. The providers are obligated to deliver a specified set of health care services. The fixed amount of income provides incentive to control expenses and costs. The HMO provides a mechanism to analyze costs, expenses and utilization of services, and affords a means to implement measures to enhance efficiency.

The problem of the quality of health care is not susceptible to an easy solution. An HMO is in a position to assess the quality of care provided since it is a closed system. It can study the health of its members, review the records of treatment and, in general, provide a monitoring mechanism.

The Need for State Authorizing and Regulatory Legislation

From 1970 to 1973, the administration and committees in both houses of Congress spent much time analyzing the health maintenance organization alternative in connection with national health insurance and federal assistance bills for HMOs. This analysis resulted in the enactment of the federal HMO Act in 1973. Since then, the number of health maintenance organizations and the number of HMO enrollees has grown rapidly. Prior to 1972, however, few states had a statutory framework tailored to the supervision of health maintenance organizations. Chartering, licensing, contract and rate regulation, and other supervision were being carried out under general insurance laws, hospital and medical service corporation statutes, other special statutes, or not at all. Because the HMO is a unique type of organization, many provisions of such state laws were inapplicable, highly restrictive or prohibitive to the formation and operation of an HMO. Therefore, in 1972 the NAIC adopted the Model Health Maintenance Organization Act which accommodates the unique features of HMOs.

Purpose of a State Model Bill

The model bill clearly authorizes the establishment and operation of HMOs. Restrictive provisions in other laws which are inappropriate to HMOs are rendered inapplicable. Appropriate grants of authority are established to enable the HMOs to fulfill the function envisioned for them. At the same time, however, the public has a vital interest in the fiscally sound, efficient and ethical operation of HMOs. As is the case with insurance and hospital and medical service corporations, HMOs are "affected with the public interest." Regulatory safeguards dovetailed to the unique nature of HMOs are essential. Thus, the purpose of this model bill is twofold.

First, it attempts to provide a legal framework enabling the organization and functioning of HMOs of a wide variety including those based upon the medical care foundation or individual practice association concept. The legal environment is designed to permit a high degree of flexibility. No one form of organization or one type of modus operandi is required. Instead the HMO concept can be refined and subjected to further experimentation. Second, the model bill attempts to provide a regulatory monitoring system not only to prevent or remedy abuse, but also to assist in the future improvement and development of this alternative form of a health care delivery system.

Of course, it is also possible that the statutes of a given state are presently broad enough to allow operation of at least certain types of HMOs and provide the commissioner with appropriate authority to regulate them. In those states, a bill such as this may be desirable in order to consolidate and define more clearly the authority for and manner of regulation of an HMO. However, it may be possible to form HMOs under existing laws in some states before passage of this model legislation and it is anticipated that such programs can develop concurrently with any legislative activity.

The model, or substantial portions of it, has been enacted in 27 states and substantial experience has been gained in implementing and regulating HMOs under its terms. In addition, as HMOs have become insolvent and commissioners have had to deal with the results of those insolvencies, the model act has been revised to reflect changes which have occurred in the federal law, to reflect experience gained in administering of the law, and to clarify and strengthen the provisions relating to HMO solvency.

It may be necessary to modify or replace certain language in the model bill prior to legislative consideration to make terminology consistent with existing law in a particular state. To simplify this adjustment, three frequently used terms known to be subject to variation from state to state are enclosed in brackets wherever used in order to facilitate necessary modification. These terms are: (1) commissioner, whose counterparts in some states are known as director or superintendent; (2) commissioner of public health, whose counterparts in other states are known as directors of public health or by some other title; and (3) hospital or medical service corporations, whose counterparts in other states may be known as health service corporations, hospital indemnity corporations, etc. Where specific reference to existing state laws is required, the nature of the citation is indicated in brackets.

The model bill provides that the principal regulator is the commissioner of insurance. It may be desirable for the commissioner to have an advisory council to advise him in carrying out his duties under the Act. Such an advisory council could be established through the promulgation of a regulation pursuant to Section 23 of the model bill or by adding a new section to the model bill.

SECTION 2. DEFINITIONS

A. "Basic health care services" means the following medically necessary services: preventive care, emergency care, inpatient and outpatient hospital and physician care, diagnostic laboratory and diagnostic and therapeutic radiological services. It does not include mental health services or services for alcohol or drug abuse, dental or vision services or long-term rehabilitation treatment.

B. "Capitated basis" means fixed per member per month payment or percentage of premium payment wherein the provider assumes the full risk for the cost of contracted services without regard to the type, value or frequency of services provided. For purposes of this definition, capitated basis includes the cost associated with operating staff model facilities.

C. "Carrier" shall mean a health maintenance organization, an insurer, a nonprofit hospital and medical service corporation, or other entity responsible for the payment of benefits or provision of services under a group contract.

D. "Commissioner" [director, superintendent] means the commissioner [director, superintendent] of insurance.

E. "Copayment" means an amount an enrollee must pay in order to receive a specific service which is not fully prepaid.

F. "Deductible" means the amount an enrollee is responsible to pay out-of-pocket before the health maintenance organization begins to pay the costs associated with treatment.

G. "Enrollee" means an individual who is covered by a health maintenance organization.

H. "Evidence of coverage" means a statement of the essential features and services of the health maintenance organization coverage which is given to the subscriber by the health maintenance organization or by the group contract holder.

I. "Extension of benefits" shall mean the continuation of coverage under a particular benefit provided under a contract following termination with respect to an enrollee who is totally disabled on the date of termination.

J. "Grievance" means a written complaint submitted in accordance with the health maintenance organization's formal grievance procedure by or on behalf of the enrollee regarding any aspect of the health maintenance organization relative to the enrollee.

K. "Group contract" means a contract for health care services which by its terms limits eligibility to members of a specified group. The group contract may include coverage for dependents.

L. "Group contract holder" means the person to which a group contract has been issued.

M. "Health maintenance organization" means any person that undertakes to provide or arrange for the delivery of basic health care services to enrollees on a prepaid basis, except for enrollee responsibility for copayments and/or deductibles.

N. "Health maintenance organization producer" means a person who solicits, negotiates, effects, procures, delivers, renews or continues a policy or contract for HMO membership, or who takes or transmits a membership fee or premium for such a policy or contract, other than for himself, or a person who advertises or otherwise holds himself out to the public as such.

O. "Individual contract" means a contract for health care services issued to and covering an individual. The individual contract may include dependents of the subscriber.

P. "Insolvent" or "insolvency" shall mean that the organization has been declared insolvent and placed under an order of liquidation by a court of competent jurisdiction.

Q. "Managed hospital payment basis" means agreements wherein the financial risk is primarily related to the degree of utilization rather than to the cost of services.

Comment: Examples of Subsection Q agreements include but are not limited to payments on a DRG or per diem basis or where there is an agreement between a hospital and health maintenance organization and which are under common ownership or control.

R. "Net worth" means the excess of total admitted assets over total liabilities, but the liabilities shall not include fully subordinated debt.

S. "Participating provider" means a provider as defined in U below who, under an express or implied contract with the health maintenance organization or with its contractor or subcontractor, has agreed to provide health care services to enrollees with an expectation of receiving payment, other than copayment or deductible, directly or indirectly from the health maintenance organization.

T. "Person" means any natural or artificial person including but not limited to individuals, partnerships, associations, trusts or corporations.

U. "Provider" means any physician, hospital or other person licensed or otherwise authorized to furnish health care services.

V. "Replacement coverage" shall mean the benefits provided by a succeeding carrier.

W. "Subscriber" means an individual whose employment or other status, except family dependency, is the basis for eligibility for enrollment in the health maintenance organization, or in the case of an individual contract, the person in whose name the contract is issued.

X. "Uncovered expenditures" means the costs to the health maintenance organization for health care services that are the obligation of the health maintenance organization, for which an enrollee may also be liable in the event of the health maintenance organization's insolvency and for which no alternative arrangements have been made that are acceptable to the commissioner [director, superintendent].

Comment: Subsection X defines uncovered expenditures for use in Section 13. They will vary in type and amount, depending on the arrangements of the HMO. They may include out-of-area services, referral services and hospital services. They do not include expenditures for services when a provider has agreed not to bill the enrollee even though the provider is not paid by the HMO, or for services that are guaranteed, insured or assumed by a person or organization other than the health maintenance organization.

SECTION 3. ESTABLISHMENT OF HEALTH MAINTENANCE ORGANIZATIONS

A. Notwithstanding any law of this state to the contrary, any person may apply to the commissioner [director, superintendent] for a certificate of authority to establish and operate a health maintenance organization in compliance with this Act. No person shall establish or operate a health maintenance organization in this state, without obtaining a certificate of authority under this Act. A foreign corporation may qualify under this Act, subject to its registration to do business in this state as a foreign corporation under [insert citation] and compliance with all provisions of this Act and other applicable state laws.

B. Any health maintenance organization which has not previously received a certificate of authority to operate as a health maintenance organization as of the effective date of this Act shall submit an application for a certificate of authority under Subsection C within [insert number] days of the effective date of this Act. Each such applicant may continue to operate until the commissioner [director, superintendent] acts upon the application. In the event that an application is denied under Section 4, the applicant shall thereafter be treated as a health maintenance organization whose certificate of authority has been revoked.

C. Each application for a certificate of authority shall be verified by an officer or authorized representative of the applicant, shall be in a form prescribed by the commissioner [director, superintendent], and shall set forth or be accompanied by the following:

(1) A copy of the organizational documents of the applicant, such as the articles of incorporation, articles of association, partnership agreement, trust agreement, or other applicable documents, and all amendments thereto;

(2) A copy of the bylaws, rules and regulations, or similar document, if any, regulating the conduct of the internal affairs of the applicant;

(3) A list of the names, addresses and official positions and biographical information on forms acceptable to the commissioner [director, superintendent] of the persons who are to be responsible for the conduct of the affairs and day to day operations of the applicant, including all members of the board of directors, board of trustees, executive committee or other governing board or committee and the principal officers in the case of a corporation, or the partners or members in the case of a partnership or association;

Comment: NAIC biographical forms are recommended.

(4) A copy of any contract form made or to be made between any class of providers and the health maintenance organization and a copy of any contract made or to be made between third party administrators, marketing consultants or persons listed in Paragraph (3) and the health maintenance organization;

(5) A copy of the form of evidence of coverage to be issued to the enrollees;

(6) A copy of the form of group contract, if any, which is to be issued to employers, unions, trustees or other organizations;

(7) Financial statements showing the applicant's assets, liabilities and sources of financial support. Include both a copy of the applicant's most recent (regular) certified financial statement and an unaudited current financial statement;

(8) A financial feasibility plan which includes detailed enrollment projections, the methodology for determining premium rates to be charged during the first twelve months of operations certified by an actuary or other qualified person, a projection of balance sheets, cash flow statements showing any capital expenditures, purchase and sale of investments and deposits with the state, and income and expense statements anticipated from the start of operations until the organization has had net income for at least one year, and a statement as to the sources of working capital as well as any other sources of funding;

(9) A power of attorney duly executed by such applicant, if not domiciled in this state, appointing the commissioner [director, superintendent] and his successors in office, and duly authorized deputies, as the true and lawful attorney of such applicant in and for this state upon whom all lawful process in any legal action or proceeding against the health maintenance organization on a cause of action arising in this state may be served;

(10) A statement or map reasonably describing the geographic area or areas to be served;

(11) A description of the internal grievance procedures to be utilized for the investigation and resolution of enrollee complaints and grievances;

(12) A description of the proposed quality assurance program, including the formal organizational structure, methods for developing criteria, procedures for comprehensive evaluation of the quality of care rendered to enrollees, and processes to initiate corrective action and reevaluation when deficiencies in provider or organizational performance are identified;

(13) A description of the procedures to be implemented to meet the protection against insolvency requirements in Section 13;

(14) A list of the names, addresses, and license numbers of all providers with which the health maintenance organization has agreements;

(15) Such other information as the commissioner [director, superintendent] may require to make the determination required in Section 4.

D. (1) The commissioner [director, superintendent] may promulgate such rules and regulations as he deems necessary to the proper administration of this Act to require a health maintenance organization, subsequent to receiving its certificate of authority to submit the information, modifications or amendments to the items described in Subsection C of this section to the commissioner [director, superintendent], either for his approval or for information only, prior to the effectuation of the modification or amendment, or to require the health maintenance organization to indicate the modifications to both [the commissioner of public health] and the commissioner [director, superintendent] at the time of the next succeeding site visit or examination.

   (2) Any modification or amendment for which the commissioner's [director's, superintendent's] approval is required shall be deemed approved unless disapproved within thirty (30) days, provided that the commissioner [director, superintendent] may postpone the action for such further time, not exceeding an additional thirty (30) days, as necessary for proper consideration.

Comment: Section 3 requires the licensing of an HMO in order to provide health care services on a prepaid basis. The legal entity in which the responsibilities imposed by this Act are vested, serves as the focus of regulatory attention to assure that the consuming public is well served.

Subsection A is intended to provide a general override to existing state laws which restrict or prevent the formation or operation of health maintenance organizations. Among other restrictions, existing state laws may:

(1) Require approval of a health maintenance organization by a medical society;

(2) Require that physicians constitute all or a majority of the governing body of a health maintenance organization;

(3) Require that all physicians or a percentage of physicians in the local medical society be permitted to participate in rendering the services of the organization.

(4) Require that such organization submit to regulation as an insurer of health care services;

(5) Require that only unincorporated individuals or associations or partnerships may provide health care services;

(6) Prohibit advertising by a professional group for recruitment of enrollees.

In addition to the general override provided in Subsection A, Section 26 specifically provides that the insurance law, the hospital and medical service corporation law and certain other provisions do not apply to HMOs.

It is assumed that, restrictive provisions of state law having been overcome, the "person" making application for a certificate of authority, if not an individual, will be created through existing state mechanisms such as the applicable non-profit corporation act, business corporation act, etc. as appropriate. Since state laws generally establish detailed procedures related to business organizations, inclusion of organizational procedures in a model act of this nature would appear unnecessary. A business having incorporated under the law of a foreign state could qualify under this act after following appropriate state procedures required of foreign corporation seeking to do business in the state.

SECTION 4. ISSUANCE OF CERTIFICATE OF AUTHORITY

A. (1) Upon receipt of an application for issuance of a certificate of authority, the commissioner [director, superintendent] shall forthwith transmit copies of such application and accompanying documents to the [commissioner of public health].

(2) The [commissioner of public health] shall determine whether the applicant for a certificate of authority, with respect to health care services to be furnished has complied with Section 7 of this Act.

(3) Within forty-five (45) days of receipt of the application for issuance of a certificate of authority, the [commissioner of public health] shall certify to the commissioner [director, superintendent] that the proposed health maintenance organization meets the requirements of Section 7 or notify the commissioner [director, superintendent] that the health maintenance organization does not meet such requirements and specify in what respects it is deficient.

B. The commissioner [director, superintendent] shall within forty-five (45) days of receipt of certification or notice of deficiencies from the [commissioner of public health] issue a certificate of authority to any person filing a completed application upon receiving the prescribed fees and upon the commissioner [director, superintendent] being satisfied that:

(1) The persons responsible for the conduct of the affairs of the applicant are competent, trustworthy and possess good reputations;

(2) Any deficiencies identified by the [commissioner of public health] have been corrected and the [commissioner of public health] has certified to the commissioner [director, superintendent] that the health maintenance organization's proposed plan of operation meets the requirements of Section 7;

(3) The health maintenance organization will effectively provide or arrange for the provision of basic health care services on a prepaid basis, through insurance or otherwise, except to the extent of reasonable requirements for copayments and/or deductibles; and

(4) The health maintenance organization is in compliance with Sections 13 and 15 of this Act.

C. A certificate of authority shall be denied only after the commissioner [director, superintendent] complies with the requirements of Section 20.

Comment: A health maintenance organization combines several characteristics of an insurance operation (including the need for financial responsibility, the assumption of risk and similarity in marketing activities) with the characteristics of a health care delivery system. Section 4 provides for the authorization and regulation of health maintenance organizations to be carried out through existing state agencies. The creation of a new agency specifically for health maintenance organizations would unnecessarily duplicate existing functions in the state insurance and health departments. It is felt that the expertise of the state insurance department on fiscal and other regulatory matters and the familiarity of the state health department with regard to health matters should both be utilized in the regulation of health maintenance organizations. To minimize administrative problems, the prime responsibility for administration is vested in one agency— the insurance department. However, to the extent possible, the responsibilities of the two agencies are clearly defined with the insurance commissioner obligated to rely on the health department with respect to the latter's sphere of expertise.

Comment: Subsection B(3) makes explicit the requirement that a health maintenance organization must provide a minimum package of services on a prepaid basis. Reasonable copayments, however, are permitted and do not violate the requirement for prepayment. Such copayments may be used to (1) reduce the amount of prepayments and (2) minimize frivolous utilization of services. In addition, a health maintenance organization may have more than one benefit package involving different levels of copayments.

SECTION 5. POWERS OF HEALTH MAINTENANCE ORGANIZATIONS

A. The powers of a health maintenance organization include, but are not limited to, the following:

(1) The purchase, lease, construction, renovation, operation or maintenance of hospitals, medical facilities, or both, and their ancillary equipment, and such property as may reasonably be required for its principal office or for such purposes as may be necessary in the transaction of the business of the organization;

(2) Transactions between affiliated entities, including loans and the transfer of responsibility under all contracts (provider, subscriber, etc.) between affiliates or between the health maintenance organization and its parent;

(3) The furnishing of health care services through providers, provider associations or agents for providers which are under contract with or employed by the health maintenance organization;

(4) The contracting with any person for the performance on its behalf of certain functions such as marketing, enrollment and administration;

(5) The contracting with an insurance company licensed in this state, or with a hospital or medical service corporation authorized to do business in this state, for the provision of insurance, indemnity or reimbursement against the cost of health care services provided by the health maintenance organization;

(6) The offering of other health care services, in addition to basic health care services. Non-basic health care services may be offered by a health maintenance organization on a prepaid basis without offering basic health care services to any group or individual;

(7) The joint marketing of products with an insurance company licensed in this state or with a hospital or medical service corporation authorized to do business in this state as long as the company that is offering each product is clearly identified.

B. (1) A health maintenance organization shall file notice, with adequate supporting information, with the commissioner [director, superintendent] prior to the exercise of any power granted in Subsections A(1), (2) or (4) which may affect the financial soundness of the health maintenance organization. The commissioner [director, superintendent] shall disapprove such exercise of power only if in his opinion it would substantially and adversely affect the financial soundness of the health maintenance organization and endanger its ability to meet its obligations. If the commissioner [director, superintendent] does not disapprove within thirty (30) days of the filing, it shall be deemed approved.

(2) The commissioner [director, superintendent] may promulgate rules and regulations exempting from the filing requirement of Paragraph (1) those activities having a *de minimis* effect.

SECTION 6. FIDUCIARY RESPONSIBILITIES

A. Any director, officer, employee or partner of a health maintenance organization who receives, collects, disburses or invests funds in connection with the activities of such organization shall be responsible for such funds in a fiduciary relationship to the organization.

B. A health maintenance organization shall maintain in force a fidelity bond or fidelity insurance on such employees and officers, directors and partners in an amount not less than $250,000 for each health maintenance organization or a maximum of $5,000,000 in aggregate maintained on behalf of health maintenance organizations owned by a common parent corporation, or such sum as may be prescribed by the commissioner [director, superintendent].

Comment: As an optional additional subsection, language may be included that would make the appropriate provisions of the state's insurance laws governing prohibitions or restrictions on activities of directors, officers and certain shareholders applicable to health maintenance organizations.

SECTION 7. QUALITY ASSURANCE PROGRAM

A. The health maintenance organization shall establish procedures to assure that the health care services provided to enrollees shall be rendered under reasonable standards of quality of care consistent with prevailing professionally recognized standards of medical practice. Such procedures shall include mechanisms to assure availability, accessibility and continuity of care.

B. The health maintenance organization shall have an ongoing internal quality assurance program to monitor and evaluate its health care services, including primary and specialist physician services, and ancillary and preventive health care services, across all institutional and non-institutional settings. The program shall include, at a minimum, the following:

(1) A written statement of goals and objectives which emphasizes improved health status in evaluating the quality of care rendered to enrollees;

(2) A written quality assurance plan which describes the following:

(a) The health maintenance organization's scope and purpose in quality assurance;

(b) The organizational structure responsible for quality assurance activities;

(c) Contractual arrangements, where appropriate, for delegation of quality assurance activities;

(d) Confidentiality policies and procedures;

(e) A system of ongoing evaluation activities;

(f) A system of focused evaluation activities;

(g) A system for credentialing providers and performing peer review activities; and

(h) Duties and responsibilities of the designated physician responsible for the quality assurance activities;

(3) A written statement describing the system of ongoing quality assurance activities including:

(a) Problem assessment, identification, selection and study;

(b) Corrective action, monitoring, evaluation and reassessment; and

(c) Interpretation and analysis of patterns of care rendered to individual patients by individual providers;

(4) A written statement describing the system of focused quality assurance activities based on representative samples of the enrolled population which identifies method of topic selection, study, data collection, analysis, interpretation and report format; and

(5) Written plans for taking appropriate corrective action whenever, as determined by the quality assurance program, inappropriate or substandard services have been provided or services which should have been furnished have not been provided.

C. The organization shall record proceedings of formal quality assurance program activities and maintain documentation in a confidential manner. Quality assurance program minutes shall be available to the [commissioner of public health].

D. The organization shall ensure the use and maintenance of an adequate patient record system which will facilitate documentation and retrieval of clinical information for the purpose of the health maintenance organization evaluating continuity and coordination of patient care and assessing the quality of health and medical care provided to enrollees.

E. Enrollee clinical records shall be available to the [commission of public health] or an authorized designee for examination and review to ascertain compliance with this section, or as deemed necessary by the [commissioner of public health].

F. The organization shall establish a mechanism for periodic reporting of quality assurance program activities to the governing body, providers and appropriate organization staff.

SECTION 8. REQUIREMENTS FOR GROUP CONTRACT, INDIVIDUAL CONTRACT, AND EVIDENCE OF COVERAGE

A. (1) Every group and individual contract holder is entitled to a group or individual contract.

    (2) The contract shall not contain provisions or statements which are unjust, unfair, inequitable, misleading, deceptive, or which encourage misrepresentation as defined by [cite section of state law which implements the NAIC Unfair Trade Practices Act];

    (3) The contract shall contain a clear statement of the following:

       (a) Name and address of the health maintenance organization;

       (b) Eligibility requirements;

       (c) Benefits and services within the service area;

       (d) Emergency care benefits and services;

       (e) Out of area benefits and services (if any);

       (f) Copayments, deductibles or other out-of-pocket expenses;

       (g) Limitations and exclusions;

       (h) Enrollee termination;

       (i) Enrollee reinstatement (if any);

       (j) Claims procedures;

       (k) Enrollee grievance procedures;

       (l) Continuation of coverage;

       (m) Conversion;

       (n) Extension of benefits (if any);

       (o) Coordination of benefits (if applicable);

       (p) Subrogation (if any);

       (q) Description of the service area;

       (r) Entire contract provision;

       (s) Term of coverage;

       (t) Cancellation of group or individual contract holder;

       (u) Renewal;

       (v) Reinstatement of group or individual contract holder (if any);

       (w) Grace period; and

       (x) Conformity with state law.

An evidence of coverage may be filed as part of the group contract to describe the provisions required in Paragraphs (3)(a) to (q) of this subsection.

B. In addition to those provisions required in Subsection A(3)(a) to (x), an individual contract shall provide for a ten-day period to examine and return the contract and have the premium refunded. If services were received during the ten-day period, and the person returns the contract to receive a refund of the premium paid, he or she must pay for such services.

C. (1) Every subscriber shall receive an evidence of coverage from the group contract holder or the health maintenance organization.

(2) The evidence of coverage shall not contain provisions or statements which are unfair, unjust, inequitable, misleading, deceptive, or which encourage misrepresentation as defined by [cite section of state law which implements the NAIC Unfair Trade Practices Act].

(3) The evidence of coverage shall contain a clear statement of the provisions required in Subsection A(3)(a) to (q).

D. The commissioner [director, superintendent] may adopt regulations establishing readability standards for individual contract, group contract, and evidence of coverage forms.

Comment: The commissioner [director, superintendent] may adopt standards provided for in the NAIC "Life and Health Insurance Policy Language Simplification Act."

E. No group or individual contract, evidence of coverage or amendment thereto, shall be delivered or issued for delivery in this state, unless its form has been filed with and approved by the commissioner [director, superintendent], subject to Subsection F and G of this section.

F. If an evidence of coverage issued pursuant to and incorporated in a contract issued in this state is intended for delivery in another state and the evidence of coverage has been approved for use in the state in which it is to be delivered, the evidence of coverage need not be submitted to the commissioner [director, superintendent] of this state for approval.

G. Every form required by Section 8 shall be filed with the commissioner [director, superintendent] not less than thirty (30) days prior to delivery or issue for delivery in this state. At any time during the initial thirty (30) day period, the commissioner [director, superintendent] may extend the period for review for an additional thirty (30) days. Notice of an extension shall be in writing. At the end of the review period, the form is deemed approved if the commissioner [director, superintendent] has taken no action. The filer must notify the commissioner [director, superintendent] in writing prior to using a form that is deemed approved.

At any time, after thirty (30) days notice and for cause shown, the commissioner [director, superintendent] may withdraw approval of any form, effective at the end of the thirty (30) days.

When a filing is disapproved or approval of a form is withdrawn, the commissioner [director, superintendent] shall give the health maintenance organization written notice of the reasons for disapproval and in the notice shall inform the health maintenance organization that within thirty (30) days of receipt of the notice the health maintenance organization may request a hearing. A hearing will be conducted within thirty (30) days after the commissioner [director, superintendent] has received the request for hearing.

H. The commissioner [director, superintendent] may require the submission of whatever relevant information he deems necessary in determining whether to approve or disapprove a filing made pursuant to this section.

SECTION 9. ANNUAL REPORT

A. Every health maintenance organization shall annually, on or before the first day of March, file a report verified by at least two principal officers with the commissioner [director, superintendent], with a copy to the [commissioner of public health] covering the preceding calendar year. Such report shall be on forms prescribed by the commissioner [director, superintendent]. In addition, the health maintenance organization shall file by the first day of March, unless otherwise stated:

(1) Audited financial statements on or before June 1;

(2) A list of the providers who have executed a contract that complies with Section 13(D)(1) of this Act; and

(3) (a) A description of the grievance procedures, and

    (b) The total number of grievances handled through such procedures, a compilation of the causes underlying those grievances, and a summary of the final disposition of those grievances.

B. The commissioner [director, superintendent] may require such additional reports as are deemed necessary and appropriate to enable the commissioner [director, superintendent] to carry out his duties under this Act.

SECTION 10. INFORMATION TO ENROLLEES OR SUBSCRIBERS

A. The health maintenance organization shall provide to its subscribers a list of providers, upon enrollment and re-enrollment.

B. Every health maintenance organization shall provide within thirty (30) days to its subscribers notice of any material change in the operation of the organization that will affect them directly.

C. An enrollee must be notified in writing by the health maintenance organization of the termination of the primary care provider who provided health care services to that enrollee. The health maintenance organization shall provide assistance to the enrollee in transferring to another participating primary care provider.

D. The health maintenance organization shall provide to subscribers information on how services may be obtained, where additional information on access to services can be obtained and a number where the enrollee can contact the HMO, at no cost to the enrollee.

Comment: For the purpose of this section any major change in the provider network is considered a material change.

SECTION 11. GRIEVANCE PROCEDURES

A. Every health maintenance organization shall establish and maintain a grievance procedure which has been approved by the commissioner [director, superintendent], after consultation with the [commissioner of public health], to provide procedures for the resolution of grievances initiated by enrollees. The health maintenance organization shall maintain records regarding grievances received since the date of its last examination of such grievances.

B. The commissioner [director, superintendent] or the [commissioner of public health] may examine such grievance procedures.

SECTION 12. INVESTMENTS

With the exception of investments made in accordance with Section 5A(1), the funds of a health maintenance organization shall be invested only in accordance with [cite section of law or regulation implementing the NAIC "Health Maintenance Organization Investment Guidelines"].

SECTION 13. PROTECTION AGAINST INSOLVENCY

A. Net Worth Requirements
    (1) Before issuing any certificate of authority, the commissioner [director, superintendent] shall require that the health maintenance organization have an initial net worth of one million five hundred thousand dollars ($1,500,000) and shall thereafter maintain the minimum net worth required under Paragraph (2).
    (2) Except as provided in Paragraphs (3) and (4) of this subsection, every health maintenance organization must maintain a minimum net worth equal to the greater of:
        (a) One million dollars ($1,000,000); or
        (b) Two percent (2%) of annual premium revenues as reported on the most recent annual financial statement filed with the commissioner [director, superintendent] on the first $150,000,000 of

premium and one percent of annual premium on the premium in excess of $150,000,000; or

(c) An amount equal to the sum of three months uncovered health care expenditures as reported on the most recent financial statement filed with the commissioner [director, superintendent]; or

(d) An amount equal to the sum of:

   (i) Eight percent (8%) of annual health care expenditures except those paid on a capitated basis or managed hospital payment basis as reported on the most recent financial statement filed with the commissioner [director, superintendent]; and

   (ii) Four percent (4%) of annual hospital expenditures paid on a managed hospital payment basis as reported on the most recent financial statement filed with the commissioner [director, superintendent].

(3) A health maintenance organization licensed before the effective date of this Act must maintain a minimum net worth of:

(a) Twenty-five percent (25%) of the amount required by Section 13(A)(2) by December 31, 19__;

(b) Fifty percent (50%) of the amount required by Section 13(A)(2) by December 31, 19__;

(c) Seventy-five percent (75%) of the amount required by Section 13(A)(2) by December 31, 19__;

(d) One hundred percent (100%) of the amount required by Section 13(A)(2) by December 31, 19__.

(4) (a) In determining net worth, no debt shall be considered fully subordinated unless the subordination clause is in a form acceptable to the commissioner [director, superintendent]. Any interest obligation relating to the repayment of any subordinated debt must be similarly subordinated.

(b) The interest expenses relating to the repayment of any fully subordinated debt shall be considered covered expenses.

(c) Any debt incurred by a note meeting the requirements of this section, and otherwise acceptable to the commissioner [director, superintendent], shall not be considered a liability and shall be recorded as equity.

B. Deposit Requirements

(1) Unless otherwise provided below, each health maintenance organization shall deposit with the commissioner [director, superintendent] or, at the discretion of the commissioner [director, superintendent], with any organization or trustee acceptable to him through

which a custodial or controlled account is utilized, cash, securities, or any combination of these or other measures that are acceptable to him which at all times shall have a value of not less than three hundred thousand dollars ($300,000).

(2)   A health maintenance organization that is in operation on the effective date of this section shall make a deposit equal to one hundred fifty thousand dollars ($150,000).

In the second year, the amount of the additional deposit for a health maintenance organization that is in operation on the effective date of the section shall be equal to one hundred fifty thousand dollars ($150,000), for a total of three hundred thousand dollars ($300,000).

(3)   The deposit shall be an admitted asset of the health maintenance organization in the determination of net worth.

(4)   All income from deposits shall be an asset of the organization. A health maintenance organization that has made a securities deposit may withdraw that deposit or any part thereof after making a substitute deposit of cash, securities, or any combination of these or other measures of equal amount and value. Any securities shall be approved by the commissioner [director, superintendent] before being deposited or substituted.

(5)   The deposit shall be used to protect the interests of the health maintenance organization's enrollees and to assure continuation of health care services to enrollees of a health maintenance organization which is in rehabilitation or conservation. The commissioner [director, superintendent] may use the deposit for administrative costs directly attributable to a receivership or liquidation. If the health maintenance organization is placed in receivership or liquidation, the deposit shall be an asset subject to the provisions of the liquidation act.

(6)   The commissioner [director, superintendent] may reduce or eliminate the deposit requirement if the health maintenance organization deposits with the state treasurer, insurance commissioner [director, superintendent], or other official body of the state or jurisdiction of domicile for the protection of all subscribers and enrollees, wherever located, of such health maintenance organization, cash, acceptable securities or surety, and delivers to the commissioner [director, superintendent] a certificate to such effect, duly authenticated by the appropriate state official holding the deposit.

C.   Liabilities

Every health maintenance organization shall, when determining liabilities, include an amount estimated in the aggregate to provide for any unearned premium and for the payment of all claims for health care expenditures which have been incurred, whether reported or unreported, which are unpaid and for which such organization is or may be liable, and to provide for the expense of adjustment or settlement of such claims.

Such liabilities shall be computed in accordance with regulations promulgated by the commissioner [director, superintendent] upon reasonable consideration of the ascertained experience and character of the health maintenance organization.

D. Hold Harmless

(1) Every contract between a health maintenance organization and a participating provider of health care services shall be in writing and shall set forth that in the event the health maintenance organization fails to pay for health care services as set forth in the contract, the subscriber or enrollee shall not be liable to the provider for any sums owed by the health maintenance organization.

(2) In the event that the participating provider contract has not been reduced to writing as required by this subsection or that the contract fails to contain the required prohibition, the participating provider shall not collect or attempt to collect from the subscriber or enrollee sums owed by the health maintenance organization.

(3) No participating provider, or agent, trustee or assignee thereof, may maintain any action at law against a subscriber or enrollee to collect sums owed by the health maintenance organization.

E. Continuation of Benefits

The commissioner [director, superintendent] shall require that each health maintenance organization have a plan for handling insolvency which allows for continuation of benefits for the duration of the contract period for which premiums have been paid and continuation of benefits to members who are confined on the date of insolvency in an inpatient facility until their discharge or expiration of benefits. In considering such a plan, the commissioner [director, superintendent] may require:

(1) Insurance to cover the expenses to be paid for continued benefits after an insolvency;

(2) Provisions in provider contracts that obligate the provider to provide services for the duration of the period after the health maintenance organization's insolvency for which premium payment has been made and until the enrollee's discharge from inpatient facilities;

(3) Insolvency reserves;

(4) Acceptable letters of credit;

(5) Any other arrangements to assure that benefits are continued as specified above.

F. Notice of Termination

An agreement to provide health care services between a provider and a health maintenance organization must require that if the provider terminates the agreement, the provider shall give the organization at least sixty (60) days' advance notice of termination.

SECTION 14. UNCOVERED EXPENDITURES INSOLVENCY DEPOSIT

A. If at any time uncovered expenditures exceed ten percent (10%) of total health care expenditures, a health maintenance organization shall place an uncovered expenditures insolvency deposit with the commissioner [director, superintendent], with any organization or trustee acceptable to the commissioner [director, superintendent] through which a custodial or controlled account is maintained, cash or securities that are acceptable to the commissioner. Such deposit shall at all times have a fair market value in an amount of 120% of the HMO's outstanding liability for uncovered expenditures for enrollees in this state, including incurred but not reported claims, and shall be calculated as of the first day of the month and maintained for the remainder of the month. If a health maintenance organization is not otherwise required to file a quarterly report, it shall file a report within forty-five (45) days of the end of the calendar quarter with information sufficient to demonstrate compliance with this section.

B. The deposit required under this section is in addition to the deposit required under Section 13 and is an admitted asset of the health maintenance organization in the determination of net worth. All income from such deposits or trust accounts shall be assets of the health maintenance organization and may be withdrawn from such deposit or account quarterly with the approval of the commissioner [director, superintendent].

C. A health maintenance organization that has made a deposit may withdraw that deposit or any part of the deposit if (1) a substitute deposit of cash or securities of equal amount and value is made, (2) the fair market value exceeds the amount of the required deposit, or (3) the required deposit under Subsection A is reduced or eliminated. Deposits, substitutions or withdrawals may be made only with the prior written approval of the commissioner [director, superintendent].

D. The deposit required under this section is in trust and may be used only as provided under this section. The commissioner [director, superintendent] may use the deposit of an insolvent health maintenance organization for administrative costs associated with administering the deposit and payment of claims of enrollees of this state for uncovered expenditures in this state. Claims for uncovered expenditures shall be paid on a pro rata basis based on assets available to pay such ultimate liability for incurred expenditures.

Partial distribution may be made pending final distribution. Any amount of the deposit remaining shall be paid into the liquidation or receivership of the health maintenance organization.

E. The commissioner [director, superintendent] may by regulation prescribe the time, manner and form for filing claims under Subsection D.

F. The commissioner [director, superintendent] may by regulation or order require health maintenance organizations to file annual, quarterly or more frequent reports as he deems necessary to demonstrate compliance with this section. The commissioner [director, superintendent] may require that the reports include liability for uncovered expenditures as well as an audit opinion.

SECTION 15. ENROLLMENT PERIOD, REPLACEMENT COVERAGE IN THE EVENT OF INSOLVENCY

A. Enrollment Period

(1) In the event of an insolvency of a health maintenance organization, upon order of the commissioner [director, superintendent] all other carriers that participated in the enrollment process with the insolvent health maintenance organization at a group's last regular enrollment period shall offer such group's enrollees of the insolvent health maintenance organization a thirty-day enrollment period commencing upon the date of insolvency. Each carrier shall offer such enrollees of the insolvent health maintenance organization the same coverages and rates that it had offered to the enrollees of the group at its last regular enrollment period.

(2) If no other carrier had been offered to some groups enrolled in the insolvent health maintenance organization, or if the commissioner [director, superintendent] determines that the other health benefit plan(s) lack sufficient health care delivery resources to assure that health care services will be available and accessible to all of the group enrollees of the insolvent health maintenance organization, then the commissioner [director, superintendent] shall allocate equitably the insolvent health maintenance organization's group contracts for such groups among all health maintenance organizations which operate within a portion of the insolvent health maintenance organization's service area, taking into consideration the health care delivery resources of each health maintenance organization. Each health maintenance organization to which a group or groups are so allocated shall offer such group or groups the health maintenance organization's existing coverage which is most similar to each group's coverage with the insolvent health maintenance organiza-

tion at rates determined in accordance with the successor health maintenance organization's existing rating methodology.

(3) The commissioner [director, superintendent] shall also allocate equitably the insolvent health maintenance organization's nongroup enrollees which are unable to obtain other coverage among all health maintenance organizations which operate within a portion of the insolvent health maintenance organization's service area, taking into consideration the health care delivery resources of each such health maintenance organization. Each health maintenance organization to which nongroup enrollees are allocated shall offer such nongroup enrollees the health maintenance organization's existing coverage for individual or conversion coverage as determined by his type of coverage in the insolvent health maintenance organization at rates determined in accordance with the successor health maintenance organization's existing rating methodology. Successor health maintenance organizations which do not offer direct nongroup enrollment may aggregate all of the allocated nongroup enrollees into one group for rating and coverage purposes.

Comment: Amendments to the insurance code regulating indemnity carriers may be necessary to bring the insurance carriers into the jurisdiction of this provision.

B. Replacement Coverage

(1) "Discontinuance" shall mean the termination of the contract between the group contract holder and a health maintenance organization due to the insolvency of the health maintenance organization, and does not refer to the termination of any agreement between any individual enrollee and the health maintenance organization.

(2) Any carrier providing replacement coverage with respect to group hospital, medical or surgical expense or service benefits within a period of sixty (60) days from the date of discontinuance of a prior health maintenance organization contract or policy providing such hospital, medical or surgical expense or service benefits shall immediately cover all enrollees who were validly covered under the previous health maintenance organization contract or policy at the date of discontinuance and who would otherwise be eligible for coverage under the succeeding carrier's contract, regardless of any provisions of the contract relating to active employment or hospital confinement or pregnancy.

(3) Except to the extent benefits for the condition would have been reduced or excluded under the prior carrier's contract or policy, no provision in a succeeding carrier's contract of replacement coverage which would operate to reduce or exclude benefits on the basis that the condition giving rise to benefits preexisted the effective date of the succeeding carrier's contract shall be applied with respect to

those enrollees validly covered under the prior carrier's contract or policy on the date of discontinuance.

SECTION 16. FILING REQUIREMENTS FOR RATING INFORMATION

A. No premium rate may be used until either a schedule of premium rates or methodology for determining premium rates has been filed with and approved by the commissioner [director, superintendent].

B. Either a specific schedule of premium rates, or a methodology for determining premium rates, shall be established in accordance with actuarial principles for various categories of enrollees, provided that the premium applicable to an enrollee shall not be individually determined based on the status of his/her health. However, the premium rates shall not be excessive, inadequate or unfairly discriminatory. A certification by a qualified actuary or other qualified person acceptable to the commissioner [director, superintendent] as to the appropriateness of the use of the methodology, based on reasonable assumptions, shall accompany the filing along with adequate supporting information.

C. The commissioner [director, superintendent] shall approve the schedule of premium rates or methodology for determining premium rates if the requirements of Subsection B are met. If the commissioner [director, superintendent] disapproves such filing, he shall notify the health maintenance organization. In the notice, the commissioner [director, superintendent] shall specify the reasons for his disapproval. A hearing will be conducted within thirty (30) days after a request in writing by the person filing. If the commissioner [director, superintendent] does not take action on such schedule or methodology within thirty (30) days of the filing of such schedule or methodology, it shall be deemed approved.

SECTION 17. REGULATION OF HEALTH MAINTENANCE ORGANIZATION PRODUCERS

A. The commissioner [director, superintendent] may, after notice and hearing, promulgate such rules and regulations as are necessary to provide for the licensing of health maintenance organization producers. Such rules shall establish:

(1) The requirements for licensure of resident health maintenance organization producers;

(2) The conditions for entering into reciprocal agreements with other jurisdictions for the licensure of nonresident health maintenance organization producers;

(3) Any examination, prelicensing or continuing education requirements;

(4) The requirements for registering and terminating the appointment
of health maintenance organization producers;

(5) Any requirements for registering any assumed names or office
locations in which a health maintenance organization producer
does business;

(6) The conditions for health maintenance organization producer license renewal;

(7) The grounds for denial, refusal, suspension or revocation of a health
maintenance organization producer's license;

(8) Any required fees for the licensing activities of health maintenance
organization producers; and

(9) Any other requirement or procedure and any form as may be
reasonably necessary to provide for the effective administration of
the licensing of health maintenance organization producers under
this section.

B. None of the following shall be required to hold a health maintenance organization producer license:

(1) Any regular salaried officer or employee of a health maintenance
organization who devotes substantially all of his time to activities
other than the taking or transmitting of applications or membership
fees or premiums for health maintenance organization membership, or who receives no commission or other compensation directly
dependent upon the business obtained and who does not solicit or
accept from the public applications for health maintenance organization membership;

(2) Employers or their officers or employees or the trustees of any
employee benefit plan to the extent that such employers, officers,
employees or trustees are engaged in the administration or operation of any program of employee benefits involving the use of
health maintenance organization memberships; provided that
such employers, officers, employees or trustees are not in any
manner compensated directly or indirectly by the health maintenance organization issuing such health maintenance organization
memberships;

(3) Banks or their officers and employees to the extent that such banks,
officers and employees collect and remit charges by charging same
against accounts of depositors on the orders of such depositors; or

(4) Any person or the employee of any person who has contracted to
provide administrative, management or health care services to a
health maintenance organization and who is compensated for those
services by the payment of an amount calculated as a percentage of

the revenues, net income or profit of the health maintenance organization, if that method of compensation is the sole basis for subjecting that person or the employee of the person to this Act.

C. The commissioner [director, superintendent] may by rule exempt certain classes of persons from the requirement of obtaining a license:

(1) If the functions they perform do not require special competence, trustworthiness or the regulatory surveillance made possible by licensing; or

(2) If other existing safeguards make regulation unnecessary.

SECTION 18. POWERS OF INSURERS AND [HOSPITAL AND MEDICAL SERVICE CORPORATIONS]

A. An insurance company licensed in this state, or a hospital or medical service corporation authorized to do business in this state, may either directly or through a subsidiary or affiliate organize and operate a health maintenance organization under the provisions of this Act. Notwithstanding any other law which may be inconsistent herewith, any two or more such insurance companies, hospital or medical service corporations, or subsidiaries or affiliates thereof, may jointly organize and operate a health maintenance organization. The business of insurance is deemed to include the providing of health care by a health maintenance organization owned or operated by an insurer or a subsidiary thereof.

B. Notwithstanding any provision of insurance and hospital or medical service corporation laws [citations], an insurer or a hospital or medical service corporation may contract with a health maintenance organization to provide insurance or similar protection against the cost of care provided through health maintenance organizations and to provide coverage in the event of the failure of the health maintenance organization to meet its obligations.

The enrollees of a health maintenance organization constitute a permissible group under such laws. Among other things, under such contracts, the insurer or hospital or medical service corporation may make benefit payments to health maintenance organizations for health care services rendered by providers.

SECTION 19. EXAMINATIONS

A. The commissioner [director, superintendent] may make an examination of the affairs of any health maintenance organization and providers with whom such organization has contracts, agreements or other arrangements as often as is reasonably necessary for the protection of the interests of the people of this state but not less frequently than once every three (3) years.

B. The [commissioner of public health] may make an examination concerning the quality assurance program of the health maintenance organization and of any providers with whom such organization has contracts, agreements or other arrangements as often as is reasonably necessary for the protection of the interests of the people of this state but not less frequently than once every three (3) years.

C. Every health maintenance organization and provider shall submit its books and records for such examinations and in every way facilitate the completion of the examination. For the purpose of examinations, the commissioner [director, superintendent] and the [commissioner of public health] may administer oaths to, and examine the officers and agents of, the health maintenance organization and the principals of such providers concerning their business.

D. The expenses of examinations under this section shall be assessed against the health maintenance organization being examined and remitted to the commissioner [director, superintendent] or the [commissioner of public health] for whom the examination is being conducted.

E. In lieu of such examination, the commissioner [director, superintendent] or [commissioner of public health] may accept the report of an examination made by the commissioner [director, superintendent] or [commissioner of public health] of another state.

SECTION 20. SUSPENSION OR REVOCATION OF CERTIFICATE OF AUTHORITY

A. Any certificate of authority issued under this Act may be suspended or revoked, and any application for a certificate of authority may be denied, if the commissioner [director, superintendent] finds that any of the conditions listed below exist:

(1) The health maintenance organization is operating significantly in contravention of its basic organizational document or in a manner contrary to that described in any other information submitted under Section 3, unless amendments to such submissions have been filed with and approved by the commissioner [director, superintendent];

(2) The health maintenance organization issues an evidence of coverage or uses a schedule of charges for health care services which do not comply with the requirements of Sections 8 and 16;

(3) The health maintenance organization does not provide or arrange for basic health care services;

(4) The [commissioner of public health] certifies to the commissioner [director, superintendent] that:

    (a) The health maintenance organization does not meet the requirements of Section 4A(2); or

    (b) The health maintenance organization is unable to fulfill its obligations to furnish health care services;

(5) The health maintenance organization is no longer financially responsible and may reasonably be expected to be unable to meet its obligations to enrollees or prospective enrollees;

(6) The health maintenance organization has failed to correct, within the time prescribed by Subsection C, any deficiency occurring due to such health maintenance organization's prescribed minimum net worth being impaired;

(7) The health maintenance organization has failed to implement the grievance procedures required by Section 11 in a reasonable manner to resolve valid complaints;

(8) The health maintenance organization or any person on its behalf, has advertised or merchandised its services in an untrue, misrepresentative, misleading, deceptive or unfair manner;

(9) The continued operation of the health maintenance organization would be hazardous to its enrollees; or

(10) The health maintenance organization has otherwise failed substantially to comply with this Act.

B. In addition to or in lieu of suspension or revocation of a certificate of authority pursuant to this section, the applicant or health maintenance organization may be subjected to an administrative penalty of up to [insert amount] dollars for each cause for suspension or revocation.

C. The following shall pertain when insufficient net worth is maintained.

    (1) Whenever the commissioner [director, superintendent] finds that the net worth maintained by any health maintenance organization subject to the provisions of this Act is less than the minimum net worth required to be maintained by Section 13 of this Act, he shall give written notice to the health maintenance organization of the amount of the deficiency and require: (a) filing with the commissioner [director, superintendent] a plan for correction of the deficiency acceptable to the commissioner [director, superintendent] and (b) correction of the deficiency within a reasonable time, not to exceed sixty (60) days, unless an extension of time, not to exceed sixty (60) additional days, is granted by the commissioner [director, superintendent]. Such a deficiency shall be deemed an impairment, and failure to correct the impairment in the prescribed time shall be grounds for suspension or revocation of the certificate of authority

or for placing the health maintenance organization in conservation, rehabilitation or liquidation.

(2) Unless allowed by the commissioner [director, superintendent] no health maintenance organization or person acting on its behalf may, directly or indirectly, renew, issue or deliver any certificate, agreement or contract of coverage in this state, for which a premium is charged or collected, when the health maintenance organization writing such coverage is impaired, and the fact of such impairment is known to the health maintenance organization or to such person.

However, the existence of an impairment shall not prevent the issuance or renewal of a certificate, agreement, or contract when the enrollee exercises an option granted under the plan to obtain a new, renewed or converted coverage.

D. A certificate of authority shall be suspended or revoked or an application or a certificate of authority denied or an administrative penalty imposed only after compliance with the requirements of this section.

(1) Suspension or revocation of a certificate of authority or the denial of an application or the imposition of an administrative penalty pursuant to this section shall be by written order and shall be sent to the health maintenance organization or applicant by certified or registered mail and to the [commissioner of public health]. The written order shall state the grounds, charges or conduct on which suspension, revocation or denial or administrative penalty is based. The health maintenance organization or applicant may in writing request a hearing within thirty (30) days from the date of mailing of the order. If no written request is made, such order shall be final upon the expiration of said thirty (30) days.

(2) If the health maintenance organization or applicant requests a hearing pursuant to this section, the commissioner [director, superintendent] shall issue a written notice of hearing and send it to the health maintenance organization or applicant by certified or registered mail and to the [commissioner of public health] stating:

(a) A specific time for the hearing, which may not be less than twenty (20) nor more than thirty (30) days after mailing of the notice of hearing; and

(b) A specific place for the hearing, which may be either in [location of regulatory body] or in the county where the health maintenance organization's or applicant's principal place of business is located.

(c) If a hearing is requested, the [commissioner of public health] or his designated representative shall be in attendance and shall participate in the proceedings. The recommendations and findings of the [commissioner of public health] with respect to matters relating to the quality of health care services provided in connection with any decision regarding denial, suspension or revocation of a certificate of authority, shall be conclusive and binding upon the commissioner [director, superintendent].

After such hearing, or upon failure of the health maintenance organization to appear at such hearing, the commissioner [director, superintendent] shall take whatever action he deems necessary based on written findings and shall mail his decision to the health maintenance organization or applicant with a copy to the [commissioner of public health]. The action of the commissioner [director, superintendent] and the recommendation and findings of the [commissioner of public health] shall be subject to review under the State Administrative Review Act (or other applicable statutory review process).

E. The provisions of the [Administrative Procedure Act] of this state shall apply to proceedings under this section to the extent they are not in conflict with Subsection D(2).

F. When the certificate of authority of a health maintenance organization is suspended, the health maintenance organization shall not, during the period of such suspension, enroll any additional enrollees except newborn children or other newly acquired dependents of existing enrollees, and shall not engage in any advertising or solicitation whatsoever.

G. When the certificate of authority of a health maintenance organization is revoked, such organization shall proceed, immediately following the effective date of the order of revocation, to wind up its affairs, and shall conduct no further business except as may be essential to the orderly conclusion of the affairs of such organization. It shall engage in no further advertising or solicitation whatsoever. The commissioner [director, superintendent] may, by written order, permit such further operation of the organization as he may find to be in the best interest of enrollees, to the end that enrollees will be afforded the greatest practical opportunity to obtain continuing health care coverage.

SECTION 21. REHABILITATION, LIQUIDATION OR CONSERVATION OF HEALTH MAINTENANCE ORGANIZATIONS

A. Any rehabilitation, liquidation or conservation of a health maintenance organization shall be deemed to be the rehabilitation, liquidation or conservation of an insurance company and shall be conducted under the supervision of the commissioner [director, superintendent] pursuant to the law governing the rehabilitation, liquidation or conservation of insurance companies. The commissioner [director, superintendent] may apply for an order directing him to rehabilitate, liquidate or conserve a health maintenance organization upon any one or more grounds set out in [cite sections of state rehabilitation law], or when in his opinion the continued operation of the health maintenance organization would be hazardous either to the enrollees or to the people of this state. Enrollees shall have the same priority in the event of liquidation or rehabilitation as the law provides to policyholders of an insurer.

B.   For purpose of determining the priority of distribution of general assets, claims of enrollees, and enrollees' beneficiaries shall have the same priority as established by [insert state statute for liquidation of insurers] for policy-holders and beneficiaries of insureds of insurance companies. If an enrollee is liable to any provider for services provided pursuant to and covered by the health care plan, that liability shall have the status of an enrollee claim for distribution of general assets.

Any provider who is obligated by statute or agreement to hold enrollees harmless from liability for services provided pursuant to and covered by a health care plan shall have a priority of distribution of the general assets immediately following that of enrollees and enrollees' beneficiaries as described herein, and immediately preceding the priority of distribution described in [insert citation to insurance code].

SECTION 22. SUMMARY ORDERS AND SUPERVISION

A.   Whenever the commissioner [director, superintendent] determines that the financial condition of any health maintenance organization is such that its continued operation might be hazardous to its enrollees, creditors, or the general public, or that it has violated any provision of this Act, he may, after notice and hearing, order the health maintenance organization to take such action as may be reasonably necessary to rectify such condition or violation, including but not limited to one or more of the following:

(1)   Reduce the total amount of present and potential liability for benefits by reinsurance or other method acceptable to the commissioner [director, superintendent];

(2)   Reduce the volume of new business being accepted;

(3)   Reduce expenses by specified methods;

(4)   Suspend or limit the writing of new business for a period of time;

(5)   Increase the health maintenance organization's capital and surplus by contribution; or

(6)   Take such other steps as the commissioner [director, superintendent] may deem appropriate under the circumstances.

B. For purposes of this section, the violation by a health maintenance organization of any law of this state to which such health maintenance organization is subject shall be deemed a violation of this Act.

C. The commissioner [director, superintendent] is authorized, by rules and regulations, to set uniform standards and criteria for early warning that the continued operation of any health maintenance organization might be hazardous to its enrollees, creditors, or the general public and to set standards for evaluating the financial condition of any health maintenance organization, which standards shall be consistent with the purposes expressed in Subsection A of this section.

D. The remedies and measures available to the commissioner [director, superintendent] under this section shall be in addition to, and not in lieu of, the remedies and measures available to the commissioner [director, superintendent] under the provisions of [cite law which implements Sections 9 and 10 of the NAIC Rehabilitation and Liquidation Model Act].

SECTION 23. REGULATIONS

The commissioner [director, superintendent] may, after notice and hearing, promulgate reasonable rules and regulations, as are necessary or proper to carry out the provisions of this Act. Such rules and regulations shall be subject to review in accordance with [insert statutory citation providing for administrative rulemaking and review of such rules].

SECTION 24. FEES

A. Every health maintenance organization subject to this Act shall pay to the commissioner [director, superintendent] the following fees:

   (1) For filing an application for a certificate of authority or amendment thereto, [insert amount] dollars;

   (2) For filing an amendment to the organization documents that requires approval, [insert amount] dollars;

   (3) For filing an amendment "for information only," [insert amount] dollars; and

   (4) For filing each annual report, [insert amount] dollars.

B. Fees charged under this section shall be distributed as follows: [insert dollar amount] to the commissioner [director, superintendent] and [insert dollar amount] to the [commissioner of public health].

[Alternative language to Subsections A and B above:

The commissioner [director, superintendent] shall promulgate rules for collecting fees from health maintenance organizations.]

Comment: Each state should examine its statutory authority to collect fees and select the appropriate language suggested above.

SECTION 25. PENALTIES AND ENFORCEMENT

A. The commissioner [director, superintendent] may, in lieu of suspension or revocation of a certificate of authority under Section 20, levy an administrative penalty in an amount not less than [insert amount] dollars nor more than [insert amount] dollars, if reasonable notice in writing is given of the intent to levy the penalty and the health maintenance organization has a reasonable time within which to remedy the defect in its operations which gave rise to the penalty citation. The commissioner [director, superintendent] may augment this penalty by an amount equal to the sum that he calculates to be the damages suffered by enrollees or other members of the public.

B. (1) If the commissioner [director, superintendent] or the [commissioner of public health] shall for any reason have cause to believe that any violation of this Act has occurred or is threatened, the commissioner [director, superintendent] or [commissioner of public health] may give notice to the health maintenance organization and to the representatives, or other persons who appear to be involved in such suspected violation, to arrange a conference with the alleged violators or their authorized representatives for the purpose of attempting to ascertain the facts relating to such suspected violation; and, in the event it appears that any violation has occurred or is threatened, to arrive at an adequate and effective means of correcting or preventing such violation.

   (2) Proceedings under this subsection shall not be governed by any formal procedural requirements, and may be conducted in such manner as the commissioner [director, superintendent] or the [commissioner of public health] may deem appropriate under the circumstances. However, unless consented to by the health maintenance organization, no rule or order may result from a conference until the requirements of this section of this Act are satisfied.

C. (1) The commissioner [director, superintendent] may issue an order directing a health maintenance organization or a representative of a health maintenance organization to cease and desist from engaging in any act or practice in violation of the provisions of this Act.

   (2) Within [insert number] days after service of the cease and desist order, the respondent may request a hearing on the question of whether acts or practices in violation of this Act have occurred. Such hearings shall be conducted pursuant to [cite sections of state administrative procedure act], and judicial review shall be available as provided by [cite sections of state administrative procedure act].

D. In the case of any violation of the provisions of this Act, if the commissioner [director, superintendent] elects not to issue a cease and desist order, or in the event of noncompliance with a cease and desist order issued pursuant to Subsection C, the commissioner [director, superintendent] may institute a proceeding to obtain injunctive or other appropriate relief in the [name of court of primary jurisdiction for actions of this nature].

Comment: Sections 25C and 25D authorize the commissioner to issue a cease and desist order and to apply for injunctive relief. When the commissioner is not granted such statutory powers, the language should be modified to provide for the legal steps to be taken by the attorney general or other appropriate state official.

E. Notwithstanding any other provisions of this Act, if a health maintenance organization fails to comply with the net worth requirement of this Act, the commissioner [director, superintendent] is authorized to take appropriate action to assure that the continued operation of the health maintenance organization will not be hazardous to its enrollees.

SECTION 26. STATUTORY CONSTRUCTION AND RELATIONSHIP TO OTHER LAWS

A. Except as otherwise provided in this Act, provisions of the insurance law and provisions of hospital or medical service corporation laws shall not be applicable to any health maintenance organization granted a certificate of authority under this Act. This provision shall not apply to an insurer or hospital or medical service corporation licensed and regulated pursuant to the insurance law or the hospital or medical service corporation laws of this state except with respect to its health maintenance organization activities authorized and regulated pursuant to this Act.

B. Solicitation of enrollees by a health maintenance organization granted a certificate of authority, or its representatives, shall not be construed to violate any provision of law relating to solicitation or advertising by health professionals.

C. Any health maintenance organization authorized under this Act shall not be deemed to be practicing medicine and shall be exempt from the provision of [citation] relating to the practice of medicine.

SECTION 27. FILINGS AND REPORTS AS PUBLIC DOCUMENTS

All applications, filings and reports required under this Act shall be treated as public documents, except those which are trade secrets or privileged or confidential quality assurance, commercial or financial information, other than any annual financial statement that may be required under Section 9 of this Act.

SECTION 28. CONFIDENTIALITY OF MEDICAL INFORMATION AND LIMITATION OF LIABILITY

A. Any data or information pertaining to the diagnosis, treatment or health of any enrollee or applicant obtained from such person or from any provider by any health maintenance organization shall be held in confidence and shall not be disclosed to any person except to the extent that it may be necessary to carry out the purposes of this Act; or upon the express consent of the enrollee or applicant; or pursuant to statute or court order for the production of evidence or the discovery thereof; or in the event of claim or litigation between such person and the health maintenance organization wherein such data or information is pertinent. A health maintenance organization shall be entitled to claim any statutory privileges against such disclosure which the provider who furnished such information to the health maintenance organization is entitled to claim.

B. A person who, in good faith and without malice, takes any action or makes any decision or recommendation as a member, agent or employee of a health care review committee or who furnishes any records, information or assistance to such a committee shall not be subject to liability for civil damages or any legal action in consequence of such action, nor shall the health maintenance organization which established such committee or the officers, directors, employees or agents of such health maintenance organization be liable for the activities of any such person. This section shall not be construed to relieve any person of liability arising from treatment of a patient.

C. (1) The information considered by a health care review committee and the records of their actions and proceedings shall be confidential and not subject to subpoena or order to produce except in proceedings before the appropriate state licensing or certifying agency, or in an appeal, if permitted, from the committee's findings or recommendations. No member of a health care review committee, or officer, director or other member of a health maintenance organization or its staff engaged in assisting such committee, or any person assisting or furnishing information to such committee may be subpoenaed to testify in any judicial or quasi-judicial proceeding if such subpoena is based solely on such activities.

(2) Information considered by a health care review committee and the records of its actions and proceedings which are used pursuant to Subsection C(1) by a state licensing or certifying agency or in an appeal shall be kept confidential and shall be subject to the same provision concerning discovery and use in legal actions as are the original information and records in the possession and control of a health care review committee.

D. To fulfill its obligations under Section 7, the health maintenance organization shall have access to treatment records and other information pertaining to the diagnosis, treatment or health status of any enrollee.

SECTION 29. [COMMISSION OF PUBLIC HEALTH'S] AUTHORITY TO CONTRACT

The [commissioner of public health], in carrying out his obligations under this Act, may contract with qualified persons to make recommendations concerning the determinations required to be made by him. Such recommendations may be accepted in full or in part by the [commissioner of public health].

SECTION 30. ACQUISITION OF CONTROL OF OR MERGER OF A HEALTH MAINTENANCE ORGANIZATION

No person may make a tender for or a request or invitation for tenders of, or enter into an agreement to exchange securities for or acquire in the open market or otherwise, any voting security of a health maintenance organization or enter into any other agreement if, after the consummation thereof, that person would, directly or indirectly (or by conversion or by exercise of any right to acquire), be in control of the health maintenance organization, and no person may enter into an agreement to merge or consolidate with or otherwise to acquire control of a health maintenance organization, unless, at the time any offer, request or invitation is made or any agreement is entered into, or prior to the acquisition of the securities if no offer or agreement is involved, the person has filed with the commissioner [director, superintendent] and has sent to the health maintenance organization, information required by Section [cite Sections 2(b)(1), (2), (3), (4), (5), and (12) of the NAIC Model Insurance Holding Company System Regulatory Act] and the offer, request, invitation, agreement or acquisition has been approved by the commissioner [director, superintendent]. Approval by the commissioner [director, superintendent] shall be governed by Section [cite law which implements Section 3(d)(1) and (2) of the NAIC Model Insurance Holding Company System Regulatory Act].

SECTION 31. DUAL CHOICE [OPTIONAL]

Each employer, public or private, in this state which offers its employees a health benefit plan and employs not less than twenty-five (25) employees, and each employee benefit fund in this state which offers its members any form of basic health benefit, shall make available to and inform its employees or members of the option to enroll in at least one group practice health maintenance organization and one other health maintenance organization holding a valid certificate of authority which provides basic health care services in the geographic areas in which a substantial number of such employees or members reside. Where there is a prevailing collective bargaining agreement, the selection of the health maintenance organization(s) to be made available to the employees shall be made under the agreement. No employer in this state shall be required to pay more for health benefits as a result of the application of this section than would otherwise be required by any prevailing collective bargaining agreement or other contract for the provision of basic health benefits to its employees. The employer or benefits fund shall pay to the health maintenance organization chosen by each employee or member an amount which does not financially discriminate against an employee who enrolls in such health maintenance organization. For purposes of the preceding sentence, an employer's contribution does not financially discriminate if the employer's method of determining the contributions on behalf of all employees is reasonable and is designed to assure employees a fair choice among health benefits plans.

Comment: This section, which is optional, is similar to Section 1310 of the federal Health Maintenance Organization Act, but extends the dual choice requirement to state licensed health maintenance organizations.

The purpose for this provision is to assist in the growth and development of state licensed health maintenance organizations. A state that wants to continue to promote the development of health maintenance organizations or to establish a standard on which employer contributions are made may want to enact this section.

SECTION 32. COORDINATION OF BENEFITS

A. Health maintenance organizations are permitted, but not required, to adopt coordination of benefits provisions to avoid overinsurance and to provide for the orderly payment of claims when a person is covered by two or more group health insurance or health care plans.

B. If health maintenance organizations adopt coordination of benefits, the provisions must be consistent with the coordination of benefits provisions that are in general use in the state for coordinating coverage between two or more group health insurance or health care plans.

C. To the extent necessary for health maintenance organizations to meet their obligations as secondary carriers under the rules for coordination, health maintenance organizations shall make payments for services that are: received from non-participating providers; provided outside their service areas; or not covered under the terms of their group contracts or evidence of coverage.

SECTION 33. INSOLVENCY PROTECTION; ASSESSMENT

A. When a health maintenance organization in this state is declared insolvent by a court of competent jurisdiction, the commissioner [director, superintendent] may levy an assessment on health maintenance organizations doing business in this state to pay claims for uncovered expenditures for enrollees who are residents of this state and to provide continuation of coverage for subscribers or enrollees not covered under Section 15. The commissioner [director, superintendent] may not assess in any one calendar year more than two percent (2%) of the aggregate premium written by each health maintenance organization in this state the prior calendar year.

B. The commissioner [director, superintendent] may use funds obtained under Subsection A to pay claims for uncovered expenditures for subscribers or enrollees of an insolvent health maintenance organization who are residents of this state, provide for continuation of coverage for subscribers or enrollees who are residents of this state and are not covered under Section 15, and administrative costs. The commissioner [director, superintendent] may by regulation prescribe the time, manner and form for filing claims under this section or may require claims to be allowed by an ancillary receiver or the domestic liquidator or receiver.

C. (1) A receiver or liquidator of an insolvent health maintenance organization shall allow a claim in the proceeding in an amount equal to administrative and noncovered expenditures paid under this section.

   (2) Any person receiving benefits under this section for uncovered expenditures is deemed to have assigned the rights under the covered health care plan certificates to the commissioner [director, superintendent] to the extent of the benefits received. The commissioner [director, superintendent] may require an assignment to it of such rights by any payee, enrollee, or beneficiary as a condition precedent to the receipt of any rights or benefits conferred by this section upon such person. The commissioner [director, superintendent] is subrogated to these rights against the assets of any insolvent health maintenance organization held by a receiver or liquidator of another jurisdiction.

   (3) The assignment or subrogation rights of the commissioner [director, superintendent] and allowed claim under this subsection have the same priority against the assets of the insolvent health maintenance organization as those possessed by the person entitled to receive benefits under this section or for similar expenses in the receivership or liquidation.

D. When assessed funds are unused following the completion of the liquidation of a health maintenance organization, the commissioner [director, superintendent] will distribute on a pro rata basis any amounts received under

Subsection A which are not *de minimis* to the health maintenance organizations which have been assessed under this section.

E. The aggregate coverage of uncovered expenditures under this section shall not exceed $300,000 with respect to any one individual. Continuation of coverage shall not continue for more than the lesser of one year after the health maintenance organization coverage is terminated by insolvency or the remaining term of the contract. The commissioner [director, superintendent] may provide continuation of coverage on any reasonable basis; including, but not limited to, continuation of the health maintenance organization contract or substitution of indemnity coverage in a form determined by the commissioner [director, superintendent].

F. The commissioner [director, superintendent] may waive an assessment of any health maintenance organization if it would be or is impaired or placed in financially hazardous condition. A health maintenance organization which fails to pay an assessment within thirty (30) days after notice is subject to a civil forfeiture of not more than $1,000 per day and/or suspension or revocation of its certificate of authority. Any action taken by the commissioner [director, superintendent] in enforcing of this section may be appealed by the health maintenance organization in accordance with [the administrative procedures act].

Drafting Comment: Section 33 is not recommended for all states. A state should carefully review its health maintenance organization market to determine whether the assessment procedure under this section is feasible. If health maintenance organization premium volume is small or dominated by a few organizations, a state may wish to rely solely on the protections provided under Sections 14 and 15.

For those states where an assessment is feasible, this section provides assurance that funds will be available to pay uncovered expenditures even if those liabilities have been underestimated by the organization or have significantly escalated as the financial condition of the organization deteriorated. In addition, an assessment provides a means for continued coverage for those subscribers or enrollees who are not protected under Section 15.

SECTION 34. SEVERABILITY

If any section, term, or provision of this Act shall be adjudged invalid for any reason, such judgment shall not affect, impair or invalidate any other section, term or provision of this Act; but the remaining sections, terms and provisions shall be and remain in full force and effect.

Legislative History (all references are to the *Proceedings of the NAIC*).
1973 Proc. I 9, 11, 141, 192, 202-222 (adopted).
1973 Proc. II 139 (synopsis of model).
1974 Proc. I 12, 14, 405, 413 (amended).
1982 Proc. I 19, 28, 431, 498-499, 530-554 (revised and reprinted).
1989 Proc. I 9, 22, 180-181, 327, 331-335 (amended).
1989 Proc. II 13, 25-26, 40, 51-79 (amended and reprinted).
1990 Proc. I 6, 26, 171, 374-376, 377-379 (amended).
1991 Proc. I 9, 19-20, 86, 108 (technical amendment).

Table of Cases _____

Note: Numbers indicate chapter and question numbers, not page numbers (e.g., 1:3 indicates Chapter 1, question 3).

V

W

Index _____

I

J

About the Authors

Patricia Younger, J.D., Cynthia Conner, LL.L., Kara Kinney Cartwright, J.D., and Susan Kole, J.D., are Health Law Center staff members at Aspen Publishers, Inc., where they are involved in extensive research and writing on health law issues. Among the publications these attorneys write for are the *Hospital Law Manual*, a multivolume looseleaf treatise on a full range of health law issues, such as medical records, medical staff, pharmacy, consents, reproductive issues, tax, and financial management; the *Health Care Labor Manual*, a three-volume looseleaf treatise on labor and employment issues of concern to health care providers; and the *Managed Care Law Manual*, a treatise on legal issues of concern in the managed care environment, such as antitrust, utilization management, taxation, and fraud and abuse. They have also authored another book in this series, the *Physician Credentialing and Peer Review Answer Book*, and collaborated with William H. Roach, Jr. in writing the second edition of *Medical Records and the Law*. In addition, these attorneys work with outside authors in producing the *Laboratory Regulation Manual*, a four-volume looseleaf treatise addressing legal issues of concern to clinical laboratories written by the law firm of O'Connor and Hannon; and the *Hospital Contracts Manual*, a three-volume treatise covering contracting issues relevant to health care providers, edited by the law firm of Baker and Hostetler.